TURNING POINTS
IN
Television

. . . .

LARRY BRODY

CITADEL PRESS
Kensington Publishing Corp.
www.kensingtonbooks.com

CITADEL PRESS BOOKS are published by

Kensington Publishing Corp.
850 Third Avenue
New York, NY 10022

All Kensington titles, imprints, and distributed lines are available at special quantity discounts for bulk purchases for sales promotions, premiums, fund-raising, educational, or institutional use. Special book excerpts or customized printings can also be created to fit specific needs. For details, write or phone the office of the Kensington special sales manager: Kensington Publishing Corp., 850 Third Avenue, New York, NY 10022, attn: Special Sales Department; phone 1-800-221-2647.

CITADEL PRESS and the Citadel logo are Reg. U.S. Pat. & TM Off.

First printing: June 2005

10 9 8 7 6 5 4 3 2 1

Printed in the United States of America

Library of Congress Control Number: 2004116402

ISBN 0-8065-2643-2

Tune In to This Great Advance Praise for
Turning Points in Television and Larry Brody!

"A lively and entertaining view of twenty-two great 'moments' in TV history, moments that held significance far beyond what most people realize. Brody takes readers on a roller coaster ride through TV history that they won't soon forget. This is essential reading for anyone who wants to remember—and understand."

—Tim Brooks and Earle Marsh, co-authors, *The Complete Directory to Prime Time Network and Cable TV Shows, 1946–Present*

"Set aside academic histories of TV—you'll learn more from this opinionated, iconoclastic and often hilarious look at what really shaped the shows we watched."

—Tom Hill, TV Land/Nick at Nite creative director, author of *TV Land to Go*

"*Turning Points in Television* is filled with countless surprising revelations; it's also loaded with passion, plus a considerable amount of 'deep thoughts.' That's because it seems Larry can't help himself. He's a passionate man, and hey, possibly even as smart as the network execs. . . . I suspect you're really going to enjoy this book."

—from the Foreword by Stan Lee, creator of *Spider-Man*, Marvel Comics

"A thorough and entertaining history of TV from a man who was shaped, employed and obsessed by it. Personally, I'm grateful for the turning point that caused him to move to Santa Fe and become a teacher. If I hadn't taken his class, I probably wouldn't be working in Hollywood today."

—Karen McCullah Lutz, screenwriter *(Legally Blonde, 10 Things I Hate About You)*, author of *The Bachelorette Party*

"A fascinating insider's view. A veteran writer/producer with an impressive list of credits, Brody peppers the milestones of the medium with one laugh-out-loud story after another starring an incomparable cast of true life characters. This is a must-read for any TV junkie like myself. I just couldn't put the damn thing down!"

—Rick Copp, author of *The Actor's Guide to Murder, The Actor's Guide to Adultery*, TV and screenwriter *(The Golden Girls, Wings, The Brady Bunch Movie)*

Contents

Foreword
by Stan Lee

*I*t wasn't always like this!

In the early days of comic books—and I mean way, way back—those of us who wrote and drew the strips operated pretty much on our own. The publishers who controlled the purse strings let us do pretty much as we wanted as long as the mags kept selling. That's the reason writers like me managed to sneak Spider-Man, X-Men, the Hulk, Fantastic Four, and a whole kaboodle of other characters out to the public when no one was looking.

Television, though, is a whole other animal. Although younger than comics, TV quickly grabbed a much larger audience and quickly came to represent much bigger financial investments and potential profits. Therefore, everyone, especially the money people, started paying attention right from the get-go, along with the commentators, critics, and innumerable assorted pundits.

As a reminder of how accessible television is compared to comics, readers today have to get on their bikes or into their cars and find one of the few stores that sell comic books, but once you've plunked your money down for a TV set it's right there, staring you in the face, begging you to turn it on.

Despite all the attention TV has gotten, *Turning Points in Television* is the first time I've seen both the programs and the business that creates them analyzed in terms of their contributions to contemporary culture by someone who has actually been part of the creative and the business side and knows each one from the inside out.

I like the fact that Larry Brody's book is up close and personal. It gives us a rare behind-the-scenes account of the shows and, even more, of the people who have influenced how millions of viewers dress and talk and work and play and buy and look at themselves. Even more frightening, it has so surely influenced the way we think.

Larry, who is both an award-winning television writer and producer as well as a compulsive viewer, surprised me on almost every page of this book. I certainly had never been aware that Desi Arnaz, Jr. is the reason we've got reruns—and that he caused that little phenomenon even before he was born!

Nor did I know the real reason I see big city neighborhoods and people with big city problems every time I channel surf, even though that's so unrepresentative of most of the real world. How could I? I'm from New York!

Before I read this book, could I have guessed that decisions made by a very hip TV executive named Fred Silverman in the '70s are why Suzanne Somers gets to sell us all that jewelry and exercise equipment over the airwaves today? Or, that a brilliant writer named Steven Bochco could very well be the reason that so many other terrific TV writers are out of work? Or how about the fact that Larry Brody loved a puppet named Howdy Doody so much that, just like The Who, he also wanted to "die before I get old?"

Not only is *Turning Points in Television* filled with countless surprising revelations, it's also loaded with passion, plus a considerable amount of "deep thoughts." That's because it seems Larry can't help himself. He's a passionate man, and hey, possibly even as smart as the network execs.

Larry Brody and I first met in the early 1990s, when he was writing for one of the animated television versions of *Spider-Man*. Of course, I instantly pegged him for a man of good taste and impeccable judgment when he confessed that my work had had a great influence on him. Which reminds me, one thing he modestly leaves out in this book is the fact that he became responsible for another major Turning Point in TV when we worked together again in 1998. That's when he ramrodded an animated series about one of my favorite creations, the Silver Surfer.

Before the Surfer, Saturday morning animation was all about the action. Characters ran and shouted and punched and kicked and fought their way through every episode. *The Silver Surfer* on Fox Kids changed all that. Larry's version was articulate and thoughtful, with the hero always looking for a way to avoid a fight. The Surfer soliloquized and philosophized and talked the way he did in the comic, like an intelligent adult. I'm happy to report that the show became a cult classic and seems to have led the way for other characters in many other animated shows to speak and act more intelligently than before.

Know something? I suspect you're really going to enjoy this book. After all, would a guy who's given you animated versions of Spidey and the Silver Surfer and a guy from Marvel Comics steer you wrong?

Excelsior!

Stan

Introduction

*T*elevision.

It's the medium everyone loves to hate. Remember all those tasteless jokes about relationships that made their way through the angry underground in the seventies and eighties? "Women! You can't live with 'em and you can't live without 'em!" "Men! A woman needs a man like a fish needs a bicycle!" (I always kind of liked that one.)

These same attitudes seem to apply whenever people talk about TV. Television too is something most viewers claim they can neither live with nor without. Television too often is regarded as being as necessary for human life as a bicycle is for the life of a fish.

And yet—

And yet the ratings show that tens of millions of people are watching every day. Every major daily newspaper in the United States and most not-so-major newspapers, cover the TV beat, often with a regular column or two, and television stars from broadcast and cable primetime, daytime, and news shows are among the highest paid human beings on the planet as well as staples in magazines and tabloids devoted to "celebrities."

So let's be honest with each other. Newton Minow may have called TV a "vast wasteland" in 1961, but waste or not, it's still a land just about everyone visits. And even television haters have to admit that for a medium that's been in existence for only half the time films have, and is only a blip along the bottom of the comparison chart when put up alongside the theater, there are a hell of a lot of highlights.

Big moments that have had an unforgettable impact on people and society in general abound.

The various broadcast television news divisions and cable and satellite news channels have brought us the Army-McCarthy hearings. The coverage of the assassinations of both Kennedys. All those choppers in our living rooms during the Vietnam War. The O.J. Simpson murder trial. The collapse of the Twin Towers at the World Trade Center and a host of other memorable events.

The entertainment divisions and channels have given us the birth of "Little Ricky." The resolution of *The Fugitive*. Who shot "J.R.?" *Roots. The Autobiography of Miss Jane Pittman. The Jericho Mile. Holocaust.* A myriad of memorable episodes of *Playhouse 90, All in the Family, I Spy, M*A*S*H, The Dick Van Dyke Show, The Mary Tyler Moore Show, The Twilight Zone, Star Trek, The West Wing, ER* and many, many more.

In fact, the number of big moments is so great, and the memories they've left so intense, that no research was needed to come up with this list, only a minute's reflection. And I don't think I'm exaggerating (much) when I say that just about everyone who reads this book will be able to do the same. (My wife can tell you the plot of every episode of *Bonanza* in its last three seasons and her sister still remembers the joke lyrics to the theme song.)

Some of the above are memorable for their significance, some for their triviality and ability to remove the pain of what was significant. But all of the great moments in television have at least one thing in common. They didn't spring into existence full-blown, like Athena from the forehead of Zeus. They came about as part of a historical continuum in the TV broadcasting medium. They enlightened and entertained and moved us because the way had been paved by what we can call the major turning points in television.

This book is about those turning points. It covers what I believe to be the twenty-some key events in television's sixty-plus–year history as a "mass medium"—events that reshaped the medium and were essential to its evolution into what it is today. These are the great leaps forward. Like all great evolutionary leaps, in the eyes of some people they may seem like moments of divine intervention, while in the eyes of others they appear as diabolical interference, like the Brotherhood of Evil Mutants on *The X-Men* of Saturday morning TV.

Yet leaps they are, and without them the media climate and our very culture wouldn't be the same. (Maybe worse in the eyes of the *cognoscenti*. Maybe better. But different nevertheless.)

Who is Larry Brody to pick these turning points? And why choose the particular ones that are in this book?

Sometimes I feel as though I've been around since the beginning of time, but although that may not be the case, I have been around since the beginning of the television industry. As a kid viewer in the 1940s and 50s I was entranced by everything I saw. As a writer and producer in the 60s, 70s, 80s, 90s, and into the current century, I've been a little more discriminating, but the fact is I've been there.

Sometimes as a fan.

Sometimes as a lover.

Sometimes as a critic.

Sometimes as a worker bee.

Sometimes as an exec.

Hell, I've been *immersed*.

Turning Points in Television is a product of that immersion. It's about television history as seen not from the outside (that would be the "scientific method," and we're talking about creativity here—or so those of us in television like to think), but from inside the experience. From within the creative well. In a very real sense, the phenomenological method used by great thinkers such as Aristotle, Kant, Hegel, Heidegger, Husserl, and Sartre, to name just a few, is the order of the day.

I figure if it's good enough for Jean-Paul (in showbiz we always use each other's first names as a sign of how "in" we are) it ought to be good enough for me.

The turning points presented here, then, are not only events that caused reverberating changes in television (or any number of what scholars often refer to as "paradigm shifts"), they're also those that changed my life as a viewer or a professional in the field. For me they're more than merely facts. They're war stories, from my time at the "front," which in the TV industry can be located on the stage or in the office. Or in the living room, the bedroom, at a party, or on the tennis court.

I'd love to know what readers think are the major turning points in television, so after you've read what's here feel free to drop me a line in care of the publisher with your ideas about the most meaningful mutations in TV. We can begin a fine dialogue. Or maybe a grand disputation.

(Or, as then Fox executive Jorge Seralegui—they're all "then-execs" or soon-to-be "then-execs" because the length of time people tend to hold those jobs is so short—once said to me during a pitch meeting, "Hey, Larry, we're Fox. We're eclectic. But not *that* eclectic.")

And I'm Brody. I'm open. I hope I'm *that* open, but it's difficult to be sure. After all, I do work in TV.

Some acknowledgments:

Yes, this book is phenomenological (which some people might harshly—and incorrectly—suggest means it's all about me), but there still are several people who must be thanked because I couldn't have done it without them:

June Clark, *agent provocateur*, a driving force (no, June, I didn't say "nagging") behind getting me to sit down and write.

Miles Lott, the brilliant editor who had the courage to ask me to bring my "distinct voice and point of view" to this material.

Gwen Brody, my wonderful wife, who loves me even when I'm battling against deadlines and my own inner demons (or at least fakes it very well).

And Joy Rothke, a researcher with boundless energy and the ability to dig out the facts to fit my most distant and obscure memories.

My thanks to you all.

TURNING POINTS

IN

Television

. . . .

The First Two Television Stations Are Licensed for Commercial Broadcasting (And Both of Them Are Owned by Networks)

*T*he year 1941 marked the beginning of the television industry as we know it. On July 1, the Federal Communications Commission licensed the first two stations for commercial broadcasting. Both stations were in New York City—WNBT, owned and operated by the National Broadcasting Company, and WCBW, owned and operated by the Columbia Broadcasting System.

It was official: NBC and CBS ruled the airwaves. They were the founding fathers, working ad hoc to create their own declaration of television independence and TV constitutions. The business and programming models instituted by those two companies on that day have continued into the present.

Instead of two television stations there now are thousands. Instead of two networks there are, as of this writing, seven broadcast networks, ABC, Fox, WB, UPN, and PAX having joined the fold, and almost 500 cable and satellite channels that operate, program, or otherwise represent themselves as networks as well. And the way they make and spend their money is pretty much, to quote David Byrne, "the same as it ever was."

This isn't a mistake.

The models have prevailed because, as we say in every office in the TV business when things are going right, they "work." They

NBC and CBS test patterns, circa 1941 (Cloud Creek Institute for the Arts)

earn money and they generate viewers. News, entertainment, and sports shows are created and watched.

Think about it for a minute. Networks by definition are groups of attached structures or organisms. Unlike so many solitary heroes in literature, most of the television stations that have emerged since the 1941 Big Bang don't ride alone. They ride in herds, posses. The broadcast networks have corralled a passel of affiliates so that their message can be seen and heard all over the land, and so their incomes can be generated from coast to coast and beyond. We're talking about a bumper-to-bumper, belly-to-belly kind of existence, with all the positives and negatives inherent in such a situation.

The positives first.

(1) By creating nationally broadcast networks of stations, some owned by the network parent company, others voluntary affiliates, the founding broadcasters made it possible for viewers throughout the country to benefit from a uniformity of programming.

The same shows, whether they be series or one-shot specials such as TV movies and miniseries, are seen all over the United States at the same time (plus or minus an hour or two to allow for time zones), creating a common culture. Everyone has the opportunity to see the same shows, learn the same things, be in on the same fads—instantly. Geographical and economic differences don't interfere with the communication. The country—and, thanks to cable and satellite, much of the world—becomes much smaller, closer. Becomes one.

(2) By creating nationally broadcast networks of stations, the founding broadcasters were able to earn much more money than they would have if they were merely local. Just as in radio, television income was (and is) generated by selling advertising time, or commercials, to sponsors. At first, the sponsors paid the entire budget plus some profit for whole shows. As that became more expensive, sponsors started buying limited amounts of time (called "spots"). And as of this writing, certain audiences are considered so attractive by the sponsors that they're starting to pay for whole shows again.

Just as newspapers and magazines determine their advertising prices based on their circulation—the more readers, the more it costs to reach them—so the networks could and can charge much more for their commercial spots than individual stations can. How much more? Try these numbers:

Station XL7-TV in Mountain Home, Arkansas, is a typical local station in a small market. XL7-TV broadcasts to an area where it can reach a potential audience of about 100,000 viewers. It's also carried by Cox Cable, which enables it to get into another 10,000 homes. In 2004 the price of a thirty-second spot on XL7-TV was $50.

In 2004 the CBS television network broadcast the Super Bowl to an estimated audience of 35 million people. Cost of a thirty-second spot during the game? Over $2 million. This pays a lot of salaries and definitely makes shareholders smile . . . from ear to ear.

Bottom line: Television networks reach masses of viewers never before dreamed of simultaneously, enabling them to succeed at an equally amazing economic level.

(3) By creating nationally broadcast networks of stations, the founding broadcasters made it possible to put tons of money back into programming. XL7-TV could never afford to finance and present a series like *60 Minutes,* or an expensive miniseries like *The Blue and The Gray*, or even *Survivor*.

Similarly, the vast financial resources available to the networks have enabled them to buy the best possible talent (assuming, of course, that "best" and "expensive" have a correlation—but that's for an ingenious doctoral candidate in industrial psychology to investigate and, maybe, prove). High-priced writers, producers, actors, and directors could never earn enough to pay for their cars and divorces if they only worked for one little local station at a time. And the production values that give network "product" the professional look that at best can be quite striking would be unaffordable at XL7-TV and its cousins.

Now for the not-so-positives:

(1) By creating nationally broadcast networks of stations, the founding broadcasters made it possible for viewers throughout the country to benefit from a uniformity of programming.

Yes, this was also one of the good points. But here's the down side. Uniformity is not in itself such a wonderful thing. Historically, art has thrived because of its diversity. Cutting edge has its place. So does middle-of-the-road. So, for that matter, does yesterday's news. But all too often in television the only thing the audience gets as it switches from channel to channel is whatever same-old, same-old the programmers have decided will attract the most viewers without, well, without *straining* them too much.

The theory here is that if viewers have to think about what

they're watching they'll resent having to put out the effort and change the channel, because they've seated themselves in front of their TV sets to relax and unwind. To keep shows in the viewers' comfort zone the networks developed research departments that developed and implemented surveys and tests and held what later became known as "focus groups" to evaluate potential programming.

My first face-to-face encounter with a network research department came in the mid-seventies, when I was a young producer and executive story consultant of an NBC series called *Police Story*. To put it simply, *Police Story* was a good show. It won a pile of awards and got rave reviews, and I loved the damn series.

I loved it so much that I stayed at the studio as late as I could every single night and woke up as early as I could the following day so I could get back there and write and cast and approve sets and costumes and do all the things writer-producers do.

What I loved most about *Police Story* was that every story was true, based on events that had happened to real L.A. cops, with twists and turns and ups and downs no one could've made up. And instead of concentrating on the cases, we concentrated on the feelings the cases aroused in the policemen and women involved. Joe Wambaugh, then a bestselling novelist and active LAPD detective, was our technical advisor, and he came up with the best description for what the show tried to do. "The cop works on the case," he said, "and the case works on the cop."

Police Story was an anthology. It had no recurring characters. Since we didn't have to worry about continuity, we could have our characters grow and change within an episode. We could have downbeat endings where cops who were heroic on the job lost their wives and families because of the obsessions they took home with them. Endings where the heroes were killed, or where the pressures they were under caused them to quit, or even commit suicide.

Shortly after I signed on, NBC summoned us to a meeting with the research department to talk about "a new direction" for the series. Since *Police Story* had been on the air for a couple of seasons (during which I'd been one of its freelance writers), I was surprised that NBC was talking about changing it now.

The meeting was held in a conference room at NBC in Burbank.

The table we sat at was round but still managed to give the illusion of having sides. On one side sat the *Police Story* contingent, consisting of Cal Clements Jr., the story consultant, myself, and our boss, David Gerber.

At the time, David Gerber had three things going for him. He was executive producer of the show, president of the studio that made it (Columbia Pictures Television), and a genuine TV legend at the time—in much the same way that Dracula was a famous monster of filmland.

The Gerb was tough. He was big and beefy. He talked a million miles an hour, always at top volume, and ranted about anything that came to mind. His professional goal seemed to be to create a sort of "creative intimidation" in which people who worked for him did the very best they could in order to escape his wrath.

Gerber caused chaos on every creative level, forcing the ideals of his writers to crash head on into the often sordid cliches he demanded, the result being a hybrid of both that almost always was very moving to the audience, sometimes to the point of being overpowering.

On the other side of the table sat the NBC contingent: one lone, hardy soul, Richard Lindheim, the soft-spoken, white-bearded, Amish-looking vice president for research. Period. No backup. I felt kind of sorry for him. Until he cleared his voice and spoke.

"We've been audience testing your episodes and discussing upcoming premises with test groups. There's a problem. The audience finds *Police Story* disturbing." He passed over a pile of reports. "See where the graphs go up? Those are points in the shows where viewers had a big emotional reaction. That isn't a good sign."

"I thought we were supposed to get an emotional reaction," I said. "I thought that making people feel something was the sign of a good show."

Dick Lindheim handed over more paperwork. "If you look there you'll see that the reaction was a negative one. The audience pushed the 'No' button instead of the 'Yes.' They didn't like what they were feeling."

Dick showed us more test results and concluded with, "We think you're going to have to make a few slight changes in your presentation. Go for more upbeat endings, stay away from the kind of personal jeopardy that the audience identifies with too strongly, be more like our other successful shows—"

That was as far as Dick got. Beside me, Gerber had taken several deep breaths, as though inhaling ammunition. Now he let it all out with a roar that seemed to hurl Dick back from the table and pin him up against the wall. The poor guy never knew what hit him.

"What the fuck're you talking about!" Gerber yelled. He machine-gunned along. "We're a fucking hit! We give you the goddamn numbers you need on Thursday night! You can take your tests and shove 'em up NBC's ass! Those people don't watch television! They hang out on Sunset Boulevard looking for action while you're sitting in your elephant tower scribbling stupid notes and praying for a Ph.D.! Nobody's changing a fucking thing!"

Gerber got up so hard and so fast that his chair went crashing down behind him. He hurried to the door. All Cal Clements Jr. and I could do was follow.

The Gerb raved all the way down the elevator and out to the parking lot. Then, as we neared our cars, he whirled, glaring at me.

"You! Baby producer! Little genius! You fucking listen to what I say!" He pointed to his Gucci shirt, which in typical Gucci fashion was patterned with a dozen letter Gs. "See these goddamn Gs? They're silk and they stand for Gerber. Me. The Gerb. That's how goddamn important I am. And the goddamn important goddamn Gerb's on the line for you now! You give me good shows and get us into the Top Ten, or I'll personally drive you over to Universal and make you work on the crap NBC's got going there!"

And with that the Gerb turned again and yanked open his door. He pushed his way behind the wheel, slammed the door, and backed out of the space, tires squealing, barely missing both Cal and me.

In the TV business that's called being a mentor.

(2) By creating nationally broadcast networks of stations, the founding broadcasters were able to earn much more money than they would if they were merely local.

Yes, this too was mentioned before as a plus, and it too has also proven to be a minus. High earnings tend to cause companies to behave more conservatively and think in terms of protecting what they have instead of expanding, and the television networks have reacted the same way.

Research and testing and focus groups have become more important every year since 1941. The development of new programming has become the development of "product" instead. Literally, that's what it's referred to as: "product." And the minute anyone starts thinking about creative output as product instead of art, and developing it in terms of what consumers say they want instead of what creators are driven by their inner demons to communicate, well, then, you've got problems in River City, boy. And Rockefeller Plaza and Studio Center as well.

In the feature film business the desire to maximize profits, to keep building so that motion picture studios make more and more money each year, has led to the "blockbuster mentality" where it's considered more desirable to open a few films with hundred-million-dollar budgets and watch them make hundreds of millions of dollars more each year than it is to roll out inexpensive smaller films that might take longer than a few weeks to turn a small profit. The result has been that the business is dominated by films aimed at the teenaged audience, making them into self-proclaimed "thrill rides" that can be seen (ridden?) over and over again. Intimate films, films with adult themes, have become a distinct minority.

In television, something similar has occurred. In the name of maximizing profits not only has the "lowest common denominator"—as it's been referred to in article after article since the 1960s—prevailed, but network authority over every aspect of television production has become stronger and stronger.

In the forties, fifties, and sixties, the networks were actively involved as upper echelon administrators. As Herbert F. Solow, an early head of daytime programming at both NBC and CBS and vice president of television production for both Paramount and MGM, points out, "In the old days the networks bought programming from various production companies based on the perceived needs of their programming schedules. Each network developed certain guidelines, usually unwritten but still delineated clearly enough so that their suppliers pretty much knew what was acceptable to say and show. But how those guidelines were met was left up to the professional production people putting on the show."

By the time I became a producer in the seventies the idea of "leaving it up to the professionals" had had its day. My experience at that time was mostly with the primetime current programming executives at NBC. Every series on NBC had someone from "current," usually a fortyish Caucasian male, whose job it was to oversee each episode of the series from start to finish.

These execs had the power to approve or disapprove every premise, outline, and script, and every continuing star and guest star of every series. They also saw the dailies (footage shot and printed from the day before) for every episode of every series, and every cut of the episode after it had been put together. And no show was aired unless the current guy approved the final cut.

In the eighties their power broadened. To become supervising producer of *The Fall Guy* on ABC, I had to be approved by not only the current guy but also his boss, and his boss's boss. So did the story editors who worked with me. So did the individual directors who were brought in for each episode. And instead of merely approving or disapproving the premises and outlines and scripts and stars and guest stars, the current guy and his bosses were also suggesting premises, coming up with new twists and turns for the outlines and new dialogue for the scripts, and offering casting suggestions of their own, even for smaller parts. In the late eighties when I was supervising producer of *Mike Hammer* on CBS, the current guy and his bosses expanded their purview still further. Each individual writer for each episode had to be approved, and "acceptable" writers were often suggested to us. Our current guy even suggested himself! (And got the job because executive producer Jay Bernstein knew how to read the handwriting on the wall.)

By the nineties and into the next century network representatives from the current guy (they were still almost always guys, but now they were usually in their early thirties and occasionally African American or Hispanic or Asian) on up to the president of the network were micro-managing everything, picking producers, writers, and directors, casting even the smallest parts, and dictating story lines, revising dialogue, and supervising the film editing as well.

What qualifications did they—do they—have?

That's not the question. Qualifications matter when you view yourself as engaged in the creative process known as television production.

But when all you're doing is making "product" the question isn't one of qualification but of enablement. When your job is to maximize profits you look at it much differently than would someone who is putting on a show. You look at it in terms of the assembly line, and what you can do to speed that line up. The hell with the craftsman carving his wooden sculpture, get a mold made (via research) and if you don't like the way your workers are pouring in the resin, well, go ahead, dude, pour it in yourself.

Which brings us to another positive turned negative element in the network paradigm.

(3) By creating nationally broadcast networks of stations, the founding broadcasters made it possible to put tons of money back into programming.

In the words of Cyndi Lauper, "Money changes everything."

Making tons of money and needing to improve the balance sheet every year by making megatons more aren't the only reasons networks have become ever more controlling of their content. The fact that everything they're making costs an arm and a leg figures into it as well.

Look at it this way. The budget for one half-hour episode of *I Love Lucy* in 1951 was $25,000. The budget for one half-hour episode of *Frasier* in 2004 was *$5,000,000*. No matter how much you play with statistics and inflation adjustments, nothing can change the fact that five million bucks is one Acme Huge Mountain O'Money, and if you're the head of a network spending that much week after week you'd be the most irresponsible CEO since the last most irresponsible CEO if you didn't maintain an enormous amount of oversight over the situation.

Although many other ongoing series cost less than *Frasier*, there are some that cost even more. Primetime network shows these days pay out huge amounts in fees and salaries. Stars are paid $1,000,000 and more per episode. Producer-writer-creators who have achieved major player status in the TV industry can receive from $100,000 to $500,000 per episode for their efforts.

Everyday costs are sky-high as well. When you figure in a rerun or two the price of a script for one television episode is in the neighborhood of $50,000, whether the writer is an experienced professional or a newcomer. The fee a director gets for one episode is about the same. A staff writer or director or a producer who is paid $15,000 per week (the writer and director receive fees for writing and directing in addition to these salaries) are at the low end of the scale. Supporting actors on a series are often paid in the $50,000 to $100,000 per episode range. And we haven't even gotten to the office staff and members of the crew who physically and practically get a show done—men and women with the titles of production manager, assistant director, production assistant, director of photography, gaffer, grip, and a host of others.

And stages! Stages cost a small fortune to rent. In 1982 the cost of shooting on a soundstage at Twentieth Century-Fox Studios was in excess of $30,000 per day—and that was just for the bare floor and four walls. Twenty years later the price is, well, let's forget the number and substitute the letters u-n-c-o-n-s-c-i-o-n-a-b-l-e instead, a word that to my way of thinking only approaches being strong enough.

When you're spending this kind of bucks, you can't afford to take any chances. Tried and true talent. Tried and true concepts. Tried and true production techniques. These must be the order of the day. There's no better way to keep your product under control and protect your investment.

At least not on a ledger sheet.

And ledger sheets are what networks are all about.

Which is as it has to be. They don't call it "show *business*" without a reason.

Even the lowest paid writer-producer knows when to cut to the chase, especially when there's a current guy (or a good editor) to help him. So here's what I'm getting at:

The major turning point in television in 1941, the network paradigm, like so many other things in this world, both giveth and taketh away.

Its great strength is its ability to bring massive quantities of slick, polished, professional entertainment to viewers not only in the United States but all over the world.

Its great weakness is its creative conservatism, its desire for a uniform, all-encompassing appeal.

We've lived with network-think for sixty-plus years. We can keep living with it. Or, as we become more aware of other turning points, past, present, and future, we can embrace new alternatives and become part of the engine that will propel the television world, the media world, the creative world, into its next phase.

"Puppet Playhouse" Airs Its First Episode and Howdy Doody Is Born

*C*hicago. A blustery December day in 1948. One year to the month after the television debut of a People-and-Puppet Show that was renamed *The Howdy Doody Show* after its first week on the air, a four-year-old boy sat on the floor of his living room, looked up at the tiny (but oh, it seemed sooo *big*) screen of his family's TV set, and watched Clarabell the Clown sneak up on Bob Smith (who hadn't yet become the legendary "Buffalo Bob") and get ready to blast him—and anything or anyone else within range—with seltzer water.

Also watching the action, but from his vantage point on the puppet stage that was part of the set, was the marionette star of the show, Howdy Doody himself. Howdy's mouth opened. He was about to shout a warning. But Clarabell put his finger to his lips and shook his head pleadingly, his entire demeanor wordlessly saying, "No, please, let me do it, just this once. . . ."

It was Big Decision Time for Howdy, but he never had to commit. Because from the "Peanut Gallery" of kids from toddlers through pre-teens who comprised a live audience that was also part of the show, shouts went up. "Look out!" "Duck!" "Oh no!" and Bob Smith whirled and saw what was about to happen and did look out and duck—just in time for the spray to shoot out over his head and almost hit Howdy!

The Peanut Gallery went wild, and on the floor of that Chicago living room the four-year-old looked up at the ceiling and prayed. "Please, God, don't make me get older than four. Because when I'm

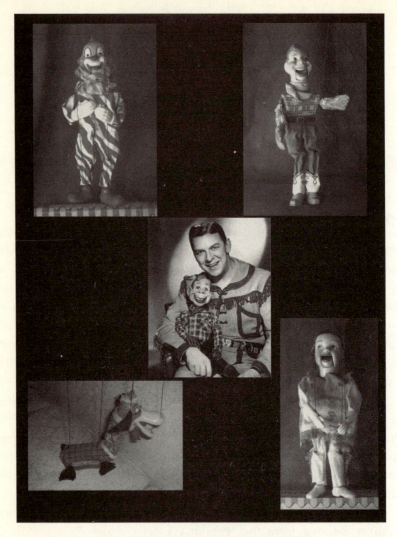

Howdy Doody and merchandise, circa 1947
(Cloud Creek Institute for the Arts)

older I won't like *Howdy Doody* anymore. And I love him so much
I don't ever want to lose him!"

That's how much this seminal television children's show meant
to that four-year-old boy.

That's how much it meant to *me*.

But although *The Howdy Doody Show* had a huge effect on its viewers, it had an even bigger effect on television, an effect that's still reverberating through the medium—and our culture as a whole.

The Howdy Doody Show was one of those legendary rarities, an instant success. Starting as a one-hour show on Saturday mornings, it soon became a half-hour show on every weekday afternoon from 5:30 to 6:00 Eastern time. This made it the first television show ever "stripped," as this kind of programming is called in TV land, by NBC, and it couldn't have found a better time slot.

Children had the perfect activity to engage in while waiting for dinner. What could be better for any kid than watching—no, hanging out with, because that's what it felt like—a bunch of crazy folks like Howdy, Mr. Bluster, Dillydally, Flub-a-Dub, Princess Summerfallwinterspring, and the rest of what became known as the "Doodyville Gang"?

And moms had the perfect babysitter so they could get that dinner made. What could be better for any dedicated homemaker (we're talking late forties and fifties here, don't forget, when being a housewife was an honored profession, with no mockery or irony along for the ride) than to bear down on your pot roast knowing her child was safe, sound, and delighted—and quiet!—in the living room while she worked?

An argument might even be made that Howdy, who was created, voiced, and owned by Buffalo Bob, was the lynchpin in a sociological turning point: the much-mocked and even more abused grand tradition of parking your kids in front of the TV set so you can get a few moments' respite from the responsibilities of parenthood.

Other societal effects of the popularity of the show are easier to pinpoint. *The Howdy Doody Show* proved that television commercials worked, with the sales of its best-known sponsor, Bosco (a chocolate syrup to be added to the kids' milk), skyrocketing. Especially direct, personal commercials, integrated into the show and featuring its puppet star.

The FCC later banned this practice on children's shows,

acknowledging that four-year-olds like Little Chicago Brody were defenseless prey. However, *The Howdy Doody Show* also proved that prey or not, we, the youthful Baby Boomers, had more than our share of marketing muscle. Looking back at my beloved show I see it as the beginning of what became a regular Baby Boomer practice—the manipulation of our loving parents into buying whatever we wanted.

The kid clout of the time was so obvious that in the early days of *Mad*, before it became a magazine and was still a comic book, the group the masthead called "the usual gang of idiots" ran a parody called *Howdy DoIt*, featuring a commercial where the camera moved in ultra close on Howdy's freckled, All-American face as he exhorted his viewers to scream and shout and hold their breaths and make their parents "BUY!!!"

Modern merchandising, the morphing of TV shows into products, began with the Doodyville Gang as well. There were Howdy Doody coloring books and Howdy Doody dolls and clocks and drinking glasses and mugs. My personal favorites were the inexpensive little marionettes based on the puppet characters. My collection today, inconveniently stored at the bottom of a pile of boxes in a shed on my property, consists of Howdy, Clarabell, Dilly Dally, Flub-a-Dub, and Princess Summerfallwinterspring. Are these pristine, in-the-box collectors' specials? Hell, no. They're used. Played with. Faded. And beautiful nevertheless. (I still long for an affordable version of Mr. Bluster!)

There were even 78 rpm *Howdy Doody Show* record albums, presenting full-length adventures from the show. The highlight of my sixth year of life was going to a *Howdy Doody* stage show at a local movie theater, where Buffalo Bob, et al. (the real deal, not imposters), spun their web of enchantment over 700 wide-eyed, wider-mouthed kids who knew, really knew, that their lives could never get any better.

The child audience and its potential buying power was immediately recognized as possibly the most important advertising discovery since pyramided newspaper ads. More and more children's shows were developed over the next few years and are being developed still, creating and expanding a genre that has become not merely a staple, but a major portion of all television programming.

The Howdy Doody Show begat *Romper Room* in 1954 and *Captain Kangaroo* (whose creator and star, Bob Keeshan, was the original Clarabell the Clown) in 1955. Other early (in terms of television history) high-profile kids' shows included *The Mickey Mouse Club, Disneyland* (later *Walt Disney's Wonderful World of Disney*), even the incomparable and still very much alive and kicking classic, *Sesame Street,* as well as shows starring the likes of Pinky Lee, Soupy Sales, and folks with monikers like Uncle Johnny Coons and Sheriff John. Bozo the Clown found a home on television and became the obvious inspiration for everyone's pal, Ronald McDonald.

But from my current vantage point, the most important development in children's programming was the creation of various "children's blocks," half-hour after half-hour upon half-hour of series designed to zero in on and take advantage of kid clout.

The earliest children's blocks were local. In the late forties in Chicago *The Hopalong Cassidy Show* would start the ball rolling on Saturday mornings, followed by old Western movies featuring Buster Crabbe, Ken Maynard, Hoot Gibson, Harry Carey, and Bob Steele, with Tom Mix, Tim McCoy, and other pioneers who spanned silent films and early talkies thrown in.

Sunday mornings would be more "high tech," featuring old episodes of various serials made by Republic Pictures and originally shown during Saturday matinees at the same local theater where I'd gone to see Howdy. The most dynamic of these serials, the ones we world-wise first graders would talk about at school on Mondays, were the Flash Gordon and Buck Rogers films. Since they also starred Buster Crabbe, he became my numero uno role model.

By the early fifties Sunday afternoons had become my generation's version of primetime. Sure, there were a few kids' shows on the networks on Saturday afternoons, most notably *Smilin' Ed McConnell and his Buster Brown Gang,* but there was something weird and off-putting about its featured player, a giant squeaky toy frog named Froggy the Gremlin whose greeting, "Hiya, kids, hiya, hiya," in a cigarette-dosed, whiskey-soaked voice struck terror into my heart. But Sunday was where the action was, with *The Adventures of Kit Carson* and *Wild Bill Hickok* airing back to back.

Hopalong Cassidy, The Adventures of Kit Carson, and *Wild Bill Hickok* were a small step forward for your local merchant and a giant leap forward for the concept of merchandising. Hoppy had a full clothing line, with shirts, sweaters, pants, belts, hats, holsters, and guns, all of which were strewn around the bedroom I shared with my toddler sister.

I didn't like the white-haired man in black all that much. He seemed old and ran with a posse, which went against my loner nature, but my mother was absolutely sure I'd love all this stuff and nothing could keep her from getting me more. Somehow I was the prime mover in Mom's personal shopping equation. More kid clout, however misunderstood.

Wild Bill Hickok and Kit Carson took another direction that is still very much in practice. Pictures of Wild Bill and his sidekick Jingles adorned boxes of Kellogg's cereal and Bill Williams, who played Kit, hawked Coca-Cola.

Today, of course, every children's show on television has its own branded merchandise and licensing tie-ins with previously existing products. But this was the beginning. And Kid Brody, continuing to pray that he wouldn't get older, was there for the next big step.

This was the creation of the block that became known as Saturday morning cartoons. Saturday morning cartoons started appearing on the then three major networks, NBC, CBS, and ABC, in the late sixties, when I was beginning my career as a primetime writer, and over the decades new networks and cable channels including Fox Kids Network, the Kids WB, and Nickelodeon joined in until the end of the Saturday morning cartoon age in the early 2000s.

From 9 a.m. to 11 a.m. or noon a variety of half-hour animated programming battled for top position in the field of kid clout. Baby boomers were the parents when Saturday morning cartoons began, and baby boomers' children were doing the child raising (and television parking of their children) when it ended. The variety of programming was unsurpassed. For the most part the cartoons were based on existing properties—animated characters imported from films, from comic books, and based on toy lines—and many of the characters appeared in several different variations—and at several different ages.

Following is a partial listing of those I actually watched, either with friends' children or my own. It's in no particular order other than that of my memory, which probably means that those making the biggest impression on me as a viewer, writer, or parent are first. (That whole inverted pyramid way of writing they used to teach in college just doesn't work when you're dealing with something as personal as the satisfaction engendered by arrested development.)

So here we are with *Bugs Bunny and Friends, Muppet Babies, Animaniacs, Casper the Friendly Ghost, Spider-Man, The Hulk, Super Friends, Justice League, Batman, Earthworm Jim, The Tick, Hong Kong Phooey, Jonny Quest, Scooby Doo, The New Scooby Doo, Shazam!, Speed Buggy, Superman, Teenage Mutant Ninja Turtles, X-Men, He-Man and the Masters of the Universe*, and on and on.

I also worked on some of these shows as a writer, and that's when I saw how much further the merchandising had progressed.

The stakes were so high that on my shows, at least, the tail was wagging the dog. That is, even though we were supposed to be creating entertainment for millions of child viewers—a max of about 20 million viewers a pop in the seventies when I wrote for *Star Trek: The Animated Series* and a minimum of about one million viewers an episode at the turn of the 2000s, as reported to me by my friends who are still involved—our television efforts were considered second in importance to the toys, clothes, and dolls.

I first got the word on this from *Spider-Man* executive producer Avi Arad in the mid-nineties. I'd been hired to write the first of what turned out to be several episodes, and was meeting with Avi, comics legend Stan Lee, who was also an executive producer, and other members of the staff. I was fairly familiar with the comic book—my first published work was a letter to the editor in an early issue of *The Amazing Spider-Man*—but when Avi started talking about the "Spider-Mobile" I was thrown.

"What Spider-Mobile?" I said.

"The one he drives in the comics," Avi said.

"Spidey swings from rooftop to rooftop in the comics," I said. "He doesn't drive around."

"He does now," Avi said. "I had them write it in."

"I thought the series was following the comic, not leading it," I said.

"Oh it is," Avi said. "But they're both following ToyBiz, the toy company."

"Which," Stan Lee added, "Avi owns."

"Before you begin work on this series," Avi went on, "you have to understand the ground rules. This isn't entertainment, it's an infomercial. We create toys and then we write episodes showing how the kids can use the toys. And since the toys are action toys, this show is an action show."

"But Spidey's always been a more sensitive, introverted kind of hero."

"And he still is." Avi smiled. "As long as he moves around fast enough to show off the toys."

A year later, I was co-creator (with Stan Lee) and writer of all the episodes of a television version of his even more sensitive and introverted hero, the Silver Surfer. At this point not only was Avi an executive producer of the series and CEO of the toy company selling all the Silver Surfer goodies, he was also working on a buy-out of the entire Marvel Comics publishing entity.

At our first meeting to plan the new series Avi's assistant passed out a pile of character and toy designs, and a list of potential episodes that could incorporate them. Avi held up each drawing, speaking only to me although there were about a dozen people in the room. "Larry," he said, "this is the creative challenge of your lifetime."

Avi tapped the bottom edges of the designs on the conference table. "Action figures that are variations of the hero are always the best-selling toys. If you can find a way to introduce the Red Silver Surfer, the Blue Silver Surfer, and the Gold Silver Surfer into the storyline, and also give us this beautiful Silver Surfer Space Station, I'll know you're a genius."

He tossed the pictures aside and sat back. "And if you can't, well, maybe I'll run into you on the street or at a ballgame sometime."

I shoehorned the space station into a couple of episodes but never could figure out what to do with the Red, Blue, and Gold Silver Surfers. The series was canceled after twelve episodes ("The ratings are fine," Sidney Iwanter, then vice president of programming for the Fox Kids Network that carried the show, told me, "But Marvel's in bankruptcy and can't pay its percentage of the production costs anymore." Avi's toy company, Iwanter informed me a couple of years later, also went out of business.)

Since that time the Saturday morning cartoon block has been replaced by cable channels entirely devoted to children's programming, with Nickelodeon, the Cartoon Network, and several variations of the Disney Channel leading the pack. All three companies offer live-action children's programming as well as animation, and most of the shows are original concepts instead of adaptations of previously existing material. All the programming is directed unrelievedly at children, counting on the kids' ability to "scream and shout and hold their breaths and make their parents *buy*!!!" to make buying spots on these shows worth the advertisers' while.

Although most of the shows on Nick, Cartoon Network, and the Disney channels have inspired lines of merchandise the merchandise seems truly to stem from the shows instead of vice versa. Could the financial problems that beset Marvel and ToyBiz have taught the executives and programmers a lesson? It's hard to say. Avi Arad's takeover of Marvel did finally go through, and it emerged from bankruptcy to scale new heights—although those heights weren't in television or comic books but in the world of feature films.

Business is one thing, but cultural events stemming from the success of *The Howdy Doody Show* and its successors may be even more important. The cultural significance of singling out the baby boom generation and its children and grandchildren as consumers to be targeted and courted cannot be overestimated. As far as I can tell my generation was the first in this country—possibly the first anywhere—to be raised with an awareness that the fulfillment of its every desire was the avowed purpose of the wealthiest and most powerful people and corporations on the planet.

It was also the first—but not the last, not yet—to have its every desire suggested to it (some might say "dictated") by the tube. At four years old I was already going through life counting on the fact that my parents wanted more than anything else to please me. As I saw it, their struggle to move up the professional, social, and financial ladder wasn't so they could lead better lives but so my sister and I could have the water bazooka with He-Man's picture on it, the lunchbox bearing the likenesses of Roy Rogers and Trigger, or—let's face it—*any other damn thing we wanted!*

Spoiled? You bet. But in an environment of spoiled children, who of us would notice? And who of those noticing would want to screw things up for themselves by agitating for change?

Before my parents or their parents or my parents' parents' generation could have a say about what they wanted out of life and the power to demand and obtain it, those people had to grow up. But as I look back on my childhood it seems to me that the main lesson I learned was that I could have it all just by asking. My generation and those that have followed have learned the power of apparent entitlement. And all we've got to do to remain entitled is to remain children so we can exercise our kid clout forever.

Now if you'll excuse me, I've got to dig through my storage shed and find those marionettes from *The Howdy Doody Show*. Time to make Flub-a-Dub fly!

"Texaco Star Theater"
Hits the Airwaves and Milton Berle
Conquers the World

*A*s this is written the only remnants of the once-powerful television variety show are *Saturday Night Live*, reruns of *The Carol Burnett Show* on cable, and clips from *The Sonny and Cher Comedy Hour, The Donny and Marie Show, The Glen Campbell Goodtime Hour*, and other seventies exercises in a music-dominated version of the genre shown on various celebrity biography series that have proliferated in our TV sets like field mice hiding from a country winter's cold.

Once upon a time, though, primetime television programming was divided more or less equally between dramatic series (most of which were and are really "action" shows, but no one in television has ever gotten rich worrying about semantics), sitcoms, and what programmers liked to call "variety hours."

And once upon an earlier time variety shows ruled.

They bestrode early television like so many tricked-out Collassi of Rhodes.

All because of Uncle Miltie.

Mr. Saturday Night.

Howdy Doody sold tons of Bosco in the course of his career, but Milton Berle sold flatcar-loads of TV sets.

His popularity made advertisers and pundits, reporters and social critics stand up and take notice. *Television is real. Television is here to stay.*

Classic Milton Berle, circa 1949 (Jerry Ohlinger's Movie Material)

Yes, Virginia, back in the early days of TV, Luddites and naysayers abounded. They said television was a fad people would soon tire of. They said the audience would return to its "proper" sources of entertainment—radio and, of course, theatrical films.

Milton Berle, whose televised behavior often looked more chimp-like than human, made monkeys out of them all.

Texaco Star Theater starring Milton Berle moved from CBS radio to NBC television in June of 1948 (about six months after the debut of *The Howdy Doody Show* but before I saw *Howdy* for the first time). I was introduced to *Texaco Star Theater* in the fall of '48, at the home of my Aunt Dorothy and Uncle George—at the same time I was introduced to television itself. Aunt Dorothy and Uncle George have never struck me as the pioneering type, but they were the first people I knew who had a TV set and my first television viewing experience was in their living room after a family dinner.

My cousin Janie and I were either playing together or fighting with each other. (It's difficult to remember which because our families were very close and we spent so much time together that the two activities were interchangeable.) Suddenly Aunt Dorothy's voice broke through our noise. "Oh, my God! It's seven o'clock. Somebody turn on the TV!"

Uncle George took up the cry. "Hurry! Turn it on! Turn it on!"

Janie's sister Ila, who was several years older than we were and closing in on adolescence, joined in. "What're you waiting for, Larry? Turn the television on!"

I didn't know what she was talking about, but Janie did. "I'll do it!" She shoved me aside and ran to a big box up against the wall behind me. I hadn't noticed it before, but now I realized, *This thing is big*.

I was thinking about the TV set, which was a looming presence in spite of its small screen. I didn't know how big what we were going to see was, and of course I had no idea of how big the whole television medium would become.

At one end of the room someone switched off the overhead light. At the other end Janie turned one of the thick dials below the screen with a *ka-chung* and slowly but surely the TV screen rezzed to life, its darkness replaced by the illuminated man who created what two generations later was called "Must See TV."

How can I describe this iconic presence?

How about this:

A hulking troglodyte in a long blonde wig, his face heavily rouged, his lips darkened and made enormous by thick lipstick, his body covered from chest to foot by a ruffled evening gown whose design emphasized padded breasts that strove to create an illusion only a starving baby hippo could love.

That was Uncle Miltie in drag. Traipsing around and smacking people. Being smacked and tripping and falling and bouncing back onto his feet—just in time to catch a pie with his monstrous parody of a woman's face while the studio audience howled.

If Howdy Doody was to become my childhood savior, then Milton Berle for me was the Anti-Christ. The terror I felt later at the sight of Froggy the Gremlin was a pale shadow of the sheer horror struck into me by my first look at television's first major star.

But all around me my family was laughing. My mother, my father, Aunt Dorothy, Uncle George, Cousin Janie, and Cousin Ila were having even more fun than the folks in New York City who were at that very moment, *live*, falling out of their tiered seats.

I'd never seen anything like it. A grown man acting dumber than any dumb kid, doing things that, if I had done them, more than likely would've resulted not in gales of laughter but in a spanking. Even though I was grossed out I was fascinated. There was something truly enchanting about the experience. Every mind in my vicinity was captured in a way I'd never seen before. Everyone I loved most was being sucked into the *Texaco Star Theater* world, along with a whole crowd of strangers.

What power!

What excruciating delight!

For the first time in my short but alienated life I saw a way to belong. I didn't have to be alone. All I had to do was let go of my fear and let myself become part of the Milton Berle Overmind and I'd be one of the family, finding comfort and hilarity as a member in good standing of the greater whole.

I admit it. I succumbed. Not even in kindergarten yet, and I was already selling out. I sat down between my parents and giggled and chortled and barked.

Two weeks later the Brody family had a TV set of its own.

Literally millions of people across the country were introduced to television this same way and bought sets of their own so they could introduce others. Apocrypha based on Uncle Miltie's popularity abounded. No, it was more than mere "popularity." It was total *dominance*.

Restaurants in cities across the U.S. closed Saturday nights because no one was going out to dinner. Instead they were staying home to watch you know who.

High schools switched basketball games from Saturday night to Friday night for the same reason. No one wanted to leave the house.

Movie theaters came up with outrageous giveaways to try to lure film fans in after five or six in the afternoon on Saturdays. And failed.

Saturday night bridge parties were either cancelled or held with the TV set on. Businesses that had been open Saturday nights to gain an edge over the competition gave up the attempt. Even crime, it was rumored, went way down.

Bottom line: For three hours every Saturday (an hour before the show to settle in, the hour of being caught in the spell of the show, and an hour afterward to unwind) America stood still.

And it didn't end there.

On Sundays friends talked to each other about Uncle Miltie's antics the night before, sharing their impressions and feelings about what they liked most. These conversations were held before church. After church. In church.

On Mondays co-workers went at it, reminiscing and acting out their own versions of the skits in which Uncle Miltie, ever the victim, performed pratfall after pratfall for our sins.

On Tuesdays everyone was still feeling the reverberations of the latest show, and making plans to watch together the coming Saturday night so that those poor unfortunates who didn't yet have TV sets wouldn't be deprived.

To be sure, variety shows weren't new. The basic format of stand-up comedy, skits, songs, dances, and more comedy and skits (and songs and dances) was as old as the English music hall and a staple of American vaudeville and even radio. But never had this kind of entertainment—or any other, succeeded on such a large scale.

So, yes, we can truthfully say that *Texaco Star Theater* (which itself lasted only six years, from 1948 to 1953, though Berle did go on for a while after) is the proud progenitor of television shows ranging from *Your Show of Shows, The Ed Sullivan Show, The Jackie Gleason Show*, and *The Steve Allen Show*, through *The Dinah Shore Chevy Show, The Perry Como Show, The Smothers Brothers Comedy Hour, Rowan and Martin's Laugh-In, The Dean Martin Show* and the other shows already mentioned here, to *The Flip Wilson Show, The Mike Douglas Show, The Merv Griffin Show*, and other shows that should have been mentioned.

But—

What's more significant is that *Texaco Star Theater* caused a social revolution. The magic of the Uncle Miltie mindmeld extended the power of the television medium from purely economic to outrageously cultural. Watching the same show at the same time and then discussing it the next day became a way of life in this country.

Over the decades the variety show lost its luster, the presence and influence of the genre diminishing considerably after the seventies, but the behavior pattern merely shifted its focus and grew stronger.

Instead of laughing together about what had happened to Jackie Gleason's Poor Soul character or Sid Caesar's Progress Hornsby over the weekend, or the weirdness inflicted on her children by Mama on *The Carol Burnett Show* last night, viewers lost themselves in the unreal lives of the lawyers on *The Defenders*, the astronauts on *I Dream of Jeannie*, and the determined fugitive on *The Fugitive*.

As college curriculums went spinning into a constant state of flux based on shifting educational standards (or was it simply kid clout rearing its "entitled" head in a newer realm?), many of the benchmarks of Western culture lost their significance—because how can something be a benchmark, a standard, if no one knows about it anymore?

Was this "the big one," as Fred Sanford on *Sanford and Son* would have said? The decline and fall? The end of civilization as we know it?

To quote *Star Trek's* Mr. Spock, "Negative, Captain."

Philosophy got you down, bunky? Literature wilting? Painting and sculpture dying uneaten on the vine? Classics of all kinds lying fallow?

In the oft-repeated words of Dorothy on *The Golden Girls*, "Not to worry." Television was ready. Like Fonzie on *Happy Days*, the medium stopped hanging out in the garage and took the dominant place at the country's dining room table.

Generations that no longer read Aristotle or Plato or Spenser or Milton or Wordsworth or Keats or Carlyle or Tennyson or Thoreau or Emerson or Eliot or Frost or Fitzgerald or Hemingway, who had never seen a canvas by Michelangelo or Da Vinci or Rembrandt or Van Gogh or Monet or Matisse or Chagall were still able to share a common vision, a worldview based on a mutual understanding of the personalities and adventures of:

Ozzie Nelson, the Beaver, Lucy Ricardo, Sergeant Friday, Samantha Stevens, James Kirk, Barnaby Jones, Marcia Brady, Andy Taylor, Rob Petrie, Gilligan, Herman Munster, McGarrett, Mannix, Archie Bunker, Baretta, Mary Richards, Richard Kimble, Keith Partridge, Jean-Luc Picard, Seinfeld, Sam Malone, Frasier, Rachel Green, Chandler Bing . . .

And on . . .

And on.

Hundreds, no, *thousands* of characters functioning as glue to keep us together. To serve as reference points for our lives. As objects of comparison in observation and conversation and social interaction of all kinds.

The return of the benchmark.

As the variety show once ruled television, so television's latest rulers, the sitcoms and dramas (*action* shows, dammit, Jim!) began ruling—

Real life.

(What's that you say? You're suggesting that maybe—just maybe—television didn't just step in to fill the culture vacuum but *created* the vacuum first?

(Could be . . .

(But you never got that from me.)

The television audience has always shared the values portrayed on successful television shows, otherwise they wouldn't be successful. As time moved on, the sharing became mutual in the sense that real world attitudes and behaviors created the attitudes and behaviors of the characters inhabiting television's fictional world, and in turn the fictional portrayal of these attitudes and behaviors started reshaping the real deal.

For years what Glen A. Larson, one of the most successful writer-producer-creators in television history (over thirty series and still counting) called "real reality" has been interacting with "television reality," like two recombinant strands of cultural DNA.

Each influences the other.

Each imitates the other.

Old Culture:

In Greece during the third century B.C., human beings struggle to lead lives that are rich and fulfilling.

To the watchful Aristotle, those who are most successful at it seem to be those whose lives are guided by a principle of moderation. So in his writing Aristotle defines and glorifies this principle.

Afterward, the Greeks honor this approach by veering from their original path and questing toward the achievement of the "golden mean."

Television Culture:

In the United States during the nineteen seventies, a great social upheaval alters the lives of urban middle-class youth. The sexual revolution, peer acceptance of casual recreational drug use, and a rise in the rate of street crime that may or may not be linked to the behavior of young people become leading news of the day.

The watchful television industry sees a chance to increase its audience by creating what it designates "relevant programming." This programming consists of cop shows, lawyer shows, and medical shows featuring urban middle-class youths who often are sexually open, drug-using perps or victims of street crime.

For one of those shows, CBS's *Hawaii Five-0*, Larry Brody, grown up and no longer afraid of Milton Berle, writes an episode about a troubled teenage couple who kidnap an infant between bouts of sexual activity (or what passed for it on TV at the time) and drug use. A few days after the episode airs, an infant is kidnapped exactly the way the fictional infant was. A week later, the baby is found unharmed and a teenage couple is arrested. During questioning, the young man and young woman claim that they're not responsible for what they did. They got the idea, they say, from—that's right—*Hawaii Five-0*.

In the heart of this definitive interaction between real reality and television reality, am I thinking about the cultural significance of it all?

Hell no.

I'm not thinking about anything. I'm feeling.

Like shit.

Ah, but let's move forward a decade. The year is 1980, and I'm standing in the lobby of the Mark Hopkins Hotel in San Francisco on a cloud-enshrouded Saturday night, having a little not-so-friendly discussion with the manager because I've come to the city on a whim only to find that there are no rooms at the inn. *Any* inn, including this one, where I've stayed a million times before.

I feel foolish as hell, so I hide it with anger and a voice loud enough to be heard across the Bay. Having grown from a Chicago kind of kid to a Hollywood kinda guy, I'm screaming my credits at the manager in the firm belief that they'll cause him to cough up a place I can stay.

It doesn't work, of course, but my recitation of what people used to call "ego-boo" attracts the attention of the clerk at the magazine stand off the lobby. The clerk, who's in his mid-twenties and taller than I am, still manages to look up at me in awe.

"I heard you talking to the manager," he says.

I say, "Uh-huh."

"Did you really write *Baretta*?"

"I was the second writer to work on the show," I say as though that means anything. (Aunt Dorothy and Uncle George were impressed, so, hell, why not lay it on this guy?)

"*Baretta* saved my life," the clerk says.

"*Baretta*?" I say. "Robert Blake?"

He says, "Who's Robert Blake? Baretta's my guy."

"What do you mean?"

The clerk looks around to make sure the manager has moved far enough away so that he won't be able to hear. Then he leans forward confidentially.

"When I was sixteen I ran away from home," the clerk says, "and went to the Tenderloin. Did a lot of drugs. Lost it completely. One day I come down from my room in this flophouse hotel and I see this guy on the television in the lobby. His name's Baretta and he's a detective but he talks like a junkie. He's grabbing some guy and pounding the crap out of him and telling him he's got to straighten out and get off the drugs. He tells the guy he's supposed to take him to jail but he doesn't want to because he loves him so he's giving him one more chance. Then he lets the guy go and the guy runs away.

"A week later I'm coming downstairs again, wasted, and I see Baretta on TV with another guy, screaming at him to kick the habit, and then going back to the station house and throwing his badge down on his boss's desk because he'd rather quit than have to take the guy in. And I think, 'Wow, Baretta really does love this guy. He loves him enough to put his own ass on the line.'

"And I think, 'Wow, I'm just like that guy. Baretta loves me.'"

The clerk straightens up and looks me in the eye with pride. "I figure that if Baretta loves me that much, then I can't let him down. I've gotta get straight. It was hell, but every time I wanted to give up and go back to the dope I thought about Baretta and how it'd kill him to see me get all fucked up again. So I stayed with it and I've been straight for five years and I'm the night manager of the News Nook over there."

Now the clerk reaches into his pocket and pulls out a set of keys. He presses them into my hand. "I'm working 'til eight tomorrow morning," he said. "Nobody's at my place so you won't be bothered if you stay there. Can't do anything less for a friend of Baretta."

He writes his address down on a little slip of paper, puts it into my hand with the key. "It's a nice little place on Haight Street. If you leave before I get home just put the key under the mat outside the door."

I don't know what to say. Finally: "Sure you want to do this?" I say.

"Gotta do it," says the clerk. "Did I tell you how Baretta saved my life?"

Almost sixty years ago *Texaco Star Theater* changed television. Through the years since then its legacy has changed the very fabric of American life.

Twenty-five years ago that legacy worked a new kind of enchantment on me.

Television ain't Aristotle, but for me miracles beat philosophy any day of the week.

Especially Saturday night.

CHAPTER 4: July 23, 1950

"The Gene Autry Show"
Brings New Made-for-TV Action
to Kids of All Ages

*H*oppy and Ken Maynard and the rest of the Western movie gang may have beaten him to the television screen, but once Gene Autry arrived it was no contest. Roy Rogers may have billed himself King of the Cowboys, but Clean Gene was the real deal. He was the most popular by far.

As he deserved to be.

Because when he made his foray into the field, Gene Autry did it in a way every American has been raised to respect. He entered the medium of television not as an employee, fattening himself up with a weekly paycheck written by studio moguls or television executives, but as an entrepreneur.

That's right. He broke the unwritten (although it may well have been set down somewhere by now) First Rule of Show Business: Thou shalt not use thine own money.

Gene took on the responsibility—and the risk—of paying for his show himself. And took on more risk by setting up his own distribution outlet to boot.

Melody Ranch, later renamed *The Gene Autry Show* when his riding and fighting and roping and shooting proved more popular than his singing, was profitably syndicated all around the country, and those profits went straight to Gene. Not even his expanding waistline (by the end of the show's five-year run Gene wore his cowboy outfit like a too-tight second skin ready to burst at the seams

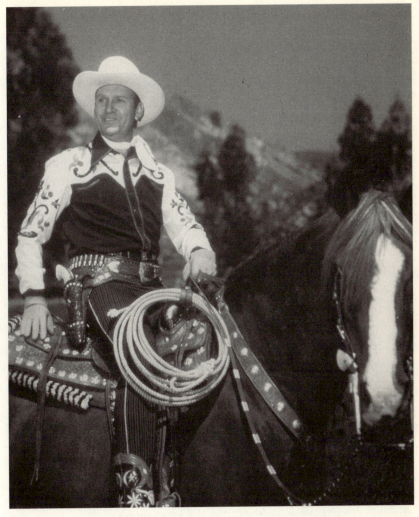

Gene Autry and Champion, circa 1949 (Still Things)

in all the wrong places) could keep up with his ever-enlarging money belt.

Making this success story all the more impressive is the fact that as a producer, Gene took another big financial risk as well. Storywise, he stuck to one basic variation of the tried and true B Western format, which went something like this:

Good Rancher is out doing good rancher thing.

Good Rancher sees trouble.

Good Rancher stops the trouble and rescues the victim.

Good Rancher learns that this is just a drop in the bucket of the big trouble being planned by a nameless bad guy.

Good Rancher figures out who the bad guy is and shows up just in time to stop the big trouble and nail the bad guy, saving any and all vics who may happen to be around.

Technically, however, *The Gene Autry Show* was much more adventurous. Under Genial Gene's supervision a major innovation leapt into television production like Gene's beloved horse Champion jumping over the treacherous boulders on location at Vasquez Rocks. And it put him in just as good a position with the television business as being atop the rocks put him with the bad guys—

In command.

Because Gene Autry, like any good businessman, saw a need. And filled that need.

And his series became the first show anywhere to be shot on film specially optimized for TV.

Before July 30, 1950, every show on television was either shown live or via kinescope (a grainy, sort-of-filmlike process in which a live performance was recorded as it was broadcast so that it could be re-shown, usually within another hour or two in another time zone), or on the same kind of film stock Kodak had created for motion picture theater screens.

What Gene did made a difference. Not only to film and television professionals and aficionados and early fifties tech geeks, but to the one who really counted—the average viewer.

The elementary school kid who had seen just about every cowboy do just about everything.

That's right. I'm talking about guys like me.

I saw Milton Berle for the first time at Aunt Dorothy and Uncle George's apartment. I saw my first episode of *The Gene Autry Show* at the apartment of another aunt and uncle, Uncle Morrie and Aunt Anne. It was 1951, and their four sons ranged in age from about fifteen years old down to, I think, four.

My cousins were wild boys. Active boys. Boys on the run. They were with-it boys who knew what was what, and on the afternoon after my grandmother and theirs was buried I was sent home with them so my father and my mother and my father's sisters, and the rest of that side of the family could go to the oldest sister's house and grieve.

My cousins, known as "The Smileys" because that was their last name, ran me through their bedrooms and their living room and into the street. We played baseball while dodging traffic and vied to see who could climb over the front hedge and up the wall to their third floor unit first. (I barely got two feet off the ground. The oldest Smiley—also named Larry—won. He'd been climbing in and out of his bedroom window for years so he could smoke without getting caught. He also had a skinny little mustache, an act of pure teenage defiance in this, the Truman era.)

Only after we were totally exhausted, and equally tired of watching our heaving bellies distend and return as we panted and sucked for air, did we call it a day and trudge inside. Allan, the Smiley who was nearest to me in age, turned on the TV set, and after the usual warm-up wait and a couple of cartoony singing commercials, the opening titles of what was at the time still called *Melody Ranch* hit the screen.

"This show is great," Allan said. "They hardly ever stop moving for anything."

He was right. It started with a chase. A little later there was a fight. Then another chase. Then a shoot-out. And then a last shoot-out *and* chase followed by Gene singing—but still moving because he was riding his horse ("The horse's name is Champion," the second youngest Smiley, Bobby, sighed) across the ranch with sidekick Pat Buttram and "good pal" Gail Russell riding at his side.

The show was half an hour long, and during that half hour the wild boys stayed motionless on the floor, paying their returning energy no heed. None of them even spoke except Bobby, who was about six, and the only words he uttered were, "Look at that. . . . Look at that. . . ."

But he uttered them non-stop.

And was echoed, every time, by the youngest Smiley wild boy, "Little Gary." "Look a'dat. . . . Look a'dat. . . ."

The show was worth looking at. This was the first time in my life as a television viewer that I paid as much attention to the *image* on the screen as I did to the story—okay, the action—and the words. (In fact, until I became a television producer responsible for how a show looked, the only time I ever watched a TV screen as closely as I did on the day my grandmother was buried was years later when I saw *color* TV for the first time.)

What, you ask, was the big deal about this particular image? What made *The Gene Autry Show*'s version of black-and-white so much better than that of any other show on television?

Definition, for one thing. For the first time on television, things looked crystal clear. The foreground was sharply delineated. And the background, instead of being a mist or a blur, was just as crisp.

Contrast, for another. Blacks were blacker and whites were whiter and each shade of gray was distinguishable from each other shade of gray. Between the contrast and definition there was a vividness that hit me like a hammer.

The new film was so much *more* of what we'd already seen that it heightened every aspect of the episode. It wasn't in 3D, but it felt like it. Especially because instead of just setting up the camera and letting things unfold before it, the cinematographer actually moved the camera around a little, showing the vistas that were supposed to be part of Gene's ranch.

Imagine living with a filter over your eyes, always wearing cheap sunglasses. Now take off those sunglasses and look all around you. What reaction can you have other than "Look at that. . . ." Or, "Look a'dat. . . ."

As Steven Poster, former president of the American Society of Cinematographers, once said to me, "Technological advancement is a lot like teenage sex. Once you've gotten so far you can't go back. You need more . . . more. . . ."

Television had become, literally, a brighter place. There was no going back. All filmed children's shows switched to the new stock, as did all filmed shows targeting adults.

Could *Dragnet* and *Father Knows Best* put out shows of lesser visual quality than a show starring a feature film cowboy who'd been considered washed-up just a few years before?

Could their producers allow *Maverick* and *Gunsmoke* and *Have Gun Will Travel*, all three of them featuring major new television stars and garnering heavyweight reviews, to be muddy, imperfect productions?

Could television shows continue to rack up big points with viewers and big victories over motion picture attendance if they looked as though their negatives had been dragged through the mud?

Early television producers and directors had often expressed contempt for their own productions, but Gene's film stock revolution changed that. Marc Daniels, who directed everything from *I Love Lucy* to *Hogan's Heroes* to *Star Trek* and more, once told me, "Before Gene Autry filmed television was nothing but talking heads separated by action. After Gene we were more willing to move the camera around because what we shot would actually be seen."

If this was all *The Gene Autry Show* accomplished it would be well worth remembering—and celebrating. But like most of what we've talked about here so far, the show had an effect that reached beyond television and into the daily lives of its watchers.

I know it had that kind of effect on me.

The Gene Autry Show was first and foremost an action show. Stuff happened. All the time. And not just any stuff—Fights, chases, shoot-outs, running, leaping, crouching, pummeling, riding, chasing, fleeing without a thought of standing still.

There's another name for these activities.

A politically incorrect name.

A name that causes metaphorical hisses and boos and the throwing of equally metaphorical tomatoes.

That name is:

Violence.

Gene's show was violent as hell. All the Westerns directed at kids in the late forties through the fifties were violent. Bad guys robbed stagecoaches, chased innocent women in buggies (the women were the ones in the buggies), and started fights in bars by throwing glasses of beer or smacking good guys over their heads with chairs.

Bank safes blew up. Horses ran off cliffs. Good guys and bad guys walked slowly and deliberately down the only street in town and then drew their .45s to see who was faster—and deadlier. Ambushes were commonplace. So were pretty young women tied to chairs in buildings about to be set afire.

Blazing lead filled the air as six-shooters fired dozens of rounds without reloading.

People died, both the good and the bad—and most of them were pretty ugly. They fell off buildings or out of stagecoaches or off mountaintops. They were trampled in stampedes of cattle. Knifed in the back. Set up and bushwhacked in box canyons. Flattened by man-made landslides. Bucked off horses who had had burrs placed under their saddles.

People died. Not only in Gambolin' Gene's adventures, but also in those of Buster Crabbe, Ken Maynard, Hoot Gibson, Harry Carey, Bob Steele, Tom Mix, Tim McCoy, Roy Rogers, and Annie Oakley (the show featuring her character was produced by Gene), and Range Rider (so was his), and in just about every other filmed show of any genre aimed at M-m-m-my G-G-G-Generation and me.

From the sixties through the early 2000s the effect of television violence on children has been a major issue, and righteously indignant groups from the PTA to the Billy Graham Crusades to the U.S. Congress have investigated and condemned—or not investigated and condemned—television as a medium for causing all those wild boys to not just walk the streets but rock them, literally as well as figuratively.

Near as I can figure, as someone who has been responsible more or less firsthand for family-shattering copycat crime, the argument *for* the idea that television violence breeds violence in our kids (which they of course carry into adulthood so they can engage in all that sex and drugs and street crime stuff we've talked about before) is as follows:

Television is a powerful and effective medium for getting one's message across and influencing human behavior. It is so powerful that its economic model is based on that fact. Why, after all, would sponsors pay exorbitant rates for commercials if those commercials didn't convince viewers to buy, buy, buy, buy, buy!!!?

And near as I can figure, as someone who has been responsible firsthand for the dread "Copycat Crime," the argument *against* the idea that television violence breeds violence in our kids goes something like this:

Television's power to get its message across and influence human behavior is vastly overrated. If it was as powerful as its critics say we'd be a nation of gun-totin' outlaws settling all our scores with Colts and Smith & Wessons. Besides, look at all the testing that's been done by respected authorities. Ain't a one of 'em that proves nuthin' either way, pard.

I can't speak for the studies. I haven't seen them and probably wouldn't understand how to interpret them anyway. My personal experience, however, shows that television definitely influences *adult* behavior. Well, young adult behavior, anyway. And every television writer or producer or director I've ever talked to about this has had the same kinds of experiences, some positive, some negative.

In the realm of science this is called anecdotal behavior and it's usually ignored or dismissed as uncontrolled and unscientific. In the realm of everyday life, though, my unscientific self finds it pretty damn conclusive. What interests me the most about this "evidence" of the television medium's power to get into people's minds and stir up things is that in the stories the connection is always immediate.

Someone sees something on television. Someone does something based on what they saw. Right now. I can almost hear the robot from *Lost In Space* explaining: "*Cannot-stop-myself-Will-Robinson. Must-go-to-the-mall-and-do-evil. Must-go-to-the-mall-and-do-good.*"

But what about long-term effects? What about kids like the wild Smileys whose minds really were open and impressionable and impressed upon for years by TV? What about yours truly staring at all that fist and gun and knife play from the time I was four until . . . well, until this very day?

What about our whole generation? And subsequent ones as well?

Have we been damaged?

Maybe permanently?

Has all that TV violence for kids changed the course of history? Made our country and our world a tooth-and-talon jungle it otherwise wouldn't have been?

To my knowledge, there are no studies on that. If there are, I'd like very much to see them.

But here's some anecdotal evidence for an anecdotal surmise.

From the time I was a four-year-old TV watcher until I was about eleven and discovered rock 'n' roll, the drums, and, a little later, girls and cars and the amazing thrills to be experienced by becoming hands-on with both, my favorite game to play was "Cowboys."

It wasn't an alienated loner thing, either. The whole neighborhood took part. Boys and girls alike would be out on the street, deciding which of them would be the good guys and which the bad, and then we'd start confronting and accusing and pushing each other. We'd throw wild, roundhouse punches, and we'd chase each other around the block, sometimes on foot and sometimes on our bikes. Those of us who had cap guns used 'em (although usually without the caps, which were a bitch to put in, and besides, the loud *bang* attracted adult attention, which no kid ever wanted to do), and those of us who didn't have them learned how to point our fingers and make a harsh, grating noise with our mouths that to us sounded just like a shot.

We clobbered each other with flying fists, but no one wanted to admit being hurt because on the TV shows we all knew and loved no one ever did. Not the good guys. Not the bad. And when someone yelped we were astounded. "That hurt? Range Rider got kicked in the face by a real big guy last week and he didn't feel a thing!" Even when the someone yelping was me I was taken aback—and angry with myself. *What kind of a hero are you? What kind of big, tough baddie? Don't you dare cry over that scraped knee!*

We "shot" each other full of holes too, and for the most part handled the consequences by refusing to acknowledge being hit. Kids shot other kids with their fingers from two inches away, and the vic would just make a face and say, "Missed me!"

(When I played a good guy and shot a bad guy at this range, this response really pissed me off, and yet I expected it because who ever thought a bad guy would play fair? On the other hand, when I was a good guy who'd been filled with invisible lead from two inches I never accepted death either. I *knew* in every fiber of my being that the universe didn't allow bad guys to kill good guys. It couldn't happen so it hadn't happened. Period.)

Generally speaking, then, very few of us ever went down and none of us stayed down. And we knew that was how it should be. My playmates and I were convinced that we were doing exactly what we saw the cowboys doing on TV, and none of us ever felt anything about it but "Hey, this is fun!"

When I was older, during Larry Brody's Golden Age of Girls and Cars, that way of thinking was still with me even though I was no longer watching the shows that had instilled it. Television now had its "adult Westerns," which were supposed to be rebellions against the kid westerns of what was rapidly becoming yore, and punches and bullets now had consequences.

For which I had no patience.

I mean it, none at all.

Have Gun Will Travel's hero Paladin just got shot? He's wincing with pain and struggling not to cry out as he sneaks around to take out the bad guy from behind? *What a jerk! Who's he kidding? I know that stuff doesn't hurt!*

During this period I experienced real-life carryover as well. My father, who owned a used car lot in what was considered a "rough neighborhood" on the South Side of Chicago, was held up in the office at closing time one night. At gunpoint.

He came home late, and he came home upset. Hell, he came home more terrified than anything or anyone on or off television had ever made me. He was the kind of man who didn't talk much, and certainly didn't talk about his feelings. But on this night the whole story came pouring out to my mother, my sister (poor thing, she was born after Howdy Doody had lost his weekday timeslot and his charm, and was growing up with *Romper Room* instead) and me. In fact, he told it twice.

And in both tellings he described how one of the two bad guys held the gun pointed at him and how the other marched him over to the safe and made him open it. And how he'd done what they said and handed over the cash inside.

I was bugged. *Kee-rist!* Was I ever bugged. Finally, my fifteen-year-old self could stand it no more.

"Wait a minute!" I said. "Didn't you even try to struggle? Didn't you try to grab the gun and take it away?"

"Take it away? A loaded gun? What're you talking about?"

"It's easy. You just reach out and grab the barrel and push it up so if the guy pulls the trigger the bullet goes into the ceiling, and then you—"

I saw the look on his face and I stopped. "Sorry," I said.

But I thought: *What a jerk!*

That's the evidence. Now here's the surmise. A question I've been asking myself for some time.

I'm a (relatively) normal human being. An artist, even, specializing in TV. I haven't shot anyone or become an axe murderer or otherwise killed another human being. I haven't thrown myself headlong into a life of crime. Neither, to my knowledge, have any of the wild Smiley boys.

Television violence witnessed in my youth didn't up my—our—violence quotient and cause us to wreak havoc upon the law-abiding land.

But I know it desensitized me.

I know that even now it's difficult for me to, in the words of Bill Clinton, "feel your pain." Sometimes—and this is the confession of a deep, dark secret, I'm even a little eensie weensie bit entertained by it.

I know I'm not alone. The murders of Nicole Brown Simpson and Ron Goldman were *real*. The pain of their survivors was *real*. But before you could blink an eye, or yell "Run, O.J., run!" it became entertainment for millions. The same thing happened with the Laci Peterson murder. Instead of empathizing with the pain of what had happened, people—the audience—treated the investigation (as of this writing the trial hasn't yet been completed) as a spectator sport.

So tell me, what's up with that? What's up with the fact that as the twentieth century rolled into the twenty-first we were treated to behavior that amounted to insensitivity on a mass scale: Corporate shenanigans that even if they weren't illegal caused widespread pain and suffering. Millions of investors wiped out. Millions of jobs terminated. Insider trading. Downsizing. Outsourcing.

And who was responsible for all this pain? Baby boomers. My generation. (Don't worry, I won't inflict my version of Roger Daltrey's stutter on you again.) Is this because we and those we've raised and those they're raising don't care? Is it because as children we were all desensitized? And are we, like so many victims of genuine childhood abuse, continuing the sorry tradition? Passing it on?

Want to know what the rules for animation writing were when I worked on *The Amazing Spider-Man* and *The Silver Surfer*? What just about everyone—writers, animators, executives—thought made a script "good"?

Three lines of dialogue and a fight.

Three more lines of dialogue and another fight.

Three more lines and the beginning of a fight, interrupted by a commercial.

Then the end of the previous fight and the same thing all over again.

As a professional in the television industry I've got a vested interest in the answer to my question being *No*. In my surmise being all wrong. Someone show me a study. Any study, as long as it proves I'm all wet.

Otherwise I'd have to become violent and direct that violence at myself out of grief and shame over what the shows I've not only seen but also written and produced have wrought. I'd have to put that Glock my buddy the child psychologist gave me for Christmas in my mouth and do my bit to end the cycle.

After all, isn't that what an honorable man would do on TV?

"See It Now" Begins Broadcasting, Creating the Force We Know as Television News

*J*anuary 2002. John Tyson, full-time rancher in Virginia City, Nevada, and part-time newsman in nearby Reno, Nevada, gets up early, feeds his horses, puts on a snappy suit complete with tie, and as the sun comes up he drives his truck to town to take part in a taping of a live news show about the state of television. He's sleepy and isn't even being paid, but "it's the news, dammit. Gotta be here."

April 1981. Maria Shriver, correspondent for NBC News working out of the L.A. office, drives to Santa Monica, California, to be at a baby shower for a friend. In the car she hears some late-breaking news, and as soon as she gets to the friend's house she asks if she can use the phone (these were pre–cell phone times!), and spends the next four hours calling coast-to-coast to amass the info she needs so she can contribute to the story. It's Saturday, her day off, but she's at it, saying later, "What was the shower like? Oh, I haven't a clue. Are you sure I was there?"

May 1968. After a day of student rioting in Mexico City during which an NBC News cameraman was accidentally shot and killed, a group of newspeople preparing the evening's broadcast watch the footage shot during the violence. Suddenly, an image panning the students jerks upward and becomes an image of the sky, then tilts down to ground level. One of the newspeople leaps from his seat, exclaiming, "What a great shot—!" and then breaks off, realizing it's

Edward R. Murrow, circa 1951 (Jerry Ohlinger's Movie Material)

the last footage that will ever be taken by the fallen cameraman, whom he considered a good friend.

November 1951 through the spring of 1957. Edward R. Murrow, the top radio newsman (they called them reporters then) hosts the television series *See It Now* on CBS. Unlike other news shows, this one is more than just a talking head report of events. Murrow's innovations, aided and abetted by co-producer Fred W. Friendly, include actually going out and showing what's happening—often through the eyes of folks who are more like his viewers than the usual newsmakers—and then doing some genuine analysis of what it all means.

Think of the above as a fifty-plus-year trip through time, peeling backward from the *result* to the *cause*. Television news in all its glory. Television newspeople in all their luminous dedication.

And dedicated they are, to a degree that can astound an outsider. Each and every TV newsperson sees him- or herself as the heir to a proud tradition. Just about every book ever written about TV news proclaims *See It Now* as the seminal television news series, and Murrow as the archetypal reporter, indomitable and committed, the combination an inspiration for all who came after.

Even the tabloid TV specialists and the "celebrity celebrants."

'Tis a worldview devoutly to be envied, Horatio, especially by those of us on the "entertainment" side of the business, who never forget for a minute that we're descended from tightrope walkers and fortune tellers and vagabond players. Showbiz. As in "the show biz." As in the circus and wagons pulled by swift, strong horses because they all too often had to rush like hell out of town.

So the people who bring you primetime and not so primetime entertainment are, in a manner of speaking, the riffraff.

And the people who bring you the primetime and not so primetime and the beyond primetime news are the idealists.

It's official.

And for those of us who watch television news, kind of comforting.

Not that you could get me near a TV newscast when I was a kid. The only thing I remember Edward R. Murrow from was the series *Person to Person*, in which he sat in a big easy chair in the studio, smoking away on a cigarette (and I mean *smoking*; the dominant image on the screen when the camera was on Murrow wasn't his face but the plume of smoke moving upward like an Indian fakir's rope alongside it), and led the audience on a tour of celebrities' digs, guided by the celebrity.

Occasionally I watched another newsman slum: Walter Cronkite on *You Are There*. The original version of this show ran from 1953 to 1957 and was made for kids. In it, Cronkite, the most respected anchorman on television during his heyday (and probably well beyond it; people still speak of him with awe otherwise reserved only for Murrow), anchored a mock newscast, covering a historical event reported by other newspeople, who were presented as though in the field.

I still remember the episode about the Piltdown Man. Unfortunately, about halfway through that one something distracted me—dinner, I think, because the show aired early Saturday evenings—and I missed the end of the show, where the hoax was uncovered. For years I thought we'd found the Missing Link!

(Notice how I refer to both Edward R. Murrow and Walter Cronkite as Murrow and Cronkite instead of Ed and Walter, which is what I'd automatically call them if they were actors starring on sitcoms or dramas or action shows? In fact, I have to force myself not to call them *Mr.* Murrow and *Mr.* Cronkite. That's how ingrained my respect for them is—even though I was never a fan of their true callings.)

As I grew up I began to appreciate news more. In the mid-fifties I discovered my parents' subscription to *Time* magazine and even read the front page of the morning paper—*The Chicago Sun-Times*—a couple of times a week, a major expansion from my previous newspaper experience, which had been confined to the Sunday comics.

Then, in 1956, I saw parts of the political conventions as covered by Chet Huntley and David Brinkley, which led to my sporadic viewership of *The Huntley-Brinkley Report*, the NBC evening news show the two men co-anchored. During the sixties I was reading just about every news magazine I could get my hands on as well as the daily paper, but I became aware of the fact that more and more people I knew were getting most of their news from TV.

The battle for viewership at the time was between Huntley and Brinkley on NBC and Cronkite (Oh, how I want to say *"Mister!"*) on CBS. No one in my circle, which was comprised of my family and various high school, college, and beginning-of-career friends) bothered with ABC's news offerings and most had hardly heard of ABC's longest-employed anchorman during that era, Peter Jennings.

I didn't understand how anyone thought they were getting a full report from any of the evening news shows. They seemed more like headlines to me, and not all that many of them. But as social upheaval became the order of the day and my emotional investment in what was happening in Vietnam and the changing of the very moral, ethical, religious, and sexual standards by which we lived grew stronger and stronger, television news became the place to turn for daily gratification.

The protests.

The speeches.

The carnage.

The footage from the cameraman shot dead in the middle of the Mexico City student riots didn't merely "find" its way into our living room screens, it was thrust at us.

Grim-faced American grunts peered into our eyes as we cut our steaks and ketchupped our fries.

Choppers filled the air.

And body bags.

Furious students ran through streets in all the major cities of the United States, and NBC, CBS, ABC, and the new kid on the block at the time, PBS, panned from them to the equally angry police officers and National Guard members who were trying to keep the action down.

It was all there on film, yes, but *alive* in the way film (and video now) brings things to life by giving them motion and immediacy. The news footage carried a power, an intensity, that for a large part of the audience made it more real than real, that heightened television reality that my generation had grown up with reaching its overwhelmingly agonizing apogee.

Grim-faced grunts.

Choppers.

Body bags.

Terrified Vietnamese peasants.

Impassive Vietnamese generals (from both sides).

Ho Chi Minh.

Anxious wives and parents of MIAs.

Activist motion picture and rock stars.

Politicians whose body language screamed their frustration.

Teenagers, young adults, and grandfatherly pediatricians whose bodily movements signified their feelings of betrayal.

Grim-faced grunts.

Choppers.

Body bags.

No matter what your opinions were, whether you were pro- or anti-war, pro- or anti–free love and pot, for or against Brit and U.S. rock 'n' roll, your nightly adrenaline rush was on standby all day, eagerly awaiting its chance to get in your face five nights a week, at 7:00 p.m. Eastern time. (6:00 central. Consult your TV listings for other time zones.)

The sixties exploded into the seventies, and the protests, the speeches, and the carnage continued. So did the coverage, a barrage of images that flayed raw the psyches of all who saw it.

At the end of *Apocalypse Now* Brando speaks to no one and everyone. The world? God? Francis Coppola? "The horror," he says. "The horror . . ."

I think he was talking about the television news of the time. Because it sure as shootin' brought the hell of both the military and civilian conflicts directly to the churning guts of those who otherwise would've been nothing more than "the folks at home."

"The horror . . ."

The audience writhed, but it watched. We couldn't let it go.

We knew we were seeing the Truth.

We may not have known what it meant, but we knew the film didn't lie. It showed too many faces that were emotionally—and sometimes—physically—wide open.

TV news may have been made up of headlines, but I for one realized that was just okey-dokey with me. If the film I was seeing and those faces that were haunting me were only the surface of what was going on, then please, God, keep me from ever having to be immersed any deeper. How could I—how could anyone?—ever survive?

Not that the newspeople of the era didn't try. News "specials," documentaries that dug deeper, particularly into the causes and implications of the Vietnam War, started applying Edward R. Murrow's analysis technique, working overtime to try to explain the political and social issues inherent in such far-flung events as the My Lai Massacre, Watergate, and the struggle for racial equality.

In 1976 the Vietnam War ended, and the rest of the turmoil died down. President Richard M. Nixon had resigned. Martin Luther King had been assassinated, but Central High in Little Rock had black students and the only people in the country who rode at the back of the bus were the ones to take the last available seats.

Many commentators on the subject of media have expressed the belief that television news, with its awe-inspiring sincerity, was more than just a little responsible for how things turned out. Whether or not that is true, news ratings were up, and although they slumped a bit as we went into a less turbulent era, the numbers stayed higher than they had been before all the action began.

Respect for the news divisions of the various networks went up as well. Edward R. Murrow was long gone from the scene, but his spiritual children had done him proud. Their accomplishments at the time showed a remarkable degree of integrity. I'm not suggesting that no TV newsperson or news organization had an agenda or point of view. That would be terribly naïve. There was, however, very little criticism of TV news from its natural rivals, the print media, at the time.

It was as though even newspaper and magazine editors and columnists had to acknowledge that the most sensational elements appearing on television news shows appeared that way because they *were* sensational in and of themselves.

By the eighties surveys were making it official: More Americans got their news from television than in any other way. Television executives responded by giving us more. CBS's *60 Minutes*, which rode the crest of the wave to huge ratings success on Sunday nights starting in 1968, became the model for *Dateline, World News Tonight*, and a raft of other network and syndicated shows. Other offshoots of Murrow's original vision include *The Lehrer Report, Charlie Rose*, and even *Entertainment Tonight, Access Hollywood*, and the flood of newsmagazine and news talk shows that have filled the *TV Guide* listings for years.

In the first year of the decade the infant cable business got a shot in the arm when Ted Turner's CNN (Cable News Network) started broadcasting. All news all the time was a revolutionary concept, and it became a very successful one. Over the years since, more all-news channels have followed, including Bloomberg Television, CNN Headline News, CNBC, CNBC World, CSPAN, CSPAN2, and Fox News Channel.

Some of these shows and channels deal with so-called "hard" news—the stuff of a newspaper's first section—others with "soft" news, the equivalent of the feature and entertainment sections. Some have demonstrated very definite political biases, which always seem to be "against" the bias of whoever is complaining about it, including myself. All of them, however, are grounded in journalistic attitudes and techniques and, yes, ambitions, amassing facts, presenting facts, discussing what the facts mean.

The family tree may have grown a little twisted, and some of the limbs may be bent, but in their zeal to show and expose, probe and jab, most of these presentations are recognizable descendants of *See It Now*. Whether they do it as well as their ancestor is another matter. Over the years there have been many news presentations I didn't agree with. But I was glad they were there, giving me the opportunity to see various sides of what's going on.

Ah, but as I write this a new survey has thrown me a curve. According to Andrew Grossman of the *Hollywood Reporter*, "An increasing number of young adults are using late-night comedy and talk shows as their primary vehicle for getting their news, particularly about politics. . . ."

The article goes on to say that "Twenty percent [of the young adults surveyed] say they learned something regularly from *The Daily Show, Saturday Night Live* or shows like that."

I watch *The Daily Show*. I used to watch *Saturday Night Live*. But get my news from the entertainment side? From other mountebanks out for a laugh—like me?

Eddie! Eddie Murrow! Eddie, sweetie! C'mon home to the tube, Eddie. And please—bring back the pain!

Note: There's a coda to this chapter. Remember the guy in 1968? The one who jumped up cheering at a shot that signified the death of a friend?

Well, here's the human side of the news and those who report it on TV. The guy's name is Jim Briley, and when he realized what he was doing he stayed on his feet and walked directly out the door.

Jim went to the office of his boss, the news director, and Jim quit.

When I met Jim Briley some years later he was teaching news writing at the university level, energizing and inspiring his students.

By being a serious, dedicated, and energetic newsman.

And always telling them the truth.

"I Love Lucy" Premieres and Changes Television Entertainment Forever

I Love Lucy is the stuff of legends.

Libraries could put in whole sections devoted to books already written about this wonderful series. Type the name into any internet search engine and you'll get well over two million responses.

As entertainment, what can beat it? Over fifty years after its heyday gray-bearded men and silver-haired women of both my parents' generation and mine can still remember favorite episodes. Many of us can mentally re-create the experience of watching them.

No, my first sight of Lucy and Ricky Ricardo wasn't at an aunt and uncle's house. It was at home in our living room, on the same TV set where I watched Howdy Doody and the rest of my favorites. It was a warm surprise shared with my parents and baby sister Ava. My parents and I—at two, Ava was too young to fall victim to the hype—had been looking forward to the debut for a week. We weren't disappointed.

The last new episode of the show aired in 1957, but it's still fulfilling audience expectations to this day. For over fifty years *Lucy* has been shown almost continuously not just in the U.S. but all over the world. New viewers and those who've seen all the episodes ten or twenty or a hundred times before are still laughing at Lucy's antics as she falls behind on an assembly line, as she tries desperately to get through the "Vitameatavegamin" commercial, and as she just plain strives and strives and strives—and screws things up every time.

Lucille Ball and friends, circa 1955 (Jerry Ohlinger's Movie Material)

When you talk about *I Love Lucy*, use of the word *classic* is inevitable. So let's get that over with now. *I Love Lucy*, starring Lucille Ball and her then-husband Desi Arnaz as Lucy and Ricky and featuring Vivian Vance and William Frawley as their landlords and neighbors, Ethel and Fred, is indeed a classic. One hundred and seventy-nine episodes were produced, and there's not a clunker in the can.

We're talking about a genuine, 24-carat gold (not plate) big moment here.

And as a turning point in television history it's more than a mere home run. It's back-to-back grand slammers, hit by the same guy.

The first way *I Love Lucy* altered the medium was in its method of production.

CBS, which was broadcasting the show, signed on assuming it would be shot live in New York, like all their other primetime series. Lucy and Desi, however, had a different idea.

Here's what happened straight from the horse's mouth. At least, it's how I remember Desi talking about it when we spoke back in 1983. He'd called me from his home in Del Mar, and his first words were, "So, kid, how you treating my boy?"

Desi had never met me and had no idea how old I was. (Thirty-nine at the time. Older than he'd been when *Lucy* began.) He was talking about his son, Desi Arnaz, Jr., who was starring in a series called *Automan* that I was running (as co-executive producer with Glen Larson). After I found my voice and heaped highly deserved praise on Desi Jr. as both a person and a performer, the conversation wound its way from "my boy's" early years in television to those of Desi himself.

"People say Lucy and I were big innovators. We had to innovate. This was the beginning of TV. There was nothing else," Desi said. "We had a great life in California and weren't about to trade it in so we gave up a little money here, a little money there, to be able to shoot on the Coast.

"The only way to do things was to film the show in advance so it could be shipped to New York in time to be aired. But CBS wanted us to do it in front of an audience so we had to come up with a way so the camera could see us and we could see each other and the audience could see and laugh. If they didn't laugh we were fucked.

"We did the only practical thing. We set up three cameras so we could play to them and to the folks watching, and now all these years later kids like you make out it's a big deal."

But it was a big deal. Until *I Love Lucy* all shows that weren't action-packed were performed live (and recorded on the dreaded kinescope during the performance). And they were all produced in New York City.

Desi and Lucy and Ricky and Lucy and Ethel and Fred polished that situation off. For good.

I Love Lucy became a smash hit, and hits not only give their producers clout, they also provide credibility for everything associated with the hit. If L.A. worked for *Lucy*, the reasoning went, maybe it'll work for X or Y or Z show as well.

In short order, L.A.—Hollywood!—became the production

center. Film became the medium of choice for sitcoms (for a while after the invention of videotape, taped shows were popular, but that phase has passed), some performed before what's become known as a "live audience" (ever see a "dead audience?"), some not. The "nots" became popular after the creation of canned laughter, an event that itself may be some kind of turning point but one most people on the creative side of the television industry would rather the business had missed.

To this day all sitcoms shot before an audience are shot with three cameras, the *I Love Lucy* way. The footage from the three cameras is edited on the spot, as the show is being performed, by a director and various assistants sitting in a control room, watching the various images and committing to which one the TV viewing audience will see, just the way the *Lucy* team did it way back when.

So, Desi, you were a big innovator, kid. Yes, you had to because you had nothing to draw on. But, damn it, unlike Lucy Ricardo, the Queen of Misadventure, you strove and you *attained*.

In fact, kid, you're the reason why I went to L.A. when I decided I wanted to be a TV writer. Who knows what would've happened without *I Love Lucy*? Would everything on television—all drama as well as all comedy—have been shot in New York? Would the New York sensibility have taken over instead of the Hollywood way?

Let's face it. Hollywood and its studios and the movie biz mentality deal with life and creativity by using a system of values that's considerably different from that under which the New York stage and literary scenes operate. And a whole different business model too.

Businesswise, in New York the writer-creator is an artist who owns the creation but gives publishers or theatrical producers various rights to print, sell, or present performances of what he or she hath wrought.

In Hollywood, however, the writer-creator of movies or television shows is an employee. The Hollywood writer-creator doesn't own the creation. The copyright is even in the name of whatever company paid for it.

The New York scene is confident, sophisticated, cutting edge. Traditionally, literature and the theater have been *about something*.

Their subject matter often is just an excuse for exploring the big issues of life.

Hollywood, however, is the capital of "Uh-oh, think the audience will get this one?" Its edge is so dull it can't even make a scratch on the lowest common denominator. Traditionally, movies are an escape. Not only have most feature films not explored the big issues, they've pretended those issues don't even exist.

The more I consider the subject, the more I realize that the work that is the sum and substance of the television writer-creator would have been very different if New York had remained the TV production hub.

I wonder what that would've done to the medium of television and its acceptance by viewers. I wonder if the audience would've been larger or smaller. Most of all, I wonder if as a consequence of the more cosmopolitan New York state of mind television programming would have been "better"? Or would it be worse? (And by whose definition? That of the New York *literati*? The Hollywood moguls? The big city audience? The not-so big city audience? Academicians? The creators themselves?

But unless someone creates a machine that'll show us alternate dimensions and finds one where *I Love Lucy* went down in flames after the first thirteen episodes, or something no one right now can foresee causes a dramatic paradigm shift, making New York the Big TV Production Apple, it's safe to say that we'll never know.

The second way *I Love Lucy* changed the medium, however, is something we do know. And Desi and Lucy and the gang may well have hit this home run even farther out of the park than the previous one.

Because this homer is something every member of the viewing audience is fully aware of, even today.

Something reviled continually by most viewers, yet praised by the biz.

A necessary evil that may not be as evil as we usually think.

This in-your-face fact of TV life is:

Reruns.

I Love Lucy is responsible for the rerun?

Aargh!

And we can even make it personal.

The real culprit is Lucy and Desi's son.

Desiderio Arnaz Jr.

(Not "Little Ricky." He was the fictional son of fictional Lucy and fictional Ricky. And no, he wasn't played by Desi Jr., although Desi Jr. did play a fictional version of himself later on *Here's Lucy*.)

Desi Jr. Who wasn't aware of it at the time. How could he be? He was a fetus. It was before he was born.

That's what happens when you're born into royalty, even television royalty. You assume some big responsibilities just by being alive.

Desi Jr., one of the hardest-working actors I've ever known (and one of the few who is actually fun to be with) explained the whole thing to me one day. "Yep," he said, jabbing his own finger into his chest with his usual high spirits, "it's me everybody's got to blame. I'm the reason for all those reruns. C'mon, kick me, I'll put up the sign."

What happened, he said, was that during *I Love Lucy's* first season Lucy became pregnant, "and it wasn't going all that well." The doctors decided Lucy needed more rest, which meant she had to take time off from work. But *I Love Lucy was* Lucy.

"Everybody was freaked because they couldn't figure out how they'd get enough shows done for next season without my mom on the set," said Desi Jr. "My father and the producers had a big meeting, and somebody—Jess Oppenheimer, I think—came up with the idea of starting off the second season by rerunning some episodes from the first.

"My dad loved the idea, but the only way he could convince CBS to go for it was to say they'd add little introductions to the reruns so part of them would be new. So the second season started with I think six reruns and then 'Little Ricky' was born. It used to really bug me that people thought I was Little Ricky. Then I talked to the guy who played him and found out it bugged him even more when people thought he was Desi Jr.!"

CBS may not have been all that keen on reruns to begin with, but when the network execs saw that audiences were embracing shows they'd seen before, they embraced the concept of repeating episodes. Within a few years what had started as a pragmatic choice made out of necessity became part of the economic underpinning of the networks, saving them hundreds of thousands of dollars in production costs because they were producing fewer (and fewer, and fewer) new episodes during the season.

During the time before reruns, most programming made specially for television was shown once and then discarded. The only repeats were old movies like the ones I watched when I was a kid. The networks authorized shows in groups of thirteen, and a full season consisted of thirty-nine original episodes.

To fill up the remaining thirteen weeks of summer, when viewing was down anyway because there were better things to do in good weather than sit in a room and stare at a box, the networks would finance limited runs of other shows. If those shows were sufficiently successful in terms of generating audience (and sponsor) interest they would return in the fall with the rest of the new season. If not, that was the end of them.

Fifty-two weeks a year of original programming didn't come cheaply, so as soon as the rerun thing caught on the networks saw a chance to give themselves a break. Instead of new shows during the summer, reruns took to the air. In fact, originally they were referred to as "summer reruns" and promoted in words that translated as "the best episodes of the season, so if you missed 'em the first time around now's your chance."

Thirty-nine new episodes and thirteen reruns became the norm and stayed that way until the mid-sixties. Then the term "summer rerun" vanished from the television lexicon as the standard authorization, or "buy," for a full season became twenty-six episodes instead. In the years since then that number has dwindled, first to twenty-four, then to twenty-two.

Now, in the early 2000s many network shows are airing only eighteen or nineteen new primetime episodes each year and most cable channel series present twelve new episodes or less, with reruns appearing both as a block at the conclusion of the regular season and interspersed with the new episodes throughout the rest of the year. (This has been common in children's programming since the early nineties, when the practice began of producing thirteen new episodes and filling out the rest of the season with old ones rerun from several seasons gone by.)

Although it may sound as though this is a major financial windfall for the networks at the expense of the audience—and the talent not being paid for not making new episodes—the situation is more complicated.

Production costs have soared in recent years, while ratings in general are down, along with the income generated by selling commercial spots because no sensible business is going to pay more for ads in order to get less. Reruns aren't entirely without cost for the networks. (Can you spell r-e-s-i-d-u-a-l-s?) But they ease much of the current pain. Without reruns the networks would have to cut back in other ways, ultimately providing even less original programming than they do now.

Another positive side to reruns is, believe it or not, a creative one. Chris Albrecht, chairman and CEO of HBO, explained it to me like this:

"There's no way HBO can afford original twenty-four-hour programming seven days a week. To survive we've got to run all our originals six or seven times. But since our viewers are paying us to see what we've got to offer, we want to give them something special for their money.

"When we develop a new series we want it to be fresh and original—original enough so that it takes more than one viewing for our audience to 'get' it," he went on. "We want our shows to break new ground in terms of content and storytelling technique so that the audience will *want* to watch the same episodes over and over in order to appreciate all the nuances and layers."

The result of this outlook? Since the turn of the 21st century HBO has been the top-rated cable channel in the country and its shows have collected more Emmy nominations and awards than almost all the other networks and cable channels combined. The guy just might be on to something. (Chris, by the way, is a New York City boy. Could his approach be a wee bit indicative of what happens when television is approached in a New York frame of mind?)

Maybe Desi Jr. hasn't done us so wrong after all. Ain't no reason to kick him, sign or no sign. Creative people have always had to face financial constraints. Success comes when those constraints are turned from liabilities into assets, as HBO appears to be doing.

Thanks for the laughs, Lucy.

Thanks for the residuals, Desi.

Thanks for the pleasure of your company, Desi Jr., and for treating others like royalty instead of expecting us to bow to you.

"TV Guide" Goes on Sale Nationwide and Loglines Take Over TV

$\mathcal{D}$esi Arnaz, Jr., has another claim to fame. Not only was he a prime cause of reruns while still in his mother's womb, he also was a major contributor to the success of what was once the magazine with the highest circulation in the U.S. As an infant lovingly held by America's favorite housewife, Desi Jr. attained the pinnacle of stardom to which television series leads still aspire to this day. He was on the cover of the very first issue of *TV Guide*.

No, I didn't see it myself. I didn't snap it up at the local drugstore, where all things worth reading were sold in those days. I didn't squirrel it away in my bedroom with my Rudy Kazootie hat (don't ask!) and other television paraphernalia. (Such truck wouldn't be called "memorabilia" for another twenty years.) I missed out on my chance to sell a yellowed copy of this hallowed issue for hundreds of dollars.

But eventually *TV Guide* found its way into my life and influenced me in ways I never would've predicted.

On a personal level, the existence of *TV Guide* could very well have been responsible for the first steps up the ladder I made in my television writing career. (That's right. The television industry is so all-consuming that career moves, which would be considered professional situations in any other business, are treated as personal.)

On a professional level (or, if you prefer, on still another professional level) the existence of *TV Guide* has influenced the development, writing, and casting of every TV series I've ever been

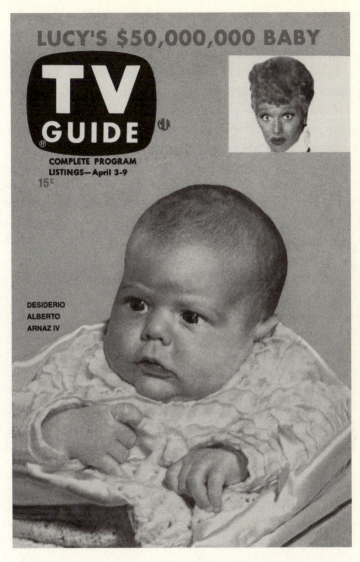

LUCY'S $50,000,000 BABY

TV GUIDE

COMPLETE PROGRAM
LISTINGS—April 3-9

15ᶜ

DESIDERIO
ALBERTO
ARNAZ IV

Desi Arnaz, Jr., April 3, 1953 (Cloud Creek Institute for the Arts)

involved in, wanted to be involved in, and just plain didn't get the chance to be involved in, from the fifties to the present day.

And the damn magazine isn't even *for* the business. It's not a trade journal like *Daily Variety* or *Hollywood Reporter*. It's a weekly paperback book–sized mag that sits there on supermarket checkout stands so shoppers can grab it at the last minute and take home to help them choose what to watch!

Be careful what you start, young entrepreneurs. To paraphrase Alexander Graham Bell, another innovator who in all likelihood was clueless about where his invention would ultimately lead, "you never know what's up the big man's sleeve. So it's not a matter of what hath God wrought, but 'What will He?'"

When *TV Guide* started, magazines giving readers their local television listings weren't unheard of. They were, however, usually free weekly inserts in the local newspaper with titles like *TV Week* or *This Week in TV*. They came out on Sunday as part of the feature package that also included the Sunday comics section, a weekly "magazine" (originally called the "rotogravure" for you fans of the film *Easter Parade*) printed on newsprint so readers could get color ink all over their hands instead of just the black stuff from the news sections, and color advertising flyers.

The newspaper *TV Week*s contained columns of small type where the names, days, and times of the various available shows were listed in a way that looked more like the Yellow Pages than anything else.

Their covers usually featured a grainy black and white photograph of a local television host. (In Chicago where I grew up, that meant someone like kids show host Uncle Johnny Coons or Morris B. Sacks, the owner of a small local chain of clothing stores who often appeared on the shows he sponsored.)

The few ads in these inserts were also for local businesses, meaning more Morris B. Sacks, whose clothes at that time carried more clout with me than did Giorgio Armani's in future more cosmopolitan days—although I eventually wore Armani, while at the age of eight I had very little need for Morris B. Sacks' 100 percent wool worsted suits.

In short, these early local attempts to service the needs of the growing number of television viewers around the country weren't very compelling. And besides, with only four channels to pick from and half a dozen shows eight-year-old LB wanted to see, I pretty much knew when I wanted to be in front of the TV set and what channel to *ka-chung* to.

TV Guide changed all that.

It was the first national publication devoted to television viewing, its various editions (which started at ten and expanded through the years to over two hundred) combining listings for the local viewing area with articles about what was happening nationwide in TV. (This gave the networks a hell of a boost, and their publicity and advertising departments twisted sideways and bent over backward cooperating with *TV Guide*'s editors and staff.)

When I discovered it (the way I discovered so many things relating to television during my childhood, at someone else's house), *TV Guide* had slick color covers featuring photos of national network stars posed in interesting locations with interesting props. It had a section of equally slick color pages at the front of the magazine featuring human interest stories about the stars and the shows, reviews of current series, even a crossword puzzle based on the reader's knowledge—or lack thereof—of what and who were on TV.

Behind all this fannish wonderment were the listings. They were still local, but set up on an easy-to-follow grid, and following the name of each show was a short paragraph giving the main star or stars and a one-sentence synopsis of what was going to happen in that particular episode.

Since *TV Guide* was a log of television shows, this one-line description became known in the trade as a "logline."

So there I was at my neighbor Neil Friedman's house for an after-school game of Ping-Pong in his basement. The year was 1955 and we were in sixth grade. Neil's parents were true television *aficionados*, with a low-slung wooden console TV with what then was the largest available screen (I think it might've been seventeen inches), a built-in radio and phonograph complete with record storage, a cover to hide everything away, and *TV Guide* sitting on the top.

Neil was stuck batting the little celluloid ball around with his obnoxious little brother that day because I picked up *TV Guide* and was hooked.

Like millions of television viewers before me.

And even millions more since.

At one point over 12 million people subscribed to *TV Guide*, which magazine publishing analysts figure probably means that almost 50 million people read each issue. Since then circulation has dipped to about 9 million, which still keeps *TV Guide* well out of the category of shopping mall throwaway. That doesn't include the hundreds of thousands of people who regularly access its website and the millions who tune in to the TV Guide cable channel. Parent company Gemstar–TV Guide International estimates that 100 million people a week avail themselves of its products and services one way or another. And even before all this expansion, Walter Annenberg, the founding publisher, retired as one of the wealthiest and most powerful men in the U.S.

Over my years as a viewer several things about *TV Guide* grabbed me.

For one thing, it evolved. Genres were added to the listings so the uninitiated would know if a new series was a drama or a comedy. (No, even *TV Guide* wouldn't just come out and say *action*. Some fictions endure.) The listing would also tell you if a show was a rerun, and if it had a special guest star. If the *TV Guide* staff deemed an episode or "Special" to be of particular significance it would identify the listing with a big star. (How they made those choices I didn't know at the time. Now I still don't know, but after over thirty years in the business I have my suspicions.)

The slick color section evolved too. There were long articles and short, snappy paragraphs of quotes and quips. The reviews became more in-depth, and more critical. (In 1971 while I was writing for a CBS series called *The Interns*, the producer, Charles Larson, opined, "We're hoping for a really bad review in *TV Guide* because that'll make us a hit. Readers know that anything Cleveland Amory [*TV Guide*'s then critic] likes will be fancy bullshit and anything he slams will be gold.")

The front section of *TV Guide* also introduced the audience to terms and procedures formerly known only within the biz. "Pilot," "pick-up," "ratings," "demographics," and "temporary hiatus" became terms used as commonly by viewers as by executives and

producers. *TV Guide* also reported on various programming decisions, some of them frivolous, some of them, well, less frivolous,
but all of them fascinating to those who were entranced by TV.
Who was the first choice for such and such a series? Why was such
and such a series renewed even though its ratings had fallen? Will
so and so stay with such and such a series even though she's pregnant? Why was so and so really fired?

This kind of information made, and still makes, television viewers feel more knowledgeable and increases their interest in the
medium, which in turn makes television itself more powerful and
effective as an entertainment and advertising tool. With me, it went
a step further. It made me want in.

By the time I was in my late teens I didn't want to just read
about television programming and television decisions. I wanted
to be part of the creation of the shows and a decision maker. I
didn't want to be on the outside looking in, I wanted to be part of
the process, to be in a world where pilots and pickups and ratings
and demographics and hiatuses were part of my everyday life.

Which is the main reason I came to L.A. at the age of twenty-
three and started shlepping my writing wares.

And in so doing encountered the most important influence *TV
Guide* has had on the television industry. That created a turning
point with a powerful effect on television professionals, feature film
professionals, and, lately, book and magazine publishing professionals as well.

It's that *logline* thing.

Today, as I write this, *all* corporate entertainment businesses
subscribe to the KISS theory of programming, production, and
publication.

Keep It Simple, Stupid.

And how do you keep it so simple?

By making sure that every creative idea can be summarized in a
short listing in *TV Guide.*

By being absolutely certain that the essence of every show,
every movie, and every book can communicated in—that's right,
you've got it!—a logline.

An exciting logline, of course.

I first encountered the logline as creative force in the early seventies when I was assigned to write an episode of ABC's *The Streets of San Francisco*. A couple of days after our first meeting to discuss the storyline, William Yates, the producer, called me excitedly. "You're in solid with Quinn now," he said, referring to Quinn Martin, the head of the production company and a very big deal TV guy with three (or was it four?) series on the air at the time.

(And who, by the way, got his start as a producer from Desi Arnaz, who upped him from film editor to take charge of the Desilu series *The Untouchables*.)

"Quinn likes the idea?" I said to Bill.

"What he especially likes about it," Bill said, "is how good it'll look in *TV Guide*. 'Stone and Keller must find a bodybuilder who doesn't know his own strength before he kills—again.'"

"That's not exactly the story you and I talked about," I said.

"It is now," Bill replied.

And it was.

A few years later while working on *Police Story* I got a more thorough lesson in the art of looking good in *TV Guide*. From David Gerber, of course.

"I need some popcorn!" he screamed one day. "Popcorn! Popcorn! Popcorn!"

His secretary scurried into the kitchen that was part of the office. "I don't think we have any," she said.

"Not that kind of popcorn!" the Gerb roared. "Popcorn casting, for *TV Guide*!" His eyes burned into mine as he pounded on his desk. "Give me some stars, dammit! A big name from the fifties that we can get cheap but who still means something to the audience. And give me a one-line description for the episode that we can give them. One line that grabs you by the goddamn throat and doesn't let go till you're dead!"

One thing you could say for Gerber. He always made his point.

By the early eighties, when I was producing both *Automan* and *The Fall Guy* on ABC, television had moved into its "high concept" era of development, which persists to this day. Suddenly network executives were tossing the phrase around as though they'd been saying it all their lives, and as though those of us being admonished to "Come up with a high concept for this episode," or to "Forget the frills, just tell me the high concept" knew what they were talking about.

It wasn't that hard to figure out, though. The network execs wanted the same thing Quinn Martin had admired and David Gerber had demanded—a short, concise description of an idea so great that it "grabs you by the goddamn throat and doesn't let go."

A logline.

To be fair, an argument can be made that all good ideas—maybe even all great ideas—can be expressed simply and concisely. That their essences can be boiled down to one direct statement communicating universal emotional truth. I've even argued that point of view myself from time to time.

But let's face it. When you're trying to earn a living and the only way you can do it is by turning out an episode a week, and one new *saleable* television series concept each year, universal emotional truth often seems too amorphous, too grandiose, too "goddamn" universal to distill and re-distill and distill again before deadline time.

So the entertainment media pro more likely than not is going to go down a more navigable route and give us something like the high concepts that follow, all of which got development deals or series on the air for their creators, who obviously had learned the trick of milking a snappy sentence for all it's worth:

"The two ex-wives of a private detective—one a ditz and the other even ditzier—inherit his detective agency when he dies and ineptly attempt to fight crime."

"He's handsome. He's rich. He's a great cop. But he can only fight crime at night—because of one other little quality. He's a vampire."

"A barbarian warrior and an apprentice thief fight evil in an alternate world."

"Two men drive around the country helping people solve their problems with the help of their monster truck."

And my favorite:

"It's already a best-selling series of books—*Mike Hammer*."

(Or, "It's already a top-selling comic book—*The Silver Surfer*."

(Or, "It's just like every old hit legal series and it features a really beloved old TV star to boot—*Matlock*, starring "Sheriff" Andy Griffith.")

Hey, admit it. These ideas all fit the bill. They're short and snappy and easy to grasp, and oh so easy to describe in *TV Guide*. (I admit it. I wrote and produced or otherwise supervised two of them.)

This particular point of view toward the creation of new material spread like wildfire. Television executives moved into feature films. Corporations that owned television networks and television and movie production companies started buying publishing houses, and what I call sideways mobility, the shuffling of executives from one branch of the entertainment business to the other, became commonplace. (Even the stage, once a bastion of complexity in terms of ideas and outlooks, has begun to succumb to corporate buy-outs and the *TV Guide* point of view. Look at all the "revivals." What could be easier to describe than a play that's already been a hit?)

Here's a high profile (similar, you could say, to high concept) example of lateral movement in the entertainment business over the past twenty-five years, typical in kind although more elevated in scope. Peter Chernin, intelligent, articulate, thoughtful (have to push those positive adjectives here; you'll soon see why), went from being a junior editor at a publishing company to David Gerber's assistant (where we worked together on a feature film project) to president of Showtime Networks to president of Twentieth Century-Fox Productions to chief operating officer of News Corporation, which now owned publishing houses much larger than the one where he'd originally worked.

With him—with everyone like him—went the Gerberian interpretation of one of the basic innovative elements that had made *TV Guide* the most successful publication in the United States for almost fifty years (until the magazine put out by the American Association of Retired People outsold it, proving once again the economic power of the now aging Baby Boomers).

Howard Stern may proclaim himself "the king of all media," but the most he can be is a crown prince.

The honor of ruling over everything goes to—

The logline.

Keep It Simple, Stupid.

Don't worry.

As things stand, it's the only way.

The Color TV Revolution Begins On "Kukla, Fran and Ollie"— A Kids' Show

*W*hen I was eight years old and not reading *TV Guide*, I learned two terrible truths.

I learned that innovation isn't always what it's cracked up to be.

And that no matter how hard you want to believe in them some things just can't live up to their hype.

I learned this from one of the most critically acclaimed children's shows of television's early days, *Kukla, Fran and Ollie.*

The show first went on the air as a local Chicago broadcast in 1947, becoming the first network show telecast live across the U.S. in 1949, and finally closing up shop in 1957. Unlike other shows from my childhood, where I have clear memories of my first encounter, *Kukla, Fran and Ollie* seems to have always been part of my life. I can't remember a time when, as a little kid, I wasn't looking forward to watching the Kuklapolitan Players on a weekday afternoon.

Unlike the puppets on *The Howdy Doody Show*, Kukla the clown, his partner Oliver J. Dragon, and the rest of their troupe (including Madame Ooglepuss the diva, Cecil Bill the stagehand, Beulah Witch, Fletcher Rabbit, Colonel Crackie, Dolores Dragon, and a few others who didn't make so big an impression on the young me) were hand puppets. They performed on a puppet stage set up at the eye level of the only human on the show, singer Fran Allison, and instead of exotic adventures or stealthy seltzer attacks, the show

Kukla, Burr Tillstrom, Ollie and Fran, circa 1953 (Jerry Ohlinger's Movie Material)

featured good conversation, mostly warm and witty arguments between the puppet cast members that were moderated by Fran.

Nothing about *Kukla, Fran and Ollie* in any way pandered to children. The issues and characters were universal and appealed to grownups and kids alike. My parents would never have thought of watching *The Howdy Doody Show* with me, nor would I have wanted them to. But my mother and I almost always watched *Kukla, Fran and Ollie* together, and on the rare occasions when my father was home at that time of day he joined us for an early version of what later would be called "quality time."

Kukla, Fran and Ollie was low key and charming, which at first glance makes it an odd choice to be NBC's selection as its color television pioneer. Where was the pizzazz? The sizzle? Where were the elements that cried out for full color enhancement?

The Howdy Doody Show had them in abundance. So did most of NBC's primetime shows, such as *Dragnet, The Colgate Comedy*

Hour, Your Show of Shows, and *Your Hit Parade.* In fact, in November of 1953 *The Colgate Comedy Hour,* which featured regular appearances by Dean Martin and Jerry Lewis, the hottest comedy team in the business at that time, became the first series to have all its episodes broadcast in color.

My impression, based on conversations with various tech whizzes of succeeding eras and my own experience with network-think, is that the fact that *Kukla, Fran and Ollie* involved almost no physical movement (other than the hand puppets gliding a foot or two in either direction on the puppet stage) was a factor because it made setting up the cameras easier and kept the color—which at the time had a tendency to become distorted if the electrons had to "paint" too quickly—under control. The fact that the show didn't air in primetime may also have been a plus because if it got screwed up the error wouldn't be noticed by too large an audience—and it wouldn't sink the rest of the schedule.

Whatever the reason, after holding private tests of a color *Kukla* over a period of several months, NBC announced that August 30, 1953, was going to be its big day, bringing color to Kuklapolitan fans.

Man, was I ready.

My mother and sister and I sat down to watch the show, and lo and behold—

We saw what we'd always seen: Kukla trying to solve the latest problem created by Madame Ooglepuss's ego, Ollie getting upset and biting Kukla's big red clown nose, Cecil Bill speaking his special "toytatoytatoytoytoy" language (forgive me, oh ghost of puppeteer Burr Tillstrom, if I've got the spelling wrong) that only Fran could understand, and Fran at last prevailing upon everyone to re-establish the peace.

Oh, yes, they also talked about the fact that they were in color and how exciting that was.

But my mother didn't see it that way.

Nor my sister.

Nor myself.

For us, everything was black and white and various shades of gray. As it had always been. As it would always be—until the family shelled out for a new RCA (they owned NBC at the time) color TV set.

Don't get me wrong. For my mother this was no big surprise. She was an adult. She'd been around. She'd read more than just the headlines of the articles heralding the great event. She knew the Brodys living over there in Chicago on the corner of Springfield and Congress wouldn't see anything new or different. No reds, no blues, no greens.

But somehow that hadn't been communicated to me.

To say I was disappointed is to understate the case. I was devastated.

I was so upset that I refused to watch *Kukla, Fran and Ollie* again. At least until the next week.

For NBC, though, the test was a great success. In addition to the ongoing *Colgate Comedy Hour* episodes NBC broadcast, it tested the use of color film for an episode of *Dragnet* in December (but broadcast it in black and white), and on January 1, 1954, the network broadcast the Rose Bowl Parade in color. Throughout the fifties NBC ramped up its colorcasts, and the rest of the industry followed.

In September of 1961, color broadcasting took a major step forward as *Walt Disney's Wonderful World of Color* joined the NBC schedule. The chance to see Mickey Mouse and Donald Duck and Goofy and footage from classic Disney animated films at home and in color proved to be a major incentive for viewers to buy color television sets, and in 1962 a million of them were sold.

In 1966 NBC started colorcasting all its shows, and CBS and ABC struggled to keep up. By the end of the sixties black and white shows were a thing of the past on network television and approximately 37 million color sets were in use in the U.S.

Even yours truly.

I wasn't living with my family anymore, and I wasn't in Chicago. I was in L.A., writing *The Interns* and *Here Come The Brides* and other such stellar fare, and in 1969 I finally broke down and bought an RCA console that, as I look back at it now, looked very much like the set in Neil Friedman's house all those years before.

The reason I waited so long—other than the fact that I was

a struggling writer who needed every penny earned from this month's assignment to pay last month's bills—-was that it wasn't until '69 that color television seemed to work properly. Which is to say that it was finally a kind of hands-off proposition, no longer in need of constant adjustment in order to keep people's complexions from being too red or too pale and changing from shot to shot.

Sixteen years after I saw that first color broadcast of *Kukla, Fran and Ollie*, they finally had it right.

Today, of course, no one would even consider having anything but a color TV set. Although when they first came out they cost the proverbial arm and a leg, they're now far cheaper than black and white sets were in the first few decades of TV.

The new dimension of reality that color added all those years ago is taken for granted. Most current television viewers have never seen TV in black and white and my children, for example, find it impossible to imagine watching any medium that doesn't have a full, rainbow palette.

Color increased production costs for the networks, studios, and production companies, but so many other factors have been added to the production expense equation since then that shooting in color means almost nothing now. (Although there's still the aggravation of having to "color correct" footage. That is, of making sure that the color of film shot in a particular place under particular lighting and atmospheric conditions on one day matches the color of film shot in the same place under different conditions on another, because within the context of the production it's all supposed to happen at the same time.)

So color's here and our home entertainment is the better for it. All's right with the world.

Except—

Letting my memory roam back to the Kuklapolitans and the color test that disappointed me so much ("But why would they say it's in color if it's not, Mom? Why would they want us to have to buy a new TV?") has caused something entirely different, and yet quite relevant, to come to mind.

Kukla, Fran and Ollie was part of at least two different important experiments in television broadcasting. It served as a stalking horse for the beginning of nationwide network transmission, and as a major test case for color TV.

And *Kukla, Fran and Ollie* was a *kids'* show.

Can you imagine something like that happening today?

Do you believe for one minute that *Sesame Street*, as celebrated and vital and long-lived as that series is, would ever be picked out as a test of any new technology for future TV?

Reading Rainbow?

Rugrats?

Justice League?

Once upon a time the field was open. There was one big arena called television. That one big arena brought us programs for children at a time when children could access the family's set, for adults at a later time ("primetime," which when you think about it really is a terrific name), for older adults (mostly syndicated fare like *The Lawrence Welk Show*), and the hip and trendy who stayed up to watch "late night" for its spontaneity and irreverence.

Now everything's compartmentalized, not just in terms of when it's on—block scheduling existed from the beginning, remember?—but in terms of how it's viewed within the business. As more specific audience groups are targeted and programming becomes more fragmented, so does the business model on which it's all based.

In the beginning was the broadcast network, the avowed purpose of which was to appeal to a "general audience," and which in the process helped create such an audience both literally and perceptually. (More on this in the next chapter.) Now niche broadcasting is coming into its own, with cable and satellite channels programming themselves in a television equivalent of what happened to magazine publishing. What was then Time, Incorporated, realized a magazine like *Life*, with its generalist skew, couldn't support itself while competing with *Dog World* and *Boy's Life* and *Ladies Home Companion* and *Doll* and *Electric Train* and all the other publications that had pinpointed their readerships to specific special interest groups.

Creatively, the still-growing pattern of niche programming is a boon, and as a professional within the business, I'm a firm advocate. But as a member of the audience I miss that general sense of community. And as both I miss the sense of programming *equality*, when an adult could watch Madame Ooglepuss give a spirited tongue-lashing to Cecil Bill and not feel that he or she was slumming, and when a child could watch *Dragnet* and follow the story because it started at the beginning of the episode and finished at the end.

Which brings me to a story. About Larry Brody's attempts to be part of innovative television, and to do it not by creating a show "for mature audiences only" so characters could say, "Fuck you" and bare butts and breasts could shake it up, baby (been there, done that, had a lot of fun), but by writing and producing a new kind of puppet show that kids and parents could watch together.

The year was 1985, and Herb Solow, then an independent producer after years of running studios (during which time he worked shoulder to shoulder with Gene Roddenberry to get the original *Star Trek* series on the air and keep Mr. Spock's ears pointed), had been contacted by the Coleco Toy Company. In the Avi Arad tradition of children's programs as infomercials, Coleco had a new line of toys coming out and wanted to create a Saturday morning cartoon series based on it.

The toys were called "Sectaurs," and they were science fiction characters on an alien planet, super scientific humans living with super strong and super huge insects. There were good humans and bad humans, good insects and bad insects, and good costumes for both. The best thing about the Sectaurs, though, was that they were just the type of toy I'd loved since the *Kukla* days.

They were hand puppets.

Designed by a young muppet maker from Jim Henson's outfit, the top-of-the-line puppet creator of its day. (Do you think for one minute that *Sesame Street* would've become the phenomenon it did if all it had were short animations and humans?)

Of course, Coleco didn't call the toys hand puppets because its research (not done by Richard Lindheim of NBC but certainly the same kind of very professional investigation in which he specialized) had showed that consumers had an active dislike for the term. Too old-fashioned. Fucking antiquated, you know?

So instead Coleco called the Sectaurs "hands in play" toys. Built 'em out of solid plastic with polyester sleeves so they looked just like accessories for Mattel's He-Man line of toys.

Except that a kid could stick a hand in that polyester sleeve and have complete control over every move the Sectaurs made, for good or for bad, as heroes or tyrants.

I hated the cowardice of not calling a puppet a puppet. Can you imagine Kukla and Ollie as "hands in play" toys?

But I loved playing with the suckers.

And I loved the truly innovative approach Herb had come up with. "There are a million Saturday morning cartoons out there advertising toys," he said as we flew to Connecticut to meet with the Coleco brass. "And there will be a lot more. [He was certainly right about that.] Why should we follow the herd?

"Instead of an ongoing cartoon series," Herb said, "let's go all out. No animation, just humans. Actors in fantastic costumes working with sensational prosthetics and props.

"And," he went on, "what do we need a series for? It'll just get lost in the shuffle. Let's do the first big event full-length, two-hour, primetime, syndicated science fiction movie! Get it on the air all around the country the night before the Sectaurs appear in the stores! It'll be a major entertainment event, a precursor of a whole new kind of presentation. And it might just sell a few toys!"

He sure as hell sold me.

And Coleco too.

Everyone involved loved the idea of doing something new, of creating something families could watch together, making this a major television presentation and blazing a trail for more.

There were, of course, a host of problems to solve.

I had to write a script that would create the kind of wonder that made the movie worth watching.

A host of technicians had to come up with ways to shoot it on an affordable budget and make it look *more* than worth watching. (And this was in the days before CGI.)

And a savvy old television biz pro had to come up with a way to implement two business firsts because:

No one had ever syndicated a television movie before.

And no one had ever coordinated the syndication of anything

so that the same show would appear on all stations at the same time.

Primetime, no less.

Then there was the need for sensational advertising to provide the finished project with the audience it needed. And, of course, the money to pay for all these different aspects. That was Coleco's department.

Herb and I went back to L.A. and got to work. We assembled a team of the best of the best—including the Muppet maker–creator and his partner. We planned and we wrote and we planned some more and we sketched and we planned even more and we built.

We had the script. We had the costumes. We had the beginnings of the props. We had stations eager to carry our "event."

But you never saw *Sectaurs of Symbion* on television, did you? Or anywhere else.

And you probably have never heard of the toys.

Because as pre-production time drew to an end and production was about to begin Coleco did what any smart company should do. It ran a cost-risk evaluation of the project.

And did more consumer/marketing research on the toys.

The good news was that the research showed that hands-in-play worked just fine. No one held the fact that they were hand puppets against the Sectaurs.

The bad news was that the research showed that consumers—both children and parents—were completely freaked out by the fact that the Sectaurs were insects.

Chitinous appendages. "Eww."

Mechanical looking spiders. "Eww. Eww."

Glowing, multi-faceted eyes. "Eww. Eww. Eww."

Family relationships (read: "sex lives") no one could relate to or even understand. "Eww. Eww. Eww. Eww."

End of *Sectaurs of Symbion*, the big event full-length, two-hour, primetime, syndicated science fiction movie.

End of *Sectaurs'* chances for being even a moderately successful line of toys. (Oh, they sold 'em all right. Dumped the buggers into stores without a peep of publicity and watched 'em gather dust on the shelves.)

End of Coleco, which went belly up, bankrupt, and closed its doors only a couple of years later.

Why did the project go crashing to the earth like this? Why did its fire dissolve, unseen, into the earth's core?

I think it's because it simply was too late. Children's shows as infomercials, segregated into the Saturday morning ghetto, were the rule and nothing was going to change it.

Herb and I were fooling ourselves.

But I like to think that if instead of those disgusting chitinous spiders we'd had, say, a clown and a dragon and a diva and a guy who went "Toytatoytatoytoytoy," we would've pulled it off.

We would've done just fine.

The Weekly Numbers Aren't Enough: Overnight Ratings Come Into Play

*W*hen writers get together to discuss their craft, the conversation often turns to whether or not a story should be what we call "character driven," which is to say that the tale is moved along by the inner needs, drives, and fears of the characters, or "plot driven," a way of writing in which what occurs does so because the writer is manipulating the characters into various pre-chosen situations.

The argument often gets quite intense, but there's one thing most people who've made their living in any aspect of the television business will agree on.

Regardless of which way they think a story *should* be written—and, by the way, I'll take a stand on it here and now, fearlessly advocating a creative and reasonable melding of both points of view (okay, so maybe that's not so fearless after all)—the fact of the matter is that just about all stories on TV, regardless of their genre or length or whether they're dramas, action shows, comedies, or a blend of all three, are in fact driven by *ratings*.

That's right. You can't get around it. Ratings are what most television is all about.

When Richard Lindheim was telling the *Police Story* squad what his research showed the audience preferred, you don't think for a minute that he was trying to make the series more creatively effective, do you?

I mean, he's a nice man, and smart as all hell, but Richard and all the other men and women I've known who work in the research departments of NBC, CBS, ABC, Fox, UPN, WB, UNAME-IT know that their purpose is to help the "talent" put out shows that will get the "best numbers," where "best" means "highest" and "numbers" means "ratings."

Ain't no way around it. Television is a popularity contest. The larger the measurable audience the fatter the purse for those putting the show on the air.

Gotta feed the beast.

And ratings are what it eats.

It's been that way since the beginning, that sultry summer day in 1941. All that's changed are the means by which the audience is measured and the specific audience being sought.

Have no doubt about it: The target audience has always been a specific one. Viewers with the most disposable income and the most open minds. Viewers who aren't set in their ways. Who can be influenced—

No, not influenced by the content of the programs.

By that stuff that comes in between the content.

The "C word."

Commercials.

Sorry. Someone had to say it. Please don't wash my mouth out with soap.

Television may be the medium everyone loves to hate, but commercials are the part of TV everyone just plain despises.

Except for the execs, of course. For the CEOs and the COOs and the CFOs and all the practical, realistically minded businessmen who fight every day to keep their companies strong, commercials are what it's all about.

And ratings and commercials are inextricably intertwined, a marriage made in financial heaven presided over, some say, by Father Mammon, while others give the nod to the much less pernicious Brother Necessity.

Here's part one of the primary way the system works today. And the only way it worked until recently.

Four-year-old Larry Brody's mother turns on the TV set, and Kid Brody raptly watches *The Howdy Doody Show*. The show is free.

It has cost the family nothing except the original investment in the set and the time spent looking at its little screen. Throughout the show Howdy Doody himself tells Kid Brody how great Bosco will make that icky white milk his mother makes him drink taste. At the end of the show, Kid Brody morphs into Kid Clout and tells his mother how much he wants Bosco. How much he needs Bosco. How much he loves Bosco.

"But you've never even tasted Bosco," Mother Brody says. She takes out a bottle of brown liquid and pours the thick, cold mess into Kid Clout's milk. "Try this Hershey's Syrup."

Kid Clout shakes his head. "I want Bosco" is all he can say.

Eventually Mother Brody buys Kid Clout some Bosco. Stirs it into his milk. Kid Clout sips. Doesn't like it all that much. But he doesn't want to tell his mother that. And later that day Howdy Doody again tells the audience how good Bosco is. So the Kid tries it again. And again. And again.

Eventually, Kid Clout really does love Bosco. Or sure as hell thinks he does. But by this time the jar is empty and Mother Brody has to buy more.

Bosco's sales go way up. The number of viewers watching *The Howdy Doody Show* rises as well. There's an easy-to-make statistical correlation between the number of kids watching the show and the number of mothers buying Bosco, and that correlation is lost on no one involved. NBC raises the amount of money it charges the makers of Bosco for Howdy Doody to tell viewers how yummy their product is.

As television becomes more established this relationship changes a bit. It becomes simpler in terms of basic assumptions. Regardless of whether the sales of Bosco go up, NBC raises the price every time the number of viewers on its number one kids' show goes up. More viewers means more *potential* sales, and potential is almost as good as actual, isn't it? I mean, look here—they're *this* close.

Eventually, if sales don't go up, the prices, like those in any market for any kind of goods or services, will level off or even go down. Bosco can end up paying less per viewing head, but the company will still be paying *per head*, as determined by the universally accepted way of counting such things in television. By *ratings*.

So that's how the audience got and for the most part still gets its television shows for free. Someone has to pay for them, and that's the advertiser. It's a sponsored medium.

Which means, as management consultant Robert Lewis pointed out in a column he wrote in *InfoWorld Magazine* (which was so elementary to him that he'd actually forgotten about it until I reminded him a few years later), that when you dig just a little into how the television business really operates you see that, although the viewers are being provided with entertainment, the viewers are *not* the customers of those providers.

The sponsors are the customers.

And the viewers are the *product*.

After all, aren't the networks really selling viewers to advertisers, with advertisers buying on the theory that pushing the right button with those viewers will enable them to sell their own product to the viewers in turn?

But if the networks are in the business of supplying heads and the sponsors are buying those heads, what are the shows the networks are airing?

Bob Lewis has the answer.

In one word.

"Bait," Lewis says. "The shows are bait to attract the viewers. They're the lure that brings the viewers into the trap so they can be sold."

Kid Clout really did have clout. He was a valuable commodity lured by Howdy Doody into a figurative box on a metaphorical shelf in an electronic store owned by NBC and sold for top dollar to the company that made Bosco.

Hmm, if I'm so damn powerful, why ain't I rich?

Why ain't you?

The people who are selling us are the ones collecting the bucks. And while they do that we, instead of standing up to be counted, are instead counted as we sit down before our TV sets.

Which brings us to part two of the primary way the system works today, etc.

The mechanism that counts viewers and thereby determines their value as a product is the ratings. The viewers of all the broadcast networks and cable and satellite channels are counted via various sampling methods. The number of viewers watching each of the networks and channels as individual entities is determined, and everything gets ranked and compared a million ways to Sunday.

When television first began there were several ratings companies, with Arbitron and A.C. Nielsen the leaders of the pack. The ratings companies came into being during the days of network radio, counting and ranking listeners, and they applied the same methods they'd been using to the new medium. This meant telephone surveys. "Hi there. Whatcha watchin'?"

Obvious questions to ask when discussing any kind of sampling used to determine what the general population is listening to or watching are "How was the sampling determined? How completely does it represent the audience?" Another is, "How do we know the people being sampled are telling the truth?"

So during the forties and fifties methods grew more refined. A.C. Nielsen took the lead in the battle for network hearts and minds when it came up with a way to record what people were watching as they watched it, and set up an elaborate process for selecting its subjects based on a proportionate re-creation of census statistics.

The Nielsen guys took this very seriously. I remember when one came to the house when I was about twelve years old and started hooking up our two televisions and two radios—then stopped, packing up and leaving us rejected because his original paperwork had erroneously stated that we had two televisions and one radio, and that was the sample he needed.

Although Arbitron ratings remain important in radio, Nielsen took complete control of the television ratings business in 1959, with the creation of what came to be called "overnights." A computer tie-in to the ratings box keeping track of the television-watching habits of what were now known as "Nielsen families" gave A.C. Nielsen the ability to provide subscribers (networks, studios, and production companies, for the most part) with a complete daily breakdown of what percentage of the total population, and of the population watching at a given time, tuned in during primetime the night before.

The catch, which proved not to be a catch at all, was that the data didn't come from the total population of the United States or even a representative sample thereof, but from the total population of the "big cities," which at that time meant the twenty largest television markets, AKA the twenty most populous metropolitan areas in the country. The overnights told those who could afford to pay for the information only what urban Nielsen families were viewing.

But that was just fine.

Because the urbanites were the ones the advertisers cared about most. They were the ones with all the disposable income, the original target audience, which could now be sold as a stand-alone product instead of as part of the "nationals."

(Which also were known for a while as the "overalls." As in the clothes farmers wear. The rural folks. The play on words was unintentional at the time. The thought behind it was not.)

What happened was that right from the get-go the research departments of advertising agencies and networks alike had determined that the urban population was the one with the clout, adult clout as well as kid. But there was no quick or efficient (and certainly no self-evident) way to see if that particular group of viewers had taken the bait until overnights.

Until overnights it took months to sift through the data and cull the target herd. But as of September 1959, when overnights went into action for the first time, spewing out the numbers for the metropolis of metropolises, New York City, the generation of data was as good as instant. This meant that advertisers could make quicker decisions about what shows to buy into next, and that networks could make quicker adjustments in their pricing.

Overnight.

The remaining nineteen big city markets were tied in as quickly as Nielsen's technicians could finish programming their mainframe. In almost no time at all the future was here. Nielsen's overnight ratings represented the first in-your-face series of demographics, directly influencing what kinds of shows networks would put on the air. Once they had immediate knowledge of what was hot and on target and what was not, network development executives could buy more suitable shows, shows similar to those already garnering a large percentage of the urban clout crowd, and tweak shows that looked like they were headed the wrong way so they could get back on track.

I first learned the importance of overnights in my David Gerber days. I wasn't quite a producer yet. I was executive story consultant on an NBC series called *Medical Story*, a critically acclaimed but ill-conceived anthology show that featured idealistic young doctor protagonists opposite burned-out or greedy older physicians. The "youth versus the rest of the world" concept was very seventies, which probably wouldn't have been a problem if the uncaring old villains the so-caring young men and women were pitted against hadn't been the nation's most beloved and highly respected professional group at the time. (This was before HMOs.)

Medical Story's berth on the NBC schedule was precarious from day one, when the two-hour pilot failed to attract the ratings numbers that the network researchers had predicted. Along about the fourth episode those of us who staffed the series began worrying about our job security. There were a few rumors that our ratings were up, and a few more that our ratings were down.

Realizing that I needed more information so I could plan my professional and financial future better, I looked up from where I was rewriting operating room dialogue based on what I had heard on a tape featuring the voice of a genuine uncaring old villain doctor secretly taped by a real so-caring young one, and went up to Gerber's office to ask his secretary how the latest episode to be aired had done.

Gerber overheard and did what he always did. He hit the roof. "What the hell do you want the goddamn ratings for?" he demanded. "What do you care how the hell many people are watching? Just write what I tell you, for chrissake. And write it damn fast."

"I want to know how many people watched the last show."

"I watched the last show," Gerber the mentor said. "You watched the last show. We watched it together at my goddamn house. And we came in nineteenth in the overnights."

"The overnights are only for the major cities. What about the rest of the country?" I said. "I used to go to school in Iowa City. How'd we do there?"

"Who the hell cares about goddamn Iowa Goddamn City?" Gerber said. "We're not making this show for Iowa Goddamn City. We're making it for L.A. and New York and Chicago and Boston and St. Louis and San Francisco. The rest of the country doesn't count."

He crouched like a football lineman and feinted left, then came at me from the right, an elbow banging my rib. "If you want to get anyplace in this business you gotta understand how it works. *Medical Story* and every other kind of story on TV's not for the rest of the country. They're for the cities, where they buy the damn sponsors' damn products, and where *Medical Story*'s number nineteen. So get the fuck out of here and write an episode that'll get us in the Top Ten or I'll tell your wife what you've been doing with my secretary."

"Larry and I haven't been doing anything—" Gerber's secretary tried to say. But Gerber held up his hand. "It's not what he's doing that counts, it's what I say he's doing."

And with that the Gerb grabbed me by the shoulders and whirled me around and pushed me through the doorway and out of the office, slamming the door behind me.

All I could think was, *lesson learned.*

A few years later, Barry Diller reputedly coined the phrase "those people we fly over" in referring to the heartland of the U.S., at whom no television shows were aimed. But I always think of that disenfranchised group as "the rest of the country," in the words of my teacher the Gerb.

For thirty years the overnights were the true, behind-the-scenes gauge of the success of a television show. From time to time a critically acclaimed series that had lousy ratings nationwide would be renewed and columnists would publicly applaud the decision, usually describing it as "taking a risk." But the Gerb had taught me better, and a little homework would invariably show that the overnight ratings for the "risky" show were high enough to make it exactly what the network needed to satisfy sponsors.

Similarly, networks would sometimes cancel shows that the nationals showed were big hits. Remember the outcry when CBS axed *The Beverly Hillbillies* and its rurally oriented cousins? Yes, they were still doing well in "the rest of the country," but their overnights in the big cities made potential advertisers sneer.

In the late eighties ratings for broadcast networks in general started to fall, nationals and overnights, and sponsors started pulling back, negotiating lower prices for their spots. The broadcast networks were in genuine danger, and they knew it. Fortunately for them, so did the people counters at A.C. Nielsen, and a new category made it into the ratings for the first time.

Viewers could now—and were now—measured by age.

The era of demographics arrived.

This direct outgrowth of overnights breaks the viewing population down into various age groups, thereby creating more ratings "winners" to make up for the decline of the total audience. A network might have lost a significant percentage (share) of viewers in the cities, but it could point to the fact that it had more viewers between the ages of fourteen and forty-seven than the next guy.

That particular age group wasn't a random choice. The more refined target audience for advertisers, as determined by the latest research, had become boys and men and girls and women from their early teens to their mid-forties living in the usual urban population centers. The definition of "urban" had also been broadened to include about forty metropolitan areas as well.

The effect of this situation on television programming is still being felt, with almost one hundred percent of the shows aired by broadcast networks and basic cable channels trying to appeal to "youth." (I have a problem figuring out what fourteen-year-olds and forty-seven-year-olds have in common, tastewise, or why the age of forty-seven—which I once was not all that long ago—is considered "young," but I'm sure that if I wanted to risk the injury to body and ego that being around the Gerb always caused he could probably set me straight.)

So the next time you turn on your TV set and flick around, finding all those young urban people whose environments and problems suggest a homogeneity that in no way reflects your own situation (unless you're watching a premium cable channel like our good friends Showtime and HBO), try not to despair. All you can do is shrug philosophically and remind yourself that you're just a victim of this particular turning point in TV.

Or look at it another way. Once you know that the channel you're watching isn't trying to entertain you but to trap you instead, show its management who's boss by clicking away.

It beats being a trapped fox, doesn't it? At least you don't have to chew off your own leg.

CHAPTER 10: 1961

Fred Silverman Begins
His Legendary Career,
Going to Work at CBS

*F*red Silverman could well be the single most influential man in the history of television programming.

Yet most people who have not toiled in the television business idea mines have never heard of him.

When Fred goes out to dinner with the star of one of the many series he has produced, it's not his autograph other patrons come to the table to get, nor is it concern about Fred's satisfaction with the food that brings the chef out of the kitchen to discuss the main course. Instead, it's the presence at the table of Andy Griffith or Dick Van Dyke or Tom Bosley or any number of others.

As executive producer of *Matlock, Diagnosis Murder, Father Dowling Mysteries, The New Adventures of Perry Mason,* and other series based as much on the repackaging of a star from an earlier era ("popcorn") as on the high concept of the show itself, Fred has followed in a tradition of showmen harkening back past the old movie studio system to the early days of vaudeville, always looking for that extra something that will attract the audience's attention.

But Fred Silverman is more than just a descendant of the likes of P.T. Barnum or Buffalo Bill Cody or MGM's founder, Louis B. Mayer. He's a kind of ancestral figure all by himself, a true original whose greatest influence comes from the policies he put into effect as the only person ever to be the head programming executive at all three major networks, CBS, then ABC, and then NBC.

Within the biz, Fred's history has been well publicized. He began his career as a television executive in 1961 when the Master's thesis he wrote while getting his degree at Ohio State University helped him get a job overseeing children's programs on WGN, a local channel in Chicago. The next year he moved to another local channel, this one in New York City, and by 1963 Fred was director of daytime programming at CBS.

Fred stayed at CBS until 1975, moving up to vice president of programming for CBS Entertainment. He followed this with a stint as president of ABC Entertainment, and then in 1978 he moved into the executive suite at NBC as president and CEO, overseeing not only programming but just about everything else there until 1981.

In an arena where meteoric rises are commonplace, this kind of longevity and lateral movement remains unique. As a young man he possessed all the qualities show business movers and shakers look for in a protégé, and stockholders reward in an executive. An avowed lover of television who closely studied the careers of the executives who preceded him (this was from Fred's lips to my ears), Fred was a master of the creative, practical, and historical or contextual elements of his chosen field from the moment he entered it. The young Fred regarded his job as the most important thing in his life, a kind of higher calling, and not only was he willing to work long hours, he was also smart as all hell.

An unusual combination of brilliant intellect and forceful personality, Fred from the very beginning had the ability to combine research conclusions with gut feelings in a way that made him simultaneously the ultimate developer and the ultimate audience. If Fred liked a show the odds were viewers would like it too. And if he *loved* it, well now you're talking major ratings numbers. Add to this the fact that *shy* and *retiring* are words that could never be used to describe him on the job (at home it seems always to have been a different matter), and you have a veritable force of nature on your hands, a guy who's just plain unstoppable.

(In fact, in the mid-nineties, when I was overseeing an animated series based on the Marvel Comics character the Silver Surfer, I based the personality of our ongoing most super of super villains and the "creator" of our hero, Galactus, partly on Fred.)

    The bottom line, then, is that Fred Silverman was and still is a
dynamo, called by *Time* magazine (in a cover story no less) "the
man with the golden gut" and referred to by others as "the mad
programmer." The occasion of his first job in television is a major
turning point in the history of the medium because this brilliant
and sensitive man created, molded, and shaped the programming
philosophy and practice that has dominated television for almost
fifty years, continuing to this day, more than twenty-five years since
he left his last network job.

And what was this mighty philosophy?

This powerful practice?

Television critics called it "jiggle."

But Fred himself coined a slightly longer phrase:

"Tits and ass."

Not that Fred Silverman started out as a full-fledged tits and ass
man. No, it took him a while. He had to work into the jiggle thing.

But the signs were there, even in his children's programming.

    The way television shows are developed is that producers, writ-
ers, and sometimes actors get ideas that they bring to "the network." That means they meet with the highest level network series
development executive they can and try to get a series commitment, or a pilot commitment, or at least a pilot script commitment,
for their idea. The meeting is usually a give and take affair, with the
network executive contributing as much as those on the other side
of the desk. When it's over the executive—if he or she is upper
management level and has the authority—gives some kind of
go-ahead or else agrees to recommend that his or her superior give
said go-ahead. (Or not, but we're being positive now.)

    After the necessary number of scripts or pilots have been writ-
ten and shot, the head of development meets with the chief programmer and together they decide which shows to put on the
air. Then the programmer decides where to put them. Many
people, even those otherwise well-versed in the business, think
that this is the point where the programmer enters the picture.
He is, however, there from the beginning, because it's the programmer's vision, developed from research and gut feeling, of what
kind of shows the network will need for the coming season

that determines which shows make it past that first development meeting. The development gang is looking for "good" ideas based on the old adage that "'good' means something my boss will like."

So as chief programmer for children's shows at CBS, Fred Silverman's definition of "good," which is to say his wants, needs, and tastes, pervaded the Saturday morning schedule throughout all development phases. And what did Fred do in terms of CBS's programming for kids?

Three things.

He developed, bought, and scheduled one-hour shows like *The Flintstones Comedy Hour* at a time when all Saturday morning kids' block shows were half an hour, thereby insuring continuity on the half-hour by making it more difficult for a young viewer to decide to change the channel. (Watch for half an hour without seeing the end? Can't do that! Gotta stick with it no matter what!)

He pioneered the scheduling of animated shows starring—well, they starred hot chicks is what they did. *Josie and the Pussycats in Outer Space* was, no matter how you look at it, about babes whose animated breasts defied gravity in a way most human women's couldn't—at least not until implants became the showbiz standard instead of the exception.

He presided over an era in which CBS's Saturday morning animation schedule went from third in the ratings to first.

Fred got 'em watching. And kept them watching.

He did the same thing for CBS primetime, putting *All in the Family, The Mary Tyler Moore Show, The Waltons, Maude, Rhoda, The Jeffersons, Phyllis,* and a slew of other innovative programs on the air.

During an era in our country's history in which political debate and dissonance created the kind of controversy and generational conflict usually reserved for matters of sex, religion, and alternate lifestyles, Fred put humorous, fictionalized versions of the debate on from 8:00 to 11:00 p.m. It was high class stuff all the way, and it got 'em watching. Kept 'em watching too.

All except Fred. Instead of continuing to turn out gemlike programming for what once billed itself as "the Tiffany of TV," Fred became president of ABC. It was here that the hints of tits and ass turned into something more substantial, as in genuine bosoms and butts.

During Fred's ABC years, the Vietnam War came to an end and idealism lost its potency, as well as its novelty. "The country needed a change," Fred told me one day a few years later. "*I* needed a change. The sexual revolution was in full swing, and I realized that people of my generation felt like they'd been left out. They were too old to be part of it so they pretended to be against it, but let's face it, all that free love was a big turn-on."

With a mind full of turn-on Fred made over his new workplace. On the plus side, he gave the U.S. the miniseries *Roots*, a drama every bit as important and highly praised as his former CBS comedies. So what if it took the stridency out of the fight for racial equality and substituted pathos instead? It got big numbers. Then there was another miniseries, *Rich Man, Poor Man*, based on a bestseller by one of the country's greatest short story writers, Irwin Shaw. To be sure, the novel was written in pure Harold Robbins mode, and it wasn't big ideas that viewers tuned in for but the sexual misadventures of the character played by a newcomer, Nick Nolte. Anyone got a problem with that?

On the series front Fred went all out, foregoing subtlety or disguise. ABC had hits with *Starsky and Hutch, Charlie's Angels, Three's Company, The Love Boat*, and *Fantasy Island*, among others. All these shows except *Starsky and Hutch* featured lots of bikini or towel-clad stars and guest stars, lots more sensuous dancing in bikinis or towels, and lots, lots more sniggering sexual innuendo. *Starsky and Hutch* made do with two swaggering macho buddies who were as deadly to bad guys as they were irresistible to women, while driving around L.A. in America's most traditional phallic symbol—a hot, brightly painted new car.

Once again, Fred got 'em watching. And Fred kept 'em watching.

ABC's ratings soared to the highest they'd been in years.

At which point Fred moved to NBC.

How could he resist? He wasn't a mere network president there—he was *CEO*.

As CEO of NBC Entertainment Fred had complete control, and used it. He hired a group of bright young executives, including

Brandon Tartikoff, who, if you had known Fred way back when—and if you squinted just right—was a hell of a lot like Fred was at that age, and he used them as sounding boards for his ideas for new shows to air, including *Supertrain; Hello, Larry;* and *Pink Lady and Jeff.*

Under Fred, NBC's programming was distinctive for what it lacked instead of what it possessed. It lacked tits and ass, and it lacked controversy and class. In fact, it lacked watchability for any reason whatsoever, as this time around Fred's attention focused on grandiose exaggeration, on big visuals shot small (because by its very nature television is always shot small), on big concepts that had no core, nothing to offer but their size.

Fred Silverman's NBC programming was, in a word, *camp.*

At their best, presented deliberately with malice aforethought, campy shows are the idiot version of post-modern reconstruction, mocking and often hate-filled parodies of beloved ancestors. At their worst, presented unknowingly, campy shows are ignorant and lifeless caricatures of outdated twaddle.

Fred's campy shows were *not* the best they could be. They were as far from deliberate re-creations as you could get.

The result was inevitable. They bombed badly, and in 1981 Fred went into the form of show business exile known as "indie prod." Independent production deals are common elements of the severance packages of studio and network executives. The exiting executive (*Daily Variety*, one of showbiz's main trade papers, likes to use the phrase "ankling exec") makes a public statement to the effect that he has resigned "to take on the challenge of independent production," and the former employer picks up the tab for an office and an assistant or two in return for a "first look" at any projects its former leader comes up with. After a year or two, the deal usually evaporates, and the severed executive is on his or her own.

But Fred wasn't even given an office for his new company. He was on his own. Most people in the know wrote him off, assuming this was the end, my friend, especially those who'd been victims of his often highhanded (admirers liked to use the term "abundantly confident") ways.

Not, however, Glen A. Larson.

It was through Glen that I met the no-longer-a-boy-genius. I was working at Glen Larson Productions, producing both *The Fall Guy* and another ABC show, *Automan*. The company had other shows on the air as well, a bunch of them. Glen's place in television history as the writer and creator of more one-hour network and syndicated television series (over thirty and still counting) than any other individual is about as secure a record as there is in any area.

And Glen's the kind of guy who never writes off anyone.

Especially not anyone as smart as Fred Silverman.

Glen had supplied Fred with several series during Fred's tenure at ABC and NBC, and had found that they had two common qualities: The love of the medium, and the love of strategizing in terms of the medium. Now that he was "down," Fred had a lot of strategizing to do, and he would come to the Larson bungalow at Twentieth Century-Fox a couple of afternoons a week to pick Glen's brain and allow his to be picked in turn.

The Fred Silverman I met was overweight and subdued. Actress Valerie Harper, who got her big break when Fred approved her for the part of Rhoda on *The Mary Tyler Moore Show*, once described him to me as "the class clown who's really the smartest guy in school." But the Fred Silverman who planned his comeback in Glen Larson's office wasn't funny at all. He was, as a matter of fact, pretty damn morose.

We had something in common, though. Our children were classmates at a private school Fred could afford much easier than could I. In between sessions where Fred advised Glen on how to handle his current success and leverage it into more, and Glen advised Fred on how to come up with ideas for series that the then-current crop of network buyers couldn't turn down, Fred and I would talk about the things dads talk about. No, not Little League. We hit the big topics: The Los Angeles social and economic environments and educational system and how they would impact his daughter Melissa and my son Jeb.

During these conversations I, like so many others before and after me, was amazed by Fred's grasp of the facts and his insight.

Which meant that I, like so many others before and after me, was also amazed by the way such a smart guy could have dedicated so much of his life to so much schlock.

I wanted to ask him about it but couldn't make myself come out with, "Hey, guy, what's with *Three's Company*? Do you realize that the success of that show has created so many imitations that it's impossible to turn on the TV and not see some smirking twenty-year-old plotting and pratfalling and bemoaning the fact that he can't get laid?" Or, "Yo, Fred, what were you thinking when you gave the go-ahead to *Supertrain*?"

After all, we were acquaintances, not close friends, and why offend him by bringing up how much his shows offended me? Not a polite thing to do. And not a smart thing to do, if all the time Fred and Glen spent together picking each other's brains paid off for this former Mr. Network Big.

Nevertheless, I did gain some insight into Fred's mindset and judgment, mostly through his reaction to problems that came up on *The Fall Guy* when he was around.

One day, for example, Glen and I had a problem with a guest star. As the star of her own series a few years earlier, she'd been quite a beauty. But when she reported to *The Fall Guy* set that beauty was hidden beneath several layers of fat. What to do?

Immediately, Fred took over the discussion. "The way to handle this," he said, "is to concentrate on Jody [our young, beautiful jiggle-character]. Show as much of her tits as you can get away with and let her shake her buns. That'll keep the audience from being disappointed. And if the character plays it like she's a little jealous of the fat old star that'll be great because it'll make it all funny."

Another day we had a scene where Lee Majors, the star, was supposed to end up dunked in a pool. But it was chilly out and we were always dunking Lee in bodies of water large and small. Lee had had it with getting wet and refused to take the plunge. "Not a big deal," said Fred, leaning back on Glen's couch with a smile. "Let Jody take the fall. And if it's cold her nipples'll get hard and it'll look even better. And her reaction to the whole thing can be pretty funny."

Sexuality. Humor. These always were the essence of Fred's suggestions. During this period I realized that he was no cynical intellectual pandering to his audience. He was his audience. He enjoyed everything he'd put on the air and was completely certain that everyone else would too.

Fred Silverman was for real.

The problem as I saw it was that as intelligent as he was, the guy simply had no taste.

But people change. What do you know?

I won't say Fred got religion, but during his period of wandering in the wilderness he became interested in exploring a new kind of show. At CBS, Fred had put on thought-provoking comedies, and in 1981 the "thought-provoking" part made a comeback in his consciousness. This time around he decided he wanted to do a thought-provoking *drama*. "It'll be a lot of fun."

Fred came up with an idea for a "high-class" one-hour dramatic series about a young female district attorney in Manhattan and asked me to write and produce the pilot, which would be made as a television movie to be shown on NBC. He had no trouble getting the commitment from his successor, Brandon Tartikoff, and within a few months the film, starring Valerie Harper as *Farrell for the People*, aired and got the kind of numbers that under most circumstances mean the project would be picked up as a series.

Only not this time.

Farrell for the People remained a one-shot, a highly rated and highly awarded MOW (Movie-of-the-Week), and nothing more.

No one involved could figure out why, although the truth finally came out a few years later when I ran into Jeff Sagansky, who'd been a vice president at NBC under Brandon. I asked Jeff, now president of CBS, what had happened to *Farrell* and he grinned. "That was a good show," he said. "Everybody liked it."

"Then why didn't it get on the schedule? It couldn't have been because it was a serious drama series because you guys put on a ton of those a year or two after."

"Hey," Jeff said, "Brandon was all for serious series. That wasn't the problem. The problem was, who wanted a serious drama from *Fred*?"

And there we have it. The Fred Silverman Legacy.

Meaningful comedy.

Tits and ass.

Unknowing parody.

Well-intended drama.

And, in his most successful indie prod phase, admiring nostalgia (in the form of all those one-hour detective shows starring aging former television leads).

But it's the tits and ass, titillate and tease, make-'em-laugh programming that overshadows everything else. It's the jiggle and sniggle, an approach so successful that it created a pit from which television still hasn't dug itself out. A pit that has spread to feature films as well.

Since the seventies, shows based on the *Charlie's Angels* formula of carefully (or should we say "gleefully?") manipulating their beautiful and sexy young female leads into situations calling for the baring of flesh and the provocative wiggle have been a staple of broadcast network, syndication, and basic cable programming. Think *Silk Stalkings. The Renegade. Baywatch. VIPs.* Even *Star Trek: Enterprise.* And of course the multiple *Charlie's Angels* films.

The number of shows and movies that have used the *Three's Company* model of puerile sex and thoughtless humor can boggle the mind. *Married with Children. Bosom Buddies. Who's the Boss? Night Court.* Anything starring Scott Baio. *Dumb and Dumber, Bill and Ted's Excellent Adventure, Dude, Who Stole My Car?* The idiot sexual comedy has become so big that it's now a highly profitable major feature film genre in itself.

Fred got 'em watching.

Fred kept 'em watching.

And, like it or not, they're watching still.

ABC's "Wide World of Sports" Premieres and Changes the Way We Regard Our Games

*F*or years social critics have been writing columns, articles, and books on the subject of television's relationship with reality. The general thrust of most of this verbiage has been along these lines:

"People have become so reliant on television as their access point to the world that we're all in danger of falling into the trap of believing that unless we see something on TV it didn't happen. It's not real."

The first time I encountered this point of view was in 1970, when as a fledgling television writer I was contacted by Michel Choquette, an editor at *National Lampoon*. Michel wanted to know if I would contribute to *The Someday Funnies*, a book about TV the *Lampoon* organization was planning. Would I write the script for a comic strip that would show all hell breaking loose around a family that totally ignored it—until they turned on their TV set and *NBC News* told them that World War III had broken out? Then they would go ballistic. (What else?)

I was impressed by this point of view. As an inveterate television watcher, I thought at the time that it made a lot of sense. I agreed to write the script. Michel told me he'd call back soon with all the details of the deal and in the meantime to work out some approaches to the material.

The publishing business being what it is (much like the television business in this regard), I'm still waiting for that follow-up call. And, from time to time, still considering some approaches to the material.

Has television become the sum total of contemporary reality? Do we really refuse to pay attention to people and events and issues, to news and politics and daily life, unless those things reach out of our home screens and grab us by the throat?

If the horrifying and tragic events of September 11, 2001, hadn't been televised, would the entire nation, the entire world, be in denial?

In the words of *Saturday Night Live* comedian-turned-socio-political-pundit Dennis Miller, "I don't think so."

If anything, the opposite may be true. How many people do you know who are firmly convinced that the Apollo 11 moon walk was faked *for television*? Or that John Kennedy and Robert Kennedy are still alive even though their assassinations have been broadcast over and over on TV?

A point of view that began as a premise for a satirical comic strip and grew to become accepted "wisdom" could well be a silly little bit of exaggeration and whimsy after all.

But if we bend the idea just a little and say that being on television makes things *important*, then I think we're onto something.

Particularly when you're talking about *sports*.

When it comes to sports, the effect of television coverage on viewers and athletes alike has been enormous.

Especially the effect of a Sunday afternoon show called *ABC's Wide World of Sports.*

Sports, of course, were hardly new to television in 1961, when *ABC's Wide World of Sports* first went on the air. Sports had been broadcasting staples—especially local broadcasting staples— from the earliest days of the medium. Back in the days when Kid Larry Brody was being dazzled by Howdy Doody and Kukla and Ollie and Gene Autry, he was also watching the Chicago Cubs play their home games at Wrigley Field. That is, the games were at Wrigley Field; Kid Larry was watching them on WGN-TV, Channel Nine. To be even more precise, I was listening to them as announced by Jack Brickhouse, one of the early masters of baseball play-by-play.

Well, okay, I wasn't really *listening* so much as just kind of *hearing* Brickhouse's excited, "Hey, hey!"

This was because by the early fifties television in the Brody house had already become our version of background music. It was always on, a continuous presence lending a soundtrack and occasional video punctuation to our lives.

This was particularly true on summer days, when our TV set was kept tuned to Channel Nine. My father was committed to watching their games when he was off work on the weekends, and my mother kept the set on "Dad's channel" on weekdays as well. A sign of respect, you could say. In the summer, when there was no school, Jack Brickhouse's voice permeated every activity I engaged in while inside.

Everything I know about baseball rules, baseball strategy, and the All-Time Chicago Cubs All-Stars I absorbed from Jack's commentary as I played cowboys, or checkers, or Monopoly, or read, or daydreamed in our Chicago apartment.

This was educational TV at its finest. Or certainly the best TV learning experience I've ever had.

As I got older my sports knowledge broadened along with my TV sports viewing experience. Baseball came to mean not only the Cubs but also the Chicago White Sox (who became my favorite team in 1959 because, by God, they *won the American League pennant!*), and sports in general came to include football, personified by the Chicago Bears and the then Chicago Cardinals; and ice hockey, via the Blackhawks.

Local teams. Local broadcasts.

But *major* sports.

By which I mean that my friends and I knew that baseball, football, and hockey (no one ever really used the "ice" part of the name) were a big deal. They were significant. They carried weight. *Gravitas*, if you will.

They *had* to be important. They had teams in Chicago. The sports, as sports, were *ours*. And we Chicagoans wouldn't settle for just anything, would we? Because Chicago itself was so "major league."

Wait, something's missing here. If we're talking about major sports, where's *basketball*?

Not in Chicago. After all, the Bulls didn't exist until 1966.

But by the late fifties my friends and I were willing to accept the existence of basketball as a big deal. A big deal of which we Chicagoans had been unfairly deprived.

By the late fifties we could acknowledge that basketball was a major sport. Because television told us it was.

The first hint was the network news. Network television news shows always gave the scores toward the end of their half hour, and there, spoken of with the same respect as major sport baseball and major sport football, and major sport hockey was—gulp—major sport basketball.

Amazing. Mind boggling.

The second sign of basketball's importance was that NBA games started showing up on TV. Again, treated with the same respect as the big three.

Those of us entering adolescence in Chicago in the fifties were forced to reorganize our sports universes, to widen our perspectives. To grow.

CBS, NBC, and ABC all had sports packages. And they didn't just show the American and National Leagues and the NFL and NHL, they brought us college football and basketball (but not much baseball and almost no hockey—why, I've always wondered, was that?) as well. But when you got down to it "major sport" still meant "team sport of the kind played in fancy stadiums for money after, or instead of, college graduation."

Until 1961, and the premiere of *ABC'S Wide World of Sports*.

The people behind the new show, ABC Sports vice president Edgar Scherick and executive producer Roone Arledge, were real pros, the kind of operators Fred Silverman was studying at the time. Without breaking a sweat, they saw exactly what was missing from television sports coverage at the time, and that's what they put on the air.

Sports from other countries.

Sports that had no professional leagues.

Individual sports.

Olympic sports.

Regional sports. (Yes, hockey was regional—but I didn't know that because I was, in effect, a regional kind of guy myself.)

Motor sports.

Without mussing a hair or having to take a shower, with the kind of originality and élan and, yes, total self-assurance that Fred would use later for entertainment programming, Edgar and Roone used television's most basic element—its amazing strength at self-promotion—to change the entire population's perception of sports.

Make no mistake about it. Self-promotion is inherent in everything involving show business, be it the entertainment side, the news side, or the sports side, but television, with its "eternal" presence in our homes and our lives (the Brody TV set was on all day long, and that wasn't unusual, not in my neck of the woods), is cloaked with the kind of authority that caused Michel Choquette and *The National Lampoon* to see it as a major reality-shifting force.

Marshall MacLuhan said, "The medium is the message." I respectfully disagree. The medium of television transcends its message because the fact that it is broadcasting something means that television has *chosen* to broadcast it. And if television can choose what and what not to broadcast, then is television not the *de facto* arbiter of what we see and hear? And what we don't see and hear? And if television is the arbiter, then television must be above the content it chooses. It's the ultimate authority figure. It has to be.

So if you see a particular sport on television often enough, how can that sport be considered unimportant or minor? How can it be considered anything but a big deal? If the TV god blesses your sport, baby, you're in.

Going against the time-honored television principle of giving the public more of what it already seems to be watching in the hope of getting even higher ratings, *ABC's Wide World of Sports* opted to give the public what it wasn't getting. In so doing, it started "making" whole sports the way established Mafiosi create "made men," simply by following its brilliant high concept as intoned by host Jim McKay at the beginning of every episode:

"Spanning the globe to bring you the constant variety of sports . . . the thrill of victory and the agony of defeat. . . ."

"Spanning the globe."

You mean the series has the whole world to choose from and it shows us this particular athletic effort? Wow, this must be hot.

"The thrill of victory."

Ah, I love to see someone win. To witness the elation. It's so darn personal, and so inspiring.

"The agony of defeat."

Now you're talking. What could be better than watching *someone else* lose? What could be more moving than to get so close you can almost feel their pain?

"The constant variety of sports."

That's the big one, that variety thing, the bright light filling the firmament of televised sports. Variety is the key to *Wide World's* success. It's what made the show different in the beginning, and what makes it different still. Variety is what overhauled my perspective as a Chicagoan—and the perspectives of millions of other sports fans as well.

What makes *ABC's Wide World of Sports* a turning point in television history is the fact that it was a kind of sports version of *You Are There*. It was the first successful regularly scheduled nationwide sports show that wasn't confined to a particular sport or league or franchise. In fact, as I write this it's the *only* "variety sports" show on the air.

Wide World knew, and knows, no boundaries. It gives us everything. Like God, it encompasses *all*. Because of that I, along with millions of others, was introduced, or re-introduced, or re-re-introduced, to the thrills and agonies of: thoroughbred racing, sports car and Gran Prix and Gran Tourisimo racing, stock car racing, drag racing, figure skating, gymnastics, Indy car racing, Japanese baseball, slalom skiing, downhill racing, ski jumping, the luge, bicycle racing, rugby, soccer, rodeo, golfing, tennis, volleyball, track and field, and a host of other sports that I had either never seen before or dismissed (even though we had to play them in school) as irrelevant, bullshit, or not worth watching.

Not all these sports became major. Their ratings didn't merit their constant repetition. But many of them scored, and scored big, because they worked and worked well on *Wide World*.

With each hot new sport came hot new heroes performing feats I could never have imagined before. Bob Hayes, Wilma Rudolph, Bjorn Borg, Roger Bannister, Casey Tibbs, Spider Savage, Nadia Comaneci, Lance Armstrong, Mia Hamm, Dale Earnhardt, Mario Andretti, John McEnroe, Billie Jean King, Bob Seagram, Arthur Ashe, Chris Evert, Jackie Stewart, Scott Hamilton, Peggy Fleming, and on and on.

Those heroes are important, key elements in the transformation of a sport from "Huh?" to major. They are champions to cheer for or root against. (Just like baseball or football or hockey or basketball stars!)

National exposure on *ABC's Wide World of Sports* brings its participants into the living rooms, dens, bedrooms, and kitchens of viewers and fans. What we can call the "television element" enhances the "sports element" enhances the "personality element" and *voilà*! The big break-out occurs.

As long as the sport continues to receive exposure on ABC's sports flagship, allowing it to stay in the audience's face.

Repetition is the key. This conclusion isn't mine. It comes straight from the heroes of the sports we're discussing. In particular, from a couple of heroes of sports who have had their chance but haven't made it. Who would know better than those who've been there?

I remember talking in the gym with Dennis Alexio in the early nineties. Dennis is a kickboxing legend who I had cast as a guest star on a syndicated series called *Super Force* that I was producing. The part hadn't made a television star out of him, and he was concentrating on what he did best, being the World Kickboxing Association heavyweight *and* cruiserweight champion simultaneously. This guy was *tough*.

In spite of his glory, Dennis was troubled. His income from kickboxing, he told me, was about the same as that of a beginning accountant. And although he and the fans knew he was "the best fighter in the world," to the general public he was "just another guy with a mustache and a thick neck.

"Kickboxing's got no meaning for the public," Dennis went on.

"It's a minor sport, and it'll stay a minor sport without more television time."

"ESPN shows kickboxing," I said.

"Yeah, for an hour a couple of nights a week. And the only people who can find the channel are those who already know they're supposed to look. We need more than that. We need *Wide World of Sports* to carry the big matches and treat the champions like real champs.

"I'm trying to get a match with Evander Holyfield," he said. "That's something *Wide World* will have to cover. It'll put us on the map."

Dennis was standing in front of the heavy bag. He frowned at it as though it were Holyfield—or maybe the unappreciative Roone Arledge—and let loose with a fury.

The bag shook and the chain holding it rattled so loudly that everyone else in the gym turned to watch. Dennis put on a hell of a show. But he didn't get the match with Holyfield and kickboxing's still a minor, non–*Wide World* sport.

Almost ten years earlier, Arnold Schwarzenegger had tried another solution to the same problem. I'd given him his first television acting part too, in an episode of *The Streets of San Francisco* I'd written, and it'd worked out pretty well for both of us. At this time Arnold and I were in Almeria, Spain, where he was shooting the movie *Conan the Barbarian* and I was hanging out for a week, visiting another friend on the set. Arnold wasn't due before the camera until later in the day, and he was relaxing at the pool of the resort that was *Conan's* HQ.

A couple of months before, he'd surprised the fans of another minor sport, bodybuilding, by unexpectedly entering its top professional competition, the Mr. Olympia contest, and winning even though he'd announced his retirement from the sport that gave him his start the previous year.

"Why'd you do it?" I said.

"For the good of bodybuilding," Arnold said. "I'm Arnold. I'm famous. Bodybuilding is bodybuilding. It's nothing. But I knew that if I made a surprise appearance we would get what we need—more television time. And I knew I had to win to make it work."

"Work?" I said. "Work how?"

"I knew that I had to win. If I won, the Olympia would be carried on *Wide World of Sports*. Not just highlights, but the whole competition, starting with my return and building up to my victory.

"And that is just what happened," Arnold said. "We had a full hour. For that week bodybuilding owned ABC Sports. Now bodybuilding has to keep the momentum going. Otherwise . . ." He gestured. "Thumbs down."

"So how does bodybuilding build on that?" I said. "How does the sport stay in the public eye?"

Arnold shrugged. "That is bodybuilding's problem. I've done what I can. If they don't come up with something, next year, without me competing, *Wide World of Sports* will cover a dog show instead."

Arnold laughed. The other cast members at the pool turned and saw him enjoying something and joined in the laughter as Arnold turned over to tan his back. Unlike Dennis Alexio, Arnold felt no fury. He'd scoped out the same situation that Alexio would later, but, hell, Arnold was just fine. *Conan the Barbarian* helped him become *Ahnold*, star and governor, even though bodybuilding, like kickboxing, is still a minor sport.

Maybe someday that'll change. Maybe someday bodybuilding's Jay Cutler and Ronnie Coleman and kickboxing's Benny the Jet Urquidez and Paul Vizzio will be as rich as Croesus and beloved by the general population. But for that to happen, you and I and that same general population are going to have to see them time after time after time on the most important sports series ever on television—*ABC's Wide World of Sports*.

"I Spy" Introduces Bill Cosby to the General Audience and a Role Model Takes Charge

$\mathcal{D}$o you know where you were at 9:00 p.m. Central time, Wednesday, September 15, 1965?

I do.

I was sitting on the couch (I'd finally outgrown the floor) in the rec room of my parents house in Skokie, Illinois (they'd moved from our so-fondly-remembered apartment when the state decided to build Chicago's first expressway directly across the street).

I was three months shy of my twenty-first birthday and no longer lived at home. I was going to Northwestern University and living in a fraternity house there. (What can I say? Fraternities were politically correct in those days.) But the Tau Delta Phi TV set was on the fritz, and nothing, but nothing, was going to stop me from seeing the most highly anticipated new series of the year.

I wasn't going to miss *I Spy*, even if it meant having to make nice to my parental authorities.

My parents didn't have a color set, so I watched it in black and white. Not that the lack of color detracted from what I saw. The debut show was still hyper real to me.

From the amazing graphics of the opening titles to the last card of the closing credits, I didn't look away. How could I? The show co-starred two of my favorites, actor Robert Culp and comedian Bill Cosby. For me it was a team-up every bit as compelling as Superman

Bill Cosby and Robert Culp, 1965 (Still Things)

and Batman teaming up in *World's Finest Comics*, or the Human Torch guest-starring in *The Amazing Spider-Man*.

At the time, Culp was my idol. He'd starred in an adult Western called *Trackdown*, where the essence of his character, Texas Ranger

Hoby Gilman, boiled down to the pure physicality of the most inso-lent walk I'd ever seen, a fluid strut that I'd practiced to high school perfection at the time and that to this day I still find myself falling into when I think people are watching me.

Culp was the essence of cool. But Cosby was red hot. I was too young to have seen his comedy act in clubs, but he was a frequent guest on *The Mike Douglas Show*, a daily afternoon talk show that was the perfect way to unwind after the morning's classes; and *The Merv Griffin Show*, an early evening talker that had replaced baseball as the perfect background show at the fraternity house, mainly because you could always count on an outrageously outfitted babe to say something that would make Merv, and anyone else over thirty, blush.

On these shows Bill Cosby was the king of fast-talking, romping through his stories with tireless energy and sending the punchlines home like the football player he'd been, crossing the goal line.

Together, these two opposites meshed like nobody's business. The formerly laconic Culp chatted it up, and as the two of them bantered and fought their way through Hong Kong that night, I was inspired to "create" the first television series of my very own.

Well, not really of my very own. It was *I Spy*, but with three spies instead of two. The spy-disguised-as-a-tennis-star, a.k.a. Culp; the spy-disguised-as-the-tennis-star's-trainer, a.k.a. Cosby; and the spy-disguised-as-a-traveling-college-kid, a.k.a. yours truly. From the very first episode I longed to hang with those two great guys. From the very beginning I wanted more than anything to banter like a sonofabitch with "Kelly Robinson" and "Alexander Scott."

That first episode was a brilliant creative achievement, the introduction of the ultimate male buddy fantasy, whether you were hetero or homo or militantly anti-homoerotic. Every week after-ward it got better.

Forget *ER*. Throw away *Hill Street Blues*. Who needs *The Sopra-nos*? For my money, *I Spy* is the single best one-hour television series ever to appear on TV. Its creator-writer-producers, David Friedkin and Mort Fine, were literally the inspiration for me to make my move into television writing and producing as a career.

But although I wish I could say that was the reason a chapter in this book is devoted to the show, the fact is that the cultural significance of *I Spy* isn't really about the writing but about the way it took Bill Cosby out of the saloons and talk show guest spots where he earned his living and made him a primetime television star.

Positioning him so he could become the cultural force he is in the U.S. today.

I Spy was the first one-hour primetime action series to have a black man as a lead. It never cracked the top twenty in the Nationals, but its overnights kept it on the air for four years. The show was a critical darling, and during its run much was written about how Cosby's character had originally been designed to be a sidekick, and how that notion had been abandoned as soon as the producers saw how well Culp and Cosby worked together.

The show's signature word, "wonderfulness," spoken ironically as in, "Ah, the wonderfulness of your smile . . ." to a villain whose face was set into a frown, became part of sixties vocabulary and the title of a Grammy-winning Cosby comedy album. (Which, although it didn't prove the word was created by Cosby, certainly testified to that idea.) Oh, and Cosby just happened to win three Best Dramatic Actor Emmys for the show, one in 1966, another in 1967, and the third in 1968.

Cosby's career was now as hot as his performances had always been. Although the same articles that discussed how Cosby had "taken over" *I Spy* from his co-star always pointed out that the episodes of the series were "colorblind," staying away from references to Cosby's race, the fact is that the articles themselves were making a big thing about what in those days would've been called his "Negritude." The implication was clear. Bill Cosby wasn't merely a terrific actor, he was a terrific black actor. He wasn't merely a highly regarded television (and recording and nightclub) star, he was a highly regarded black star.

That in turn made him a role model for black youth, a black man who was constantly questioned about his blackness, and about racial issues in general. A black man who was constantly quoted on the subject, even though most of the quotes were to the effect of "I'm a comedian, not Martin Luther King. If you want to talk about what he does, let's talk about *him.*" This seemed to be especially true after April 4, 1968, when King was killed. Journalists wanted Bill Cosby to pick up King's mantle—and Cosby refused.

After *I Spy* went off the air in 1968, Cosby went back to comedy, filling theaters instead of nightclubs, recording another Grammy-winning album, and even winning another Emmy, this time for a comedy special called, appropriately, *The Bill Cosby Special.*

In 1969 NBC broadcast Cosby's own sitcom, *The Bill Cosby Show*, in which he played an idiosyncratic high school P.E. teacher. The show itself was very unusual, from its jazz theme co-written by Cosby (with him performing what can only be called "lead grunts") to the subject matter of the episodes.

NBC's promotional material touted the show as being about the "trials and tribulations of Chet Kincaid," and emphasized the fact that Cosby's "gentle humor and philosophy" were at the core of the series. While this may have been the intention, the "achievement" fell far short. *The Bill Cosby Show* paid lip service to focusing on the usual sitcom relationships—a hero's interaction with his family and co-workers—but the episodes of the series that I saw were mostly about Chet's interaction with Chet.

In fact, the hero's emotions and internal conflicts were such key ingredients of the stories that I stopped watching because I was embarrassed. I felt like a voyeur, as though I was entering Bill Cosby's dreams in which he walked down the street or through the halls of Richard Allen Holmes High, looking straight ahead and nodding at others but seeing only himself.

(I kept hoping he'd bump into Robert Culp as Kelly Robinson and snap out of his trance, but it was never to be.)

The plain fact was that Cosby's new show wasn't funny. No Best Actor in a Comedy Series Emmys came to Bill Cosby, and *The Bill Cosby Show* was canceled in 1971. Within the television business Cosby was written off as a TV series lead.

This was more than the usual negative buzz that so often develops as a result of show business's self-destructive urge to see its stars fall. Marvin Miller, one of the producers of the series, was a true admirer of Cosby's talent, but that hasn't stopped him from telling me that "As a person, Bill was erratic, both on the show and when he was doing his act in Vegas. I ended up having to do a lot of covering up as part of my job."

Cosby starred in another series, *Cos*, in 1976. This one was a variety show and was short-lived, and he didn't star in another television series until his blockbuster hit *The Cosby Show* began in 1984. Throughout the seventies and early eighties, though, he was working his tail off, performing his stand-up comedy act; writing best-selling memoirs; starring in movies with Sidney Poitier and Harry Belafonte (and Robert Culp); starring in various television specials; becoming the spokesman for a major breakfast cereal maker; making a name for himself in the field of children's programming by creating the animated series *Fat Albert and the Cosby Kids*; appearing regularly on PBS's educational children's series *The Electric Company*; and producing educational videos.

According to the William Morris Talent Agency's official biography of this very important client of theirs, during this period Cosby donated heavily to his alma mater, Temple University, and to black colleges and civil rights organizations, and became known as "a crusader . . . for a better world and for better understanding between people. . . .

"In addition," the bio goes on, "Cosby earned his Masters degree in 1972 and his Doctorate in education . . . in 1977 from the University of Massachusetts. His [dissertation] was titled 'The Integration of Visual Media via *Fat Albert and the Cosby Kids* into the Elementary Schools Culminating as a Teacher Aid to Achieve Increased Learning.'"

Oh, and he also stayed married to his wife, Camille, and fathered two daughters in addition to the son and two daughters they already had, which is no easy task for anyone, let alone a TV star.

The result of this activity was that, even before the first episode of *The Cosby Show* was seen on NBC, Bill Cosby had expanded his reputation from that of "mere" star to "sage."

And this was just the beginning.

The Cosby Show was on the air until 1992, and unlike Cosby's previous venture into sitcom-land, it was a conservative, by-the-numbers effort. Cosby's character, Cliff Huxtable, was a doctor with a wife and a household full of children, and family interaction and family problems were at the forefront of every episode. The series was never about Cliff. Rather it was about how Cliff handled the situation of the week. What did his wife learn? His kids? What did he learn along the way?

Also unlike *The Bill Cosby Show* of the sixties, the new series was funny. It was written in an identifiable sitcom rhythm so that even though viewers thought they were watching and hearing genuine family discussions, what they were really getting was:

"Set up."

"Another set up."

"Punchline."

"Set up."

"Another set up."

"Punchline."

The voices were softer, the delivery a bit slower, but *The Cosby Show* mined the same territory staked out by *The Dick Van Dyke Show* and *The Mary Tyler Moore Show* and *All in the Family*, and mined it in just about the same way.

And struck even more gold.

The Cosby Show turned Cosby from hot to incandescent. It was a huge hit in both the overnight and the national ratings, and although as a series it won only one Emmy and one Golden Globe, from 1984 to 1992 when it went off the air, Cosby was awarded seventeen major awards for his performance, including three Golden Globes, fourteen People's Choice Awards, and an Image Award from the NAACP.

As if this wasn't enough, the series was credited with "saving" NBC by bringing the network's ratings to number one and rumored to have made Cosby one of the richest men in the world, so rich that for years reports circulated that he was going to buy NBC and establish *the* network as the place for socially conscious entertainment.

No one I know who heard this particular rumor ever doubted it.

Cosby's good works are legion. His best-selling books, including (but not "limited to" because five or ten more may be coming down the chute as I write this) *Fatherhood; Love and Marriage; Time Flies;*

Childhood; I Am What I Ate . . . and I'm Frightened!!!; It's All Relative: A Field Guide to the Modern Family; and *Congratulations! Now What?: A Book for Graduates*, are humorous, yes, but also warm, chatty volumes of advice on how to handle just about every aspect of life. His childrens' books are models of how to improve childhood self-esteem, and his most successful TV series offers more insight into human problem-solving than the most rigorously academic treatises.

All these good intentions have done more than make the network-buying rule credible. They've made it a holy grail eagerly sought by millions of admirers, even now, at a time when it's clear that NBC:

1. Isn't for sale.
2. Would cost a hell of a lot more money than one man, even a very rich one, could pony up.

I'll 'fess up. When I sat down to watch *I Spy* in Skokie on that September night I never in my wildest fantasies thought I'd be writing someday about the show being historically significant because it was the beginning of Bill Cosby's prominence as the leading black male figure of our time, a man whose screen, stage, and literary presence has influenced millions of Americans. I never thought for one minute that I was seeing the beginning of St. Bill.

But the numbers don't lie. Twenty to 40 million people watched *The Cosby Show* every damn week. Between ten and twenty percent of our population, if the Nielsens are right.

That's a lotta folks.

That's a lotta influence from the man who calls himself "Dr. Comedy." He's generating enough heat to become the core of his own planet. It's a real wonder that his halo hasn't melted down.

In fact, Bill Cosby is such a positive influence that is it all that unreasonable to say that, all things considered, he's our contemporary equivalent of Martin Luther King?

And might we go even further? Might we say that, considering all the ways in which he has been part of our lives, Dr. Comedy may possibly be even *bigger* than Dr. King?

One day in the early 2000s, in the kind of hip and trendy Beverly Hills restaurant that I only go to when other people are making the reservation and paying the check, I propounded these theories to an old friend of mine, an African-American Network Executive.

Although barely in his forties, AANE has a solid history of service in the trenches of entertainment and educational television. He's put in his time at networks, studios, and the obligatory start-up entertainment dotcom.

He's a graduate of a prestigious university who grew up in a ghetto of a mid-American city. AANE is black.

Dreadlocked, and black.

Successful, and black.

Smart as hell, and black.

Rich, and black.

So, being curious and all too often bigger of mouth than I am of mind, I asked AANE what he thought about Bill Cosby's place in social history. After he'd finished choking on his salmon he shook his head.

"Are you assuming that because I'm a black man Bill Cosby's had some effect on me? That at some point in my life I've consciously or unconsciously emulated him or the characters he's played?" AANE said. "Are you looking me right in the eyes and zapping me with that stereotype?"

"Well, if you're going to put it like that—uh, yeah. I guess I am." I tried to smile, but it was the grin of a nervous dog.

He shook his head. "Let's take that big hit show first. Cosby played an obstetrician, for Christ's sake! Hugely successful. Living in an upper middle class neighborhood. Never letting on that he was black. Never worrying about being black. Never being stopped for driving on his own street in his new BMW just because he was black. The Huxtable family was white, Larry. They just played it in blackface.

"Now let's take the books and all that," AANE continued. "Funny self-help. Big hits because they're universal. And what does 'universal' mean? 'Universal' means *white*. These books aren't crammed with wit and wisdom for black people, they're crammed with wit and wisdom for the white people who buy books. The only way you know the author is a black man is by looking at his picture on the back cover, not by anything he says."

But AANE wasn't finished. "Sure, millions of people are Bill Cosby fans. Sure, the ratings for his show, and the ratings Nielsen does on individual performer likeability, are high. Better than high—they're *huge*. But do you know what percentage of the viewing audience is black? Do you know what percentage of the population of this country is black?

"A little over twelve percent of the population is black, Larry," AANE said. "And significantly less than twelve percent of the audience. Bill Cosby's work and life are irrelevant to the average black man. His show and his books and whatever else he does wouldn't make a dent on the ratings or best-seller lists if black people were his primary audience. He's a huge hit because he's generic."

AANE leaned back in his chair. He looked thoughtful. "The truth is that you may well be right. Bill Cosby could be every bit as much a black leader and role model as Martin Luther King was.

"But not necessarily for Black people.

"More likely his real effect is on whites."

The check came, and AANE picked it up.

"Let me pay the tip," I said.

He added and signed quickly. "Too late."

Oh well, what the hell. At least I got it *half* right.

Which leads to another line of investigation.

What effect has Bill Cosby's success had on other black television performers? What effect has it had on television programming? What effect has it had on race relations in this country in general?

It doesn't take a lunch with my friend AANE to discover the answers. A simple ramble through back issues of *TV Guide* for the decade after *The Cosby Show*'s departure from NBC gives us the message, and that message is:

Not much.

The percentage of broadcast network, cable, and satellite TV series starring black people is, as the Talking Heads once put it when singing about *all* of U.S. society, "the same as it ever was." Specifically, it's the same post-*Cosby* as it was in the ten years following television's last big hits purporting to present black culture—NBC's *Sanford and Son* and CBS's *The Jeffersons* and *Good Times*, all hot items in the seventies.

No series starring a black performer has become a breakaway hit since Cosby's turn as America's favorite obstetrician. Even *Whoopi!*, a highly anticipated show starring Whoopi Goldberg, barely limped through one season before being canceled by NBC.

The Fox Network has trumpeted its attempts to program "for minorities," (hey, they put on *The Bernie Mac Show*, a black family sitcom with a difference—Bernie's a genuine ABM, *Angry Black Man*) but the ratings show no numbers that could be interpreted as genuine success. In fact, the ratings of most Fox shows came under dispute in 2004 when Nielsen attempted to switch its measurement system for local ratings from a weekly diary filled in by the viewer to real-time electronic recording and Fox's numbers went way down, indicating that some of the fine, upstanding Nielsen families that claimed to watch the Fox lineup really weren't watching it at all.

The "Cos Effect" may have shown up in the fact that almost all of the series featuring black performers in the past ten years have been family sitcoms, but that could just be coincidence. As Alvin Poussaint points out in his online article *Why Is TV So Segregated*, the first designated black TV series, *Amos 'n' Andy*, was also a family sitcom. And, like *Amos 'n' Andy*, recent black sitcoms have for the most part presented blacks living and interacting exclusively with other blacks.

Ah, AANE . . . why couldn't you be wrong?

Note: There *is* a place where television is actively being used to put across the message of racial harmony. That place, however, isn't in the United States. It's the country of South Africa.

In 2004 I went to Johannesburg as a consultant for the South African Broadcasting Corporation. Government-owned and -financed, SABC runs three broadcast networks, and its mission statement reads, in part:

"SABC2 strives to strengthen social ties beyond cultural and social divides and promote unity and nation building while acknowledging and reflecting existing diversity. . . . SABC2 strives to use its programming to create a responsible, trustworthy, safe, and stable environment that reflects hope and appeal to tradition and establish norms that reinforce and support the ideal in the face of the harsh real world."

To do this, South African television presents shows that are totally integrated, showing blacks and whites living and working together and having its characters speak as they would in real life, which means conversations where as many as eleven different languages—including English—can be used.

To say I was impressed by what the South Africans were trying to do is putting it mildly. Television with a social purpose! Art with meaning! Who could ask for anything more?

The answer to that question turns out to be the South African TV writers, that's who. No writer can ever be happy as long as there are limits or constraints on creativity, even the most well intended, and this was brought home to me by a young South African comedy writer working on the country's best sitcom.

"Meaning, meaning, meaning!" this writer erupted one day. "I'm sick of meaning. Why the fuck can't we just entertain!?"

Another note: Meanwhile, back in the world of Bill Cosby, in 1975 William F. Blinn, multiple Emmy-winning writer of *Roots* and *Brian's Song*, called me and said, "I'm producing a new series. Want to write a script?"

"What's it about?"

"Two spies who roam the world together undercover, watching each other's backs and generally having the kind of great relationship everyone who watches will wish they had."

"That sounds familiar," I said. "Reminds me of *I Spy.*"

"It *is I Spy*," said Bill. "Only it's called *Double Trouble* now. It was created by David Friedkin and Mort Fine, and it's just like their old show except for one thing."

"Which is?" I said.

"The two spies are a married couple, played by Martin Landau and Barbara Bain. So there's an underlying sexual context to the whole thing. The perfect added twist."

"Is the show on the schedule?"

"Not yet, but how can it miss?"

And so, ten years after the work of Friedkin and Fine caused me to want to write for TV, I got to write *almost* an episode of *I Spy*.

And, sadly, yes, the show did miss. It never got on the air.

What can I tell you? Martin Landau's a hell of an actor, but he's no Robert Culp. And Barbara Bain just couldn't cut it as the Cos.

"Dammit, Jim, We're a Franchise, Not a Show!"

$\mathcal{G}$ene Roddenberry was the perfect college teacher you never had.

Tall and physically imposing, with an impish gleam in his eye at all times (you know, the look that says, "I'm getting laid, my friend, what about you?"), Gene knew his stuff and he knew that he knew his stuff, and he liked nothing better than giving that knowledge to whoever was around.

When I first met him in 1972 Gene wasn't yet a legend. He was just another guy trying to survive. As a writer and producer he'd had his days of glory, but they'd ended in 1969. Since then he'd been making his living selling "genuine" *Star Trek* paraphernalia, mostly by mail, while trying to get other projects off the launching pad and into space.

"The scripts sell well," he told me, sitting at his new office at an animation studio called Filmation. "We're constantly having to mimeo new ones. The phasers are a hot item too, and the alien masks. And look how good they are. We found this great place in the Valley to make them even better than the originals were."

Yes, times were hard for Gene Roddenberry in 1972, but that was about to change. *Star Trek* was about to make a comeback on its old home network, NBC. And I was going to write an episode.

Of *Star Trek: The Animated Series*, the most adult cartoon series ever made for Saturday morning TV.

It was the beginning of the "franchise" concept in television and films.

The Transporter Room, 1966 (Still Things)

And none of us knew it at the time, not even the "great bird of the universe," as Gene liked to call himself.

The franchise, of course, was the *Star Trek* universe, which entered the American consciousness (and the *Ur* consciousness of the world) in the fall of 1966. There's not much left to say about that debut that hasn't already been said and re-said in the multitudes of books, articles, convention panel discussions, news reports, publicity handouts, and Trekkie (or "Trekker") web sites that are part of the cottage industry of *Star Trek* support.

The point here is that although the show's ratings were never even as good as those of *I Spy*, I feel quite confident that there's not a man or woman reading these words who hasn't seen at least one episode from the original three-year run of the series, and who doesn't instantly know who Jim, Spock, and Bones are.

You've probably got more than a nodding acquaintance with Uhura, Mr. Sulu, and Ensign Chekov as well. The characters from what has become known to aficionados (my cop-out word of the day so I don't have to make the "Trekkie" or "Trekker" decision) as *The Original Star Trek* have become part of Western culture, icons bearing the same importance Thor and Beowulf and King Arthur had for previous societies.

It wasn't planned that way. Gene just wanted to put on a show. My old friend Herb Solow, who ran Desilu Productions before it and *Star Trek* were folded into Paramount Studios, remembers that, "Gene had this terrific idea, but everybody was afraid of it. Sometimes he even seemed afraid.

"We had a huge fight with NBC over Spock's ears. NBC didn't want them to be pointy. For a while it looked like Gene was going to agree to this just to get the show on the air, but then I told him how terrific everything about the show was as originally conceived—because I really felt that way—and Gene got about three sizes larger and started roaring at the network in defiance. The pointy ears stayed."

Star Trek started with a bang. I was hooked even before the debut thanks to the *Today* show. Not a big *Today* fan (who got up that early?), I happened to turn it on one morning at the end of August, 1966, when the stars of the new season's shows were making promotional appearances. And there were Spock and his pointy ears. *Pointy fucking ears!* I thought. *Fantastic! This I gotta see.*

After the first few weeks, though, *Star Trek*'s numbers started to shrink, and they went down continuously, if gradually, pretty much the whole time it was on the air. As a viewer, I found the first season, with Gene Roddenberry and the very talented Gene Coon running things, to be as original and exciting as the science fiction books and magazines I was addicted to at the time.

The second season, with the two Genes still running things (the real-life incarnations of Captain Kirk and First Officer Spock) was a little weaker in terms of holding my interest. I found myself looking more closely at the scantily clad (for those days) female guest stars than at the other wonders of the future.

By the beginning of the third season of *Star Trek*, I was living in Los Angeles and starting to get work writing for TV. For this season Gene Coon was replaced by Howie Horowitz, and the stories degenerated to variations of "The Monster of the Week."

As an aspirant and a fan there was only one thing I could do and be me. I wrote my own episode of the series and had my agent, the late (and deeply missed) Sylvia Hirsch, send it in. The subject matter was as true to me as the egotism of thinking I could show Howie H. how the show should be. It was about the crew of the *Enterprise* encountering God in space.

Howie Horowitz passed on buying the script, and on meeting with me.

But three years later there I was, sitting in that Filmation office with Gene Roddenberry.

Pitching him the same episode.

"If you could write any storyline you wanted to for *Star Trek*," Gene said, "what would it be? I mean for the old show, the live show, the real show. Because even though this one's animated it's going to be the real show, with the same characters and actors and meaning and themes.

"The animated *Star Trek* will be every bit as good as the original," he said. "No, I take that back. It'll be better. Because the artists can draw more special effects!"

"If I could write any storyline I wanted for *Star Trek*," I replied nervously, unsure of whether he'd ever seen, read, or heard of my old script, "I'd write about the *Enterprise* meeting God."

Gene beamed. "Me too," he said. "I've always wanted to write about the *Enterprise* meeting God, but NBC's primetime bosses always shot it down. Let's see if we can slip it past the daytime boys."

Gene Roddenberry had always wanted to write about the *Enterprise* meeting God? And so had I? I beamed back at him. Kindred spirits! *Aww riight!*

By the end of that day I had an official deal to write an episode of the new show. I started thinking about exactly what could happen and why. I wasn't the same writer I'd been when I'd tried this before. I'd learned much more about the craft and knew that this time around the script would be a hundred times better.

When we were finished it *was* better, that I know.

Of course, it wasn't about meeting God anymore. The NBC "daytime boys" had nixed that as quickly as their primetime counterparts would've. But writing about Kirk and Spock and McCoy and the rest of the crew meeting the *Devil* in outer space was just fine. So that's what I did.

Make that ". . . what we did."

Because I can safely say that Gene and his story editor, Dorothy Fontana (working as D.C. Fontana because women weren't all that welcome as writers in those not-so-good-old-days), rewrote every word.

When they sent me the final draft of *Star Trek: The Animated Series, The Magicks of Megas-Tu*, every single description and every line of dialogue was changed. But my name and only my name was still on the cover as that of the writer. And Gene called to invite me to the voice recording session on the episode so I could meet Bill Shatner and Leonard Nimoy and the other actors.

I didn't get it. I called Dorothy Fontana and asked what I'd done wrong. If the Great Bird of the Universe hated me and my work.

"Oh, no," she said. "He loves you."

"Then why the rewrite?" I said.

Dorothy sighed. "Because that's what Gene does."

Star Trek: The Animated Series was everything Gene said it would be: a half-hour show with all the elements that had stirred the imaginations of primetime audiences from '66 through '69. I watched every episode with my daughter, Jennifer, who then was about three. To be precise, I watched every minute of every episode. Jenny, however, would be off and running in another direction by the time the opening theme (the same as that on *The Original Star Trek*) was done.

Evidently she was much more typical of the audience than was I. The animated *Trek* folded after thirteen episodes.

But Gene Roddenberry continued to survive, getting himself a development deal at Universal. A year or so after the animated series went off the air Gene called. "Want to work on a new series with me?" he said. "Want to be a story editor?"

"Who do I have to kill?"

"I'll let you know when the time comes. Meanwhile you've just got to give me enough of what I need so it's fun to rewrite."

The next day I met with Gene in his new, hippie dippie office, the two of us sitting on big cushions in the middle of the floor. He had two new series in the works. The pilot for one, *Questor*, had already been shot. Now they were trying to develop half a dozen scripts so they'd be ready when the series started production. The other series, *Genesis II*, existed only as a fifty-or-so-page-long presentation that included the setting, characters, and a long list of potential stories.

Gene wanted me on *Genesis II*.

I jumped at the chance. Armed with the presentation, I went to work on the story Gene told me was his favorite for the show: The one with alien robots coming to Earth and trying to destroy it.

The premise of *Genesis II* was that several hundred years in the future mankind was trying to recover from an apocalypse that had destroyed civilization. A super scientific enclave had been carved underground, and from its headquarters exploration teams were sent to the surface to find surviving individuals and developing cultures. The teams would reconnect the survivors to the scientists' new civilization and help them solve their problems at the same time.

The show concentrated on one of those teams, led by a father figure captain with a French-sounding name, and including a younger, dedicated, and heroic second-in-command; a doctor; a female sociologist with special "empathetic powers;" a big, tough alien warrior; and a human-looking android robot who envied the fact that people had emotions and kept trying to learn how to *feel*.

I wrote my episode, *Robots' Return*. In it we learn that the robots aren't really alien at all. They're self-replicating "descendants" of an old U.S. space probe, and after centuries of trying, they've finally found the planet they came from—Earth—and are eager to meet their creator and god—NASA. When they learn that NASA has been destroyed they interpret the situation as one of pure evil. Human beings have destroyed their god. Therefore they must destroy all human beings.

Are you with me here?

This stuff sound familiar?

Just the slightest bit?

Like Friedkin and Fine's *I Spy* clone, *Double Trouble*, *Genesis II* never got on the air, although a pilot with some big differences from the original premise was shot.

But then, in 1979, I went to the theater to see a highly publicized new movie directed by Robert Wise. It's name was *Star Trek: The Motion Picture*, and its plot was—

Robots' Return.

Gene had reworked his original *Genesis II* story.

He'd rewritten me again!

And I couldn't have been happier.

Star Trek was back. Big and bold and splashy and laden with special effects that no Saturday morning cartoon animator would ever have been able to touch.

It wasn't perfect. There were slow spots, and it was upsetting to see Kirk and the crew looking so old, but it grossed well enough for Paramount to plan a sequel.

And to start referring publicly to *Star Trek* as a *franchise*.

Think about that for a minute. In the business world, the word "franchise" has to do with the value of a brand in the minds of consumers. Jack Feldman, a professor of industrial psychology at Georgia Tech, uses Kleenex as an example in his class. Kleenex is a valuable business franchise because the name is so well known that it is commonly used in place of the generic term "tissue." Professor Feldman says, "That means that people go to the supermarket hunting for the Kleenex brand when they have to blow their noses."

So what was Paramount saying? That movie audiences were going to think *Star Trek* equaled "film"? Or *Star Trek* equaled "science fiction"?

Not quite. They were saying the equivalent of "This is our blockbuster. The name *Star Trek* in a title will automatically mean 'a movie we want to see.'"

Or to put it another way: "Whoa, baby! *Star Trek* is one hot property. We're going to promote the hell out of it and make it even hotter so we can milk it for all it's worth!"

They might even have said, "Whoa! Whoa! Why spend money on new ideas that involve the risk of audience acceptance when we can go with a sure thing? Get ready, world. Here come more *Star Trek* movies! And books! And games! And wait'll you see the toys!"

The language and thought process of the business world took complete control of the "franchise," and, like the self-replicating robots of the first *Star Trek* movie and *Robots' Return*, *Star Trek* went into heavy reproductive mode. In 1982 there was *Star Trek: The Wrath of Khan*. The year 1984 gave us *Star Trek: The Search for Spock*. *Star Trek: The Voyage Home* showed up in motion picture theaters in 1986. Then came *Star Trek: The Final Frontier*, *Star Trek: The Undiscovered Country*, *Star Trek: Generations*, *Star Trek: First Contact . . .*

Star Trek: This!

Star Trek: That!

Star Trek: The Other Thing!

On and on and on.

Gene Roddenberry the legend was born from the ashes of Gene Roddenberry the writer-producer who couldn't get anything *but* *Star Trek* into production anywhere. He was the creator of an entire universe, showered with honors and promoted even more than his characters and their ship.

But he wasn't a corporate kind of guy. He was the perfect teacher, an iconoclast who wouldn't play ball with the guys wearing the suits, so even while his face was being plastered all over the media, he was being removed from the *Star Trek: The Endless Supply of Motion Pictures* loop.

Paramount gave him a deal he couldn't refuse and sent him back to his roots. Gene the phoenix had a new mission, to boldly go where he had been before, to reconquer the lost Federation. To reclaim his due.

By bringing the next generation of *Star Trek* to TV.

Literally.

Return with us now to those thrilling days of 1986. The phone in Larry Brody's L.A. area home rings, and on the other end is—Gene.

"I hear you're a producer now," the enthusiastic voice says. "Says here you've been doing some shows for Fox and ABC." He keeps talking without taking a breath. "How'd you like to produce something good for a change?"

And that's how I found out that *Star Trek: The Next Generation* was good to go.

This time around Gene was "Gene and Company" and had a whole floor of one of the bigger buildings on the Paramount lot. I walked in the door and was surrounded by people, including Dorothy Fontana, Robert Justman, who'd been the line producer of *The Original Star Trek*, and David Gerrold, a science fiction writer who'd gotten his start while still in his teens by writing one of *Original Trek's* most beloved episodes, *The Trouble with Tribbles*.

Oh, and Gene was there too, in an inner sanctum piled high with books and scripts and drawings and scraps of costume fabric and potential pieces of sets. He was tanned and relaxed and obviously having the time of his life as he told me all about the business side of the new show. *Star Trek: The Next Generation* was being syndicated, he said. No network interference because there was no network, and the number of local stations that had signed on to carry it was greater than the number of affiliates any network had. "It's a record syndication sale," Gene said, "and we're guaranteed at least two years on the air."

He rifled through some of the papers in front of him, sending one entire pile of scripts to the floor. "Everybody wants to be part of this," he said. "Every agent is trying to get every writer in town on this show. But I need you. I need what you and only you do so well."

"Which is?"

"Get that script so close that I can have real fun when I dig in to rewrite."

Some things never change, I thought, and later that afternoon, when I got home with the hundred-plus-page pile of material Gene had given me about the creative side of the show (television series proposals had special names by 1986; they were called "writers' guides," or "bibles," the latter term seeming particularly apropos to me since Gene was being heralded as the savior of Paramount TV) I discovered another thing that had stayed the same.

The basic characters and mission from *Genesis II*.

There they were, right before me, with just a few changes.

A father figure captain with a French-sounding name.

A younger, dedicated, and heroic second-in-command.

A female doctor and her son.

A female "counselor" with special "empathetic powers."

A big, tough Klingon warrior.

And a human-looking android named Data who envied the fact that people had emotions and kept trying to learn how to *feel*.

Goddamn.

Talk about compulsive rewriting!

When it came to recombining his creative DNA, Gene Rodden-berry was the pro's pro.

All the ideas I'd had over at Universal just a few years ago flooded back into my mind, along with new ones, and I called Gene and told him I was ready to sign on. That's when he told me, "There's one catch. Before I can put you on staff I need to prove to the Paramount yahoos that you've got the necessary command of the show. I need you to take a script assignment and write an episode."

"I don't write episodes anymore, Gene," I said. "Unless I'm producing the show."

"It's just a formality," he said. "Please, consider it. Not for me but for what this show can do for *your* career."

Well, consider it I did. For about a week. But during that week, as I talked to other writer-producers about Gene's offer, I learned that every single one of them had had the same conversation with him. Twelve different writers I knew had been offered the job of producer if they would only write a script first.

Twelve top writers. Twelve top scripts. Plus, I was sure, a couple by Ms. Fontana and Mr. Gerrold. Fourteen episodes for Gene to rewrite, more than half a season's worth without committing himself to a writer-producer. Without having to pay the financial price. Or the personal one of giving up some authority to a dedicated and heroic second-in-command.

I resisted Gene's blandishments. So did all my friends. None of us wrote scripts for those first *Star Trek: The Next Generation* episodes (although I did write one a few years later, shortly before Gene's death). None of us became a producer on the show.

And every one of us has regretted it to this day.

Because *ST:TNG* stayed on the air for a lot longer than two years. It made it through eight seasons, which was and still is a miracle in a business with as high an attrition rate as television programming. That's a lot of episodes to write, a lot of stories to spin and fans to entertain and, considering the intensity of those fans, a hell of a lot of glory to revel in.

And the weekly salaries and script fees and residuals ain't bad either.

Gene died in 1991, but the franchise went on, more powerful and even more popular without its founder because now it could be promoted purely as a business entity with no consideration for, mention of, or interference by the Great God Gene.

The *Star Trek* universe took on a life of its own as the movies continued and not one, not two, but three new series sprang forth. Under the aegis of Gene's successor as executive producer, Rick Berman (previously one of those "Paramount yahoos" Gene had railed about), *Star Trek: Deep Space Nine* became the next begotten child in the line, picking up where *ST:TNG* left off in 1993. And *Star Trek: Voyager* left port a little later, premiering in 1995.

For those of us who'd known Gene Roddenberry's trials and tribulations in getting the first series launched it was strange indeed to see two *ST* children flourishing, one, *Deep Space Nine*, in syndication, the other, *Voyager*, as the flagship of the new UPN, United Paramount Network, with no Gene Roddenberry in sight. Most viewers, however, didn't seem to care. The new shows presented the audience with a continuity of execution as well as concept, with most of the writers and producers who came aboard *Next Gen* at or slightly before Gene's death continuing to guide its successors.

Unlike the writers of *The Original Star Trek*, many of these new-comers had no experience on any other television show. They were Trekkies-Trekkers-Acolytes, one hundred percent. *DS9* went off the air in 1999 and *Voyager* in 2001, but this trend toward insularity and self-reference continued into the next show, *Star Trek: Enter-prise*, in 2001. *Enterprise* was greeted with a yawn of critical apathy and a wail of dismay by the franchise's most vocal fans, and even now is still struggling to find its creative space and keep its sched-uled one.

Although *Star Trek* was the first franchise television offered it has not been the only one. In 1990 NBC scheduled a cops-and-lawyers series called, appropriately, *Law & Order*, which as of this writing has been on for fourteen years and spawned two healthy children of its own, *Law & Order: SVU* in 1999 and *Law & Order: Criminal Intent* in 2001.

The *L & O* family proved to be so healthy—and so potent in the ratings—that CBS jumped onto the franchise bandwagon in 2002 with *CSI: Miami*, a spin-off of *CSI: Crime Scene Investigation* (which has been the most popular dramatic show on television since its debut in 2000), and *CSI: New York* in 2004.

All the *Star Trek, Law & Order*, and *CSI* shows demonstrate the same good points. For the networks, syndication companies, and/or studios that make them, production is much less risky than it would be for a series based on something entirely new. The name value that makes the concepts franchises insures that a larger audi-ence than usual will sample any new spin-off, which in turn makes it more likely that the spin-off will succeed in the ratings.

For viewers, the franchise means a known commodity. As each new installment is trotted out, it can be selected for watching based on its breeding. If you like or liked a show's father or grandfather or great-grandfather, you know there's a good chance you'll enjoy the time you spend watching the new kid.

For creators, producers, writers, actors, directors, and the like, working on a television franchise means—well, more than anything it means a chance to bring home the bucks. And it's difficult to be a realistic adult trying to raise a family and say with a straight face that's not a good thing.

The downside to the franchise phenomenon, though, is stagnation. Creatively, those producing any franchise show soon have nothing new to offer, and eventually the audience will catch on (as many of those in the know say it has with *Enterprise*). As ratings go down, so do earnings generated by the show and eventually all of those people making their living from the franchise will instead be out looking for jobs.

Which brings us to another upside, because those jobs will have to be on new shows. New potential Franchises with a capital F. Created and ramrodded by new Gene Roddenberries.

And you thought I was cynical. Ha! See how much of Gene R. has rubbed off on Larry B.? I know that no matter how dull the new *Star Trek* (and *L & O* and *CSI*) shows get, a brand new, totally unrelated but equally heroic Captain Kirk will rise from out of nowhere just when we least expect it and set the hearts and imaginations of everyone on both sides of the TV screen free.

The First "Real" TV Movie and the U.S. Broadcast of the Best British Miniseries Bring Promise and High Hopes to U.S. TV

The year was 1967. It was a cold, snowy night in Iowa City, Iowa, where I was going to graduate school at the University of Iowa. In one corner of the living room of a small apartment about a mile and a half from campus, a pile of books on Celtic literature waited for me to go through it and start reading. In the other corner a portable TV set sat on top of a flimsy cart. It too was waiting for some action.

My two loves. Reading and watching television. Which would it be?

The reading was for a class; it had to get done. The TV was purely for pleasure; no rush.

There was no contest. Television won.

I clicked the set on (they didn't go *ka-chung* anymore) and there they were, the opening titles for something called *The Borgia Stick*. The scene under the titles was a funeral, and it looked different from other television opening scenes. Visually, it had scope and texture, a combination of polish and grittiness that I associated with feature films, not television.

But as I watched I was amazed at how well the structure of the movie meshed with the act structure of TV. Most feature film presentations on television went all to pieces at commercial break time.

Scenes were chopped in half, or the cut to a spot about the new
Ford or Chrysler or Norelco shaver came right after a weak spot
like two people saying, "Hi." *The Borgia Stick*, however, built to
interesting little climaxes or moments of suspense that made me sit
there impatiently, taking in everything the network, NBC, was
trying to sell me, so I could see what happened next.

Just like a television show.

Which made sense because *The Borgia Stick*, starring Don
Murray and Inger Stevens, written by A.J. Russell, and directed by
David Lowell Rich, was a television show.

And a movie as well.

It was a new twist on an old concept—the kind of thinking television does best. Old movies had been a staple of television programming from the very beginning of the medium, but television
programmers didn't start thinking of making their own full-length
feature films, intended to be viewed exclusively on TV (remember,
this was before home VCRs and DVDs, so no one was thinking
about retail sales or shelf life), until 1964 with *See How They Run*,
starring John Forsythe.

See How They Run and an assortment of films that aired on NBC
two years later, in 1966 weren't really very filmic. Their purpose
was to act as two-hour pilots, introducing viewers to potential new
series. They were constructed in the traditional television manner,
characterized a few years later by Glen Larson as "talking heads
separated by action. But mostly talking heads."

The Borgia Stick changed all that. It was meant to stand on its
own and not one second—or episode—longer. At bottom a tale
about a man and a woman who are trying to quit organized crime
before it destroys them, *The Borgia Stick* moved its camera and its
actors the way "real" movies did, and its story had more twists and
turns in two hours than the average series would have in two
years—and more characterization as well. Why, its characters even
changed, growing as people and falling in love.

NBC's little experiment got high ratings and terrific reviews,
creating the impetus for more, more, more, and a new sub-industry
was born.

And with it new aspirations.

New creative dreams.

And new creative people.

One of them was Paul Wendkos, who directed the cult favorites *Angel Baby* and *The Mephisto Waltz* for the big screen, as well as *Gidget* and a couple of its sequels. Early in his career Paul had also directed episodes of series such as *Naked City* and *Mr. Novak*, "But," he said recently during a phone call from his home on the beach in Malibu, where *Gidget* was set so many years ago, "I couldn't wait to get away. And I never would've come back to television if there hadn't been movies of the week."

Paul's return to television came in 1970, with *The Brotherhood of the Bell*, starring Glenn Ford and written by David Karp. "It was a conspiracy movie. It was about something important—business and political success and the things people will compromise to get it."

The budget was under a million dollars at a time when a theatrically released movie of this type would've cost at least five mil. "But we shot it just like a feature film. No compromises. No diminishment of the material.

"The main difference," Paul said, "was our shooting schedule. Instead of shooting it in two months we took about two weeks. And that didn't even feel like a negative at the time. Everyone on the project was feeling a very positive adrenaline rush."

The TV movie business grew steadily, and during the early seventies the networks scheduled twenty hours of original movies of the week (a term coined by the ABC publicity department that has stuck to this day) every week. (In the mid-seventies my series, *Police Story*, even changed its format from twenty-four one-hour episodes to thirteen two-hour *Police Story Movie Specials* so we could have the luxury of stretching our creative muscles.) This was more production than the Hollywood studio system had ever churned out in its heyday, which meant that more new writers and directors were needed than ever before.

Writers and directors who weren't dedicated to the conventions of television storytelling and shooting but to those of *film*.

Writers and directors like Michael Mann. Now known as the director or writer-director of *Collateral, Ali, The Insider, Heat, The Last of the Mohicans*, and other high energy movies, Michael got his start as a director in television, first on *Police Story* in 1975 and then making his real mark with the TV movie *The Jericho Mile*, starring Peter Strauss, in 1979.

When I first met Michael during our *Police Story* days he was driving a beat-up old Jag XK-E and saying things like, "Ever since I was a kid I wanted to make movies. I go without things because I've got to. You're happy in television, great. But I can't settle. Everything I see, I see on the big screen. Everything I hear, I hear on the big screen. Everything I feel, I feel *big*."

In 1984 when we encountered each other outside Anna's Italian Restaurant on Pico Boulevard in L.A., he was driving a beat-up new Ferrari and saying, "*Thief* was a great experience. I learned enough from it to make *The Keep*. But wait'll you see the next one, from a Thomas Harris novel. And then after that . . ."

It was a wonderful conversation. Michael's energy was as big as his ambition, and he was—and still is—filled with big dreams. Dreams television couldn't contain.

But that had been made possible—maybe even fueled—by TV.

The list of outstanding television movies made by equally outstanding talents is a long one. Off the top of my head, purely as a fan and in no deliberate order, I can come up with:

The Jericho Mile
The Autobiography of Miss Jane Pittman
Brian's Song
A Case of Rape
The Burning Bed
Hustling
12 Angry Men
Farrell for the People
A Christmas Story
Barbarians at the Gate
Glass Houses
A Storm in Summer
On Golden Pond
Duel

And many more, by definition ubiquitous.

At the same time television movies were undergoing this creative renaissance, another vital force entered the U.S. television scene. PBS created *Masterpiece Theater*, which brought us the best of the BBC, without question. The first season's imports included two-hour dramas and "limited series" of four to six episodes—the progenitors of what was to become the "miniseries."

The early *Masterpiece Theater* offerings had the same energizing effect on those who worked in the television industry as the movies of the week. They made all of us (I was one as of 1968) aware of what could be done, of how good—how fucking *artistic*—television could be.

Take a look at these titles broadcast by *Masterpiece Theater* from the fall of 1971 through the spring of 1972, its first season on the air:

The Last of the Mohicans
Elizabeth R
The Six Wives of Henry VIII
Cold Comfort Farm
Resurrection
The Gambler
Jude the Obscure
Père Goriot
The Possessed
The Spoils of Poynton
The First Churchills

This is heady stuff.

But the audiences weren't huge. The ratings were nothing like those for our homegrown MOWs, except for the six-episode series called *The Six Wives of Henry VIII*, starring Keith Michel. (One episode per wife. No waiting.)

Henry VIII is arguably the best series ever to appear on television in this country. Certainly the best one I've ever seen. It was superbly written, directed, and performed. It was educational yet dramatic. It dealt with life or death situations but remained literate—without being literary. Its characters came across as real human beings with the strengths and weaknesses and desires and fears that come with the human condition.

The sets gave a feeling of opulence. The costumes were museum pieces come to life. And there was nudity. Not a lot, but just enough bare breast to get people's attention.

It caused a fuss that hasn't been matched since, except maybe for Jimmy Smits' bare ass on *NYPD BLUE* in the mid-nineties. Oh, and Janet Jackson's not-really-bare-if-you-looked-close-enough-but-who-would-admit-they-did tit at halftime during *Super Bowl XXXVIII* in 2004.

U.S. critics loved *Masterpiece Theater*, and many of them made the point that we were doing nothing comparable here. Prodded by the attention and the success of our homegrown movies of the week, television's executive wizards (and "mad programmers") launched an avalanche of "miniseries," most of them with mature themes. (The nudity didn't exert a palpable influence until the nineties, when the freedom to give the audience a lingering look at a breast or a quick flash of full frontal nudity enjoyed by HBO and Showtime gave the broadcast networks the impetus to compete.)

And sure enough, just as *The Six Wives of Henry VIII* stands out for its artistry, so do a great many of our minis. Again, from my brain to your eyes, in no particular order:

Remember *Roots*?

The Thorn Birds?

North and South?

Gormenghast?

Salem's Lot?

Lonesome Dove?

Band of Brothers?

Shogun?

Andersonville?

And of course the proverbial many more.

All these productions were highly rated and highly praised. In 1977 ABC announced that *Roots* had been watched in 130 million *households* over its eight-day run.

That's a whole lotta eyes.

The perfect bait for the perfect trap.

And yet intended—as so many, if not most, of the MOWs and miniseries of the era were—so well.

My old friend and mentor, Bill Blinn, the chief writer of *Roots* in its television incarnation (it started life as a book by Alex Haley) had won an Emmy and a Peabody Award for his script for *Brian's Song*. He was at the very top of the television writing ladder at the time, and although he could've been doing other projects for more pay, he took the job, he said, "because I knew we were going to make history. The book was so damn good, so full of richness and life, that the trick was to do it justice. ABC needed somebody good for that. I figured ABC needed me."

Come to think of it, Bill felt pretty much the same when we talked right after he'd finished work on *Brian's Song*.

"It's a hell of a shot," Bill told me at lunch one day. "The minute I got the assignment I knew I was on the fifty-yard line with nobody between me and the goal. All I had to do was make sure I didn't trip and fumble the ball.

"This is the first time I've been paid to show real human emotion. To be able to literally dig down inside people and give the audience a taste of friendship and love."

High-minded thoughts from a fine writer.

(But not much of a public speaker. I still remember his acceptance speech the night he received the *Brian's Song* Emmy.

"It's late and I've got to pee, so thanks very much.")

Everyone who was involved with television benefited from the elevation of the creative perspective. The networks. The studios. The writers and directors and actors. And the audience most of all.

But nothing lasts forever.

Especially a golden age.

As more television movies were produced it became increasingly difficult to stand out in the crowded television marketplace. Venerable—and highly influential—*TV Guide* was saturated with listings for "first-run movies," and "made for television world premieres." To get the viewers loglines had to be snappier and high concepts needed to be loftier—yet also more "accessible."

For TV movies and miniseries, the term high concept came to mean, "something that worked before."

Or, "something that everyone can identify with."

Which in turn meant, "something generic."

"Issues" and "illnesses" became the order of the day for MOWs. Success in another field—as in being a best-selling book—became the criterion for minis.

Ironically, Bill Blinn's two greatest successes not only elevated television programming but turned right around and lowered it as well.

Brian's Song was about an athlete dying young of an incurable disease. It was a male buddy movie with a core of sentiment (in the best sense of the word) that attracted a huge audience of women.

Roots was an adaptation of a best-selling book. It was about generations of oppressed people fighting for empowerment. And it too attracted a huge audience of women as well as men.

So, over time, more and more television movies focused on what producers, critics, and viewers alike derisively called "the illness of the week."

More and more miniseries became television versions of best-sellers.

And more and more of both became overly sentimental tear jerkers with characters who weren't real-seeming people with their own individual stories but straw men and women created to represent specific issues that were in the news, issues that would be resolved through some sort of newfound empowerment.

The techniques of feature films remained.

But the sensibility of feature films vanished.

The polish remained, but the grittiness was AWOL. Worse than that, it received a dishonorable discharge.

I remember a meeting I had in 1978 with Deanne Barkley, vice president of long form (television-ese for television movie and miniseries) development at NBC.

I'd seen the other guys pushing down the creative barriers and letting themselves and their talents go wild in the long form field, and since *Police Story* was coming to a close I wanted to get out there and boogie too. But before I could say a word—before I could mention one idea—Deanne looked over at her assistant, a guy named Lew Hunter, who later became a screenwriting guru of sorts, then came around from behind her desk to sit on its edge and look at me hard.

"Let me stop you right there," she said. (The way I remember it, all I'd said was "Hello.") "Let's make sure that your thinking is in synch with ours. We know that a lot of audacious programming is succeeding, but NBC's research shows that's only temporary.

"We don't want to 'tell stories.' Anybody can 'tell stories.' Movies 'tell stories' all the time. We want to move on. We want to uplift our audience by presenting problems the average person faces, faced by an average person. And those stories have to have the widest possible appeal," Deanne said.

"So in other words you want something—generic?" I said.

Deanne looked thoughtful. Again she glanced over at Lew. Then she nodded at me. "'Generic,'" she said. "I like that. We're definitely in synch. What've you got that's generic enough for NBC?"

Shit! Talk about rotten luck.

Here I was just starting out in this field and it was already too late.

Throughout the eighties the good and the bad coexisted in the movie of the week and miniseries business, as they do, I am told, in all things. Viewers dwindled. Network hours devoted to television movies and such dwindled as well. This slide continued throughout the nineties, with production companies that had had thriving MOW businesses closing up shop. By 2004 there were literally *no* regularly scheduled television movies on the broadcast networks, and miniseries had become more promotable because they now were at best an annual event.

Cable channels picked up some of the slack, but far from all. Turner Broadcasting, Lifetime, and the USA Channel are the main programmers of movies of the week, with approximately six new hours of so-called product a month between them.

The old pro filmmakers like Paul Wendkos who took a flyer in television because of the chance to do something new are either dead or retired. New and aspiring filmmakers for the most part take their talent straight to home video, or walk the road of independent film. There's no room for them in TV. No need.

The Borgia Stick and *The Six Wives of Henry VIII* blazed trails, both separately and together, and our television culture is much the richer for them. But sometimes as I lie in bed at two in the morning unable to sleep, I think about what was, and what should have been. And I think about the way Bill Blinn looked at the 1972 Emmy Awards, when he was handed that statuette.

I think about how hard he worked, and how much doing the right thing meant to him.

And I wonder why, for God's sake, if the networks were going to imitate him, why those stupid, generic sons of bitches didn't all just go pee.

Note: One of the most important things about *The Borgia Stick* for me was that after I'd finished watching it that snowy night in Iowa City I had one of those great moments of clarity people are sometimes lucky enough to get. An epiphany that I've never forgotten. I thought:

I want to do that.

So, knowing absolutely nothing about movies or television or writing screenplays or teleplays, completely ignorant of form and format and how to use FADE IN and FADE OUT, I spent the next two weeks writing my own spec movie of the week.

Four months later I was living in L.A., and a new neighbor I'd met at the pool, an out-of-work former sitcom star named Sammy Jackson, was giving that completely screwed up script to a producer he knew.

One month after that I had my first Hollywood writing deal.

I guess I can't put it off any longer. I've got to break down and buy the new *The Borgia Stick* DVD.

HBO Starts Expanding, Leading Cable to Unforeseen Heights

*T*he history of cable television in the United States isn't the history of HBO.

It just seems that way.

In 1972, at a time when broadcast executives were terrified of anything resembling "pay TV," Home Box Office (the very name attests to the theater-like purpose of its programming at the company's creation) snuck in under the radar as a local provider of movies and special events in New York City. The company saw a hole in broadcast programming—the lack of uninterrupted and uncut feature films and of coverage of special, one-shot sporting events—and filled it. In November of 1972, a date that should live in infamy in the memories of broadcast network bigwigs and local station managers of the time, HBO expanded by bringing a New York Rangers hockey game played in Madison Square Garden to the small-market city of Wilkes-Barre, Pennsylvania. The cable programming giant hasn't stopped growing since.

While broadcasters fought hard and publicly, with sophisticated advertising campaigns, against the concept of pay TV by equating it with the loss of freedom and trotting out image after image of viewers who previously watched anything they wanted to for "free" now having to get up and jam coins or tokens into parking meter–like boxes attached to their TV sets, HBO and other young cable companies developed the monthly subscription system. No overt intrusion into the daily life of the viewer. Just one little payment every thirty days.

For that payment viewers got much more than the same-old same-old. They saw sporting events and concerts they would never have seen on broadcast TV simply because broadcast deals had never been struck. The broadcast networks and stations weren't ready for this no muss, no fuss approach by their competition. Instead of firing P.R. broadsides pointing out the inconvenience of having to get your service hooked up, and worse, of streets being torn up for the laying of the cable, they retreated behind a Maginot Line every bit as illusory as the one in France turned out to be at the start of World War II.

In a way, the broadcast networks' behavior was similar to that of the country dogs who bark all night at coyotes. "Get outta here!" those barks cry. "You're no good, you're no good, go away!" But then, during the day, Mr. Coyote casually saunters out of the brush and across the property line and what does the dog do? *It turns away.* The great defender of the farm, ranch, or country home doesn't see, doesn't hear, doesn't even pick up the scent of its foe and lets it pass.

The country dog turns away because it doesn't know what the hell to do now that the enemy is in its backyard, and the networks and stations did the same thing back in the seventies, probably for the same reason. They didn't know how to fight back, and they had nothing to counter with. By its very nature as a user of "public airwaves," the television broadcasting industry couldn't present the same kind of content cable channels could. They had to—and still have to—follow the Federal Communications Commission's rules. But cable, and later satellite television, did not and still do not.

Because cable outlets have from their very beginning been allowed to be more open, frank, and, yes, offensive and violent, they forever changed the viewing patterns of the nation and created a new and, believe it or not, refreshing programming paradigm, one in which viewers were treated with respect because viewers were—at last!—the true customers.

And they did it marching behind HBO.

HBO's 1976 nationwide presentation of the Ali-Frazier "Thrilla-in-Manila" heavyweight fight via satellite was a major breakthrough. Having gone national, HBO didn't look back, continuing to present boxing and other sports, uncut, unaltered feature films, and star-powered concerts to subscribers who accessed the channel via local cable providers. By the early eighties original HBO made-for-cable movies were bringing even more frankness to the small screen.

"Holy shit!" Steve Poster, a Laurel Canyon neighbor and future president of the American Society of Cinematographers said to me one night as we watched HBO's latest presentation. "They're swearing! Holy shit!" And then he realized, "They're showing her ass! And his!

"Hey," Steve said, "am I really seeing breasts in a movie made for TV?"

HBO wasn't the only cable channel offering this kind of programming, but it got there first and understood the value of advertising better than any of the others. HBO created the most aggressive marketing program of the day, doing all it could to make itself synonymous with "cable." Commercials and print ads acknowledged that you could have cable without HBO, but why on earth would you want to? Look at all you'd miss if you didn't pay the extra fee. (This approach continued well into the next century, with the slogan "It's not TV, it's HBO.")

The extra subscription fee, above and beyond what we all know today as the Basic Cable Package, is what separates the men from the boys in cable (or the bare breasts from those suspended in bikinis). HBO was and is a premium cable offering, and therein lies its strength, and the secret of its economic success and appeal to viewers as an entertainment provider.

For those who let their mates or managers or accountants or parents take care of such things, here's the (very) short course in how cable TV works:

You're a viewer living in the middle of nowhere, in an area broadcast television doesn't reach, or reaches with a pitifully weak and inadequate signal. You want to be part of your community and watch your local stations, and the networks too. So you turn to your nearest cable company, which offers as an added inducement dozens of channels available only on cable. Lots of new stuff!

So you pay your basic cable price and you're hooked in—with the option to upgrade for more.

Or maybe you're a viewer in a big city where broadcast television works perfectly, but you want to see more recent feature films on your TV set. The kinds of movies HBO and Showtime and Cinemax and others offer. And your younger kids want more shows just for them. Shows offered by the Disney Channel and Nickelodeon and the Cartoon Network. And don't forget your teenagers. They want their MTV and VH1.

So you pay for basic cable and you add extra items to it, and so does the viewer in the middle of nowhere. The two of you can now see all of the above plus a collection of sports channels and channels devoted to special interests of every shape and size.

Niche channels, as they're called in the television business, include channels for animal lovers (Animal Planet) and history buffs (the History Channel, what else?) and people who used to read *National Geographic Magazine* but now get their daily dose of Egyptian pyramids and dinosaurs on Discovery or The Learning Channel or National Geographic.

There's more, a superabundance of niches for everyone no matter how widely or narrowly focused you are. Want modern lifestyles? The E! Network's got 'em. Cooking? The Food Network's for you. Like fixing up your house? Go to House and Garden TV. Need a techno fix? Here's Tech TV. If good clean raunch is your thing, the Playboy Channel awaits. And don't forget the Video Game Channel and the Game Show Network and the Independent Film Channel, or Bravo, Arts and Entertainment, Trio, or BBC America.

The bottom line here is clear. There are literally hundreds of channels to choose from if you've got a little extra dough. Premium cable channels designed to deliver exactly what you want to see.

Premium channels that damn well better give you exactly what you want to see. Because if they don't you'll cancel 'em. And if enough viewers vote thumbs down by removing a channel from their premium package, it's gone, dude. Out. As dead as the test patterns I used to gaze at with bemusement when I was a kid.

HBO was the pioneer in acknowledging that since the audience was paying for programming, the audience was the boss. The broadcast television paradigm that makes the advertiser the client, the programming the bait, and the audience the product being sold to the advertisers who are the customers, doesn't apply in the land of premium cable. HBO, Showtime, and many other premium cable channels accept no advertising. They make their money from the subscription fees. That makes the *viewer* their customer, and having the viewer as the customer makes pleasing the viewer their number one goal.

Many premium cable channels do run commercial spots, which means they're still treating their shows as viewer bait instead of as the products. But because the channels are purchased for viewing based on the kind of content they present, there still is an implied promise of a certain level of creativity, and the bait will fail to attract its target viewers if it doesn't deliver. This keeps the adrenaline of all those involved flowing, and translates into a production philosophy in which the channels strive to give the audience the most bang they possibly can for the buck.

This sounds like no big deal. Like practical business sense. But it turns the whole television programming and business model on its head. In order to do right by their customers, cable channels have had to drop the "least objectionable program" theory of programming that has guided broadcast television from the beginning, and instead substitute a "program we really like" outlook instead.

Waitaminnit. What'd I say? *"least objectionable program?"* What in the name of socio-economic-entertainment bullshit is *that* all about?

Well, bunky, it's like this.

The least objectionable program theory came into being as an easy way out for network executives. Putting on shows that were intended to be the best possible entertainment anyone could come up with meant making judgments and commitments involving "quality," which when all is said and done is a non-measurable quality itself. When you get down to it—as everyone who works in the creative end of television eventually must no matter how hard we try to put the matter off—excellence is a matter of taste and education and experience, and whether or not what's being viewed (or read or listened to) satisfies the expectations each person's taste and education and experience have set up.

In other words, excellence is just plain non-quantifiable. Which at the dawn of television meant that the broadcast network buyer-programmers would have to go with their gut feelings about a series if their prime goal was for it to have a certain level of quality, and they knew that if you go with your gut, there's no way to cover your behind.

So some brilliant executive—quite possibly fifties and early sixties CBS vice president of programming Michael Dann, who first discussed "LOP" in an article I remember reading in *Time* magazine when I was in college—found or perhaps even commissioned some research that showed that given a specific set of choices viewers would watch whatever show they disliked the least when compared to the other shows on at the same time.

Yes, I know it sounds absurd (hmm, maybe now some of Fred Silverman's decisions as the mad programmer make more sense), but it was the way TV worked. And it really did work—as long as two conditions were satisfied.

The first condition was that television had to be so fascinating in and of itself that people would leave it on and watch it (or at least glance its way) throughout the day just in case something they disliked less than anything else came on.

The second condition was that there had to be a limited number of choices. With three networks, or three networks and maybe two or three local stations, to choose from, because only then can the choices be kept firmly in mind. Only with a small menu can the viewer's brain go through the process of thinking of each choice and deciding, "Okay, I'll go with this one. I hate it the least."

These days, both conditions are ancient history.

Our longtime love affair with the TV set seems to be over. The only way to sell new ones has been to lower the prices to almost the price range of toaster ovens and to legislate new technology making old sets obsolete. Going hand in hand with shrinking sales is the fact that according to the authorities at A.J. Nielsen and Co., the total number of people watching television just keeps on dropping.

Some television executives blame video games.

Others blame the Internet.

Others go right for the "faulty systems of measurement" jugular.

(Watch out, Mr. Nielsen. Like so many clucking parents, the guys in the suits are "disappointed in you.")

Regardless of the cause, the statistics are in. No one's watching TV anymore just because it's *there*. It's no longer enough to be merely that cute little rectangle across the room. Your set's gotta have more than a high-contrast image going for it in order to catch a human eye.

As for limited choices—whoa, HBO and the cable channels have wiped that situation all over the mat. The proliferation of cable channels in general, be they basic or premium and whether or not they run commercials, has proven to be the disaster for broadcast television that its executives feared pay TV would be.

With seven broadcast networks and twenty, no forty, make that eighty, I mean two hundred, sorry three hundred . . . okay, okay, five hundred and they're still coming, cable and satellite channels to choose from, the operative word is indeed *choice*. Being a passive viewer is a thing of the past. Even little children can grab that remote and click until they're caught by something they *like*.

That's why the percentage of total television viewers that watches cable and satellite channels is increasing every year, whether or not the audience in general is shrinking. In the late nineties HBO even had a spurt where its audience increased almost twenty percent in one year, and in the same year, 1997, fully two-thirds of all U.S. homes had at least basic cable service.

(*Two-thirds!?* Don't tell me 66 million Americans weren't getting good enough broadcast reception. It wasn't need that motivated all of those subscribers. It was *hope* for something interesting, challenging, and rewarding to watch.)

The change from a passive audience accepting the least objectionable program to an active one demanding the program we really like is why stars of shows like the Disney Channel's *Lizzie McGuire* and Nickelodeon's *All That* get as much press coverage as Britney Spears and Mel Gibson. Why the fourth season premiere of *The Sopranos* outrated its broadcast network competition.

And it's why HBO and Showtime (which has always been the

cable equivalent of Ford Motors to HBO's GM—and like Ford keeps on truckin' and tryin' nevertheless) keep going out there where no one has gone before and giving us programming that digs right in there trying to break new ground, and sometimes even succeeds. In 2001 HBO programming was nominated for an astonishing ninety-four Emmys. In 2002 the number of nominations fell by one(!) to an equally amazing ninety-three.

The film *Field of Dreams* gave us the catchphrase, "build it and they will come."

The increasing success of premium cable channels bespeaks another slogan. "Treat your audience like customers and treat your customers with respect and they'll keep coming back."

Where is the broadcast network equivalent of HBO's *Spawn*?

How about *Tales from the Crypt? Dream On? The Larry Sanders Show? Oz? Sex and the City? The Sopranos? Six Feet Under? Arliss? The Wire? Curb Your Enthusiasm? K Street?* Or *Carnivale?* Or Showtime's *Queer as Folk? The L Word? The Chris Isaak Show? Soul Food? Dead Like Me? Street Time? Jeremiah? Out of Order? Odyssey 5?* Or *Family Business?*

For that matter, where are the feature films that innovate the way these have in subject or style?

Even when the stuff on cable isn't done as well as it should be, it's still new. Even when it fails it goes down swinging for the fences.

The Cable Center of the University of Denver puts it this way: "America's thirst for quality television has been the driving force behind the cable industry's growth. The willingness to invest in new technologies and programming has made cable television more than just an antenna service. It is now an integral part of American culture."

Satellite channels, which have been increasing since the early nineties, have added more fuel to the fire. The more choice viewers have, the more "quality" and excellence will pay off.

Unless . . .

I remember a few years ago, sitting in a conference room at HBO's Century City, California, offices with the staff of the series *Spawn*, on which I was serving as creative consultant. Although animated and based on a comic book, *Spawn* was very adult in its approach to the material. In addition to demonic violence and sadism (literally because the lead character Spawn was a demon), each episode of the show featured animated nudity and sex and more "fucking" this and "fucking" that than even the most gangsta of gangsta rap tracks. In fact, the series was so adult that HBO had scheduled it to go on the air after midnight.

We were talking to Lenny Brown, a development executive in HBO's Original Programming department at the time and one of the dreaded guys in charge of our show. Not that there was much to dread. Lenny was one of the good guys who understood a little something about the creative process, even as it applied to those of us who joked about working on "the show for the damned."

"Big doings at the Home Box Office home office," Lenny said. "The suits in New York are freaking out."

"About what?" Eric Radomski, the animator, said.

"There's a rumor that we're going basic," said Lenny. "We'll be part of everybody's basic cable package in a few months."

"Hey," I said, "that's great. It'll what, quadruple your audience?"

"More than that, probably," Lenny said. He frowned.

"What's the matter?"

"If we're on basic cable we have to change our programming. Right now anybody who sees HBO has specifically selected us. They know what they're getting. They know that they'll hear a lot of swearing and see some bodies without clothes. They chose to be exposed to that.

"But if we're basic," he continued, "we have to censor ourselves. We're being thrown into people's lives whether they asked for us or not. Whether they know who we are and what we do or not. So we can't do as much. We'll have to dumb down. If we go basic we can't even do *Spawn*."

The room fell silent. Then, quietly, Catherine Winder, head of HBO Animation, spoke. "Hmm, well, does this mean it's time for me to start cleaning out my desk?"

Lenny said, "It's not definite yet. The big shots are still trying to make up their minds. I guess everything depends on which faction of geniuses prevails."

As it turned out, the group of geniuses, including CEO Chris Albrecht, who wanted HBO to remain premium cable won, and HBO has remained positioned as it was, allowing the continued development and programming of the kinds of shows that have brought it to prominence today.

To me, nothing in recent years has been more heartening than the creativity so apparent on premium cable. And nothing has been as dismaying as the broadcast networks' inability to rise to the challenge. Instead of leading, CBS, NBC, ABC, Fox, the WB, UPN, and Pax continue to look away from the coyotes, even when the critters could be on their side.

The Sopranos is a case in point. As of this writing it has won over sixty major awards in its first four seasons, for everything from Best Series to Best Actor or Actress to Best Writing to Best Costuming to Best Set Decorating and more. In short, it's been considered the best of the best for a good long while now, with Emmys, Golden Globes, even Peabody Awards.

But when it was first being developed every broadcast network that was approached turned it down.

They didn't get it.

They couldn't get it.

They didn't dare.

The nearest a broadcast network came to putting anything remotely like *The Sopranos* on the air happened more than a generation ago, back in the early seventies. I started my first ever job as a story editor on *The Magician* the same day the producer, Paul Playden, brought in another new writer to be the staff writer on the show. This writer had no credits but a great deal of enthusiasm and intelligence, and, it turned out, a hell of a lot of skill.

The staff writer's name was David Chase, and twenty-five years later he created *The Sopranos* and became its executive producer and, of course, head writer. During our *Magician* days we were under tremendous production pressure and worked side by side night and day. In the artificial world of television that means getting to know each other pretty well. Certainly better than you would if you were just, say, neighbors, instead of in the production trenches together.

David and I developed this kind of desperate relationship in which we knew we weren't all that close yet somehow *felt* close nevertheless. We talked about our personal and professional goals, and I learned that in spite of his whitebread last name, David was Italian and loved the films *The Godfather* and the just-released *The Godfather: Part II*.

I wasn't quite as crazy about them then (although now I can passionately argue that *Godfather II* is the best American film ever made), but I'd used the first *Godfather* film as partial source material for a script I'd written shortly before taking the job on *The Magician*. It was a ninety-minute pilot for a CBS soap opera about the agonies and ecstasies of a Mob family.

I mean a real family—the mothers, fathers, wives (especially the wives, this being daytime TV), children, aunts, and uncles of those in what we were forced in those days to euphemistically call "organized crime." The script was taped while David and I were working together, and we took a few moments out of our busy jobs of plotting and verbalizing unbelievable feats of stage magic that would help Bill The Magician Bixby catch weird and exotic killers to watch the pilot when it was televised one afternoon.

The show stank. Terrible acting. Terrible direction. And the script—well, since it was a soap opera, I'd written it as a weeper, and as a writer looking at my own work I definitely wanted to cry.

When this disastrous insult to the creative spirit was over I turned to David and managed to say, "What do you think?" hoping, naturally, that he would reply with a polite series of lies. Instead he played it pretty straight.

"I've always wanted to do a show like that," David said. "Well, not exactly like that. In fact, not like that at all. But a show about people like those, trapped in the Italian family outlook and in the Mob."

"What would you do differently?" I asked.

He didn't even blink. "I'd make it funny," David said.

CBS never picked up the series. Never even reran the ninety-minute tearjerker that had convinced them that the time for a Mafia soap opera hadn't yet come, and I didn't blame them a bit.

But in 1999, when I saw the first episode of *The Sopranos*, I recalled that Old Mob Try, and the conversation David and I had had, and I thought two thoughts.

Sure wish I'd been smart enough to make it funny, I thought.
And:
Sure wish I'd been smart enough to take it to HBO.

Robert Blake Becomes Baretta and the Creative Paradigm Takes a Big Shift

During much of the seventies television movies and miniseries weren't the only places where creative energy was bursting at the seams. In 1971, CBS's *All in the Family* brought contemporary life to sitcoms, which previously had been stuck in a kind of "time loop." No matter what was happening in the real world, the world of TV sitcoms gave us fifties family attitudes, fifties family problems, even fifties kids who called adults "Sir" and "Ma'am" and who always said "Yes" after an adult told them what to do.

For a while *All in the Family* was unique. Then Fred Silverman cloned it, again and again, and CBS had a stable of comedies where racial strife, unemployment, and disagreement about economic and ecological policies and the Vietnam War provided the context for the humor. NBC and ABC loosened up as well, and the sitcom genre became a rowdy and wondrous place, a funhouse mirror image of reality in keeping with the tone and spirit Aristophanes' plays had shown more than two thousand years before.

It took one-hour shows, the dramas and the action vehicles, a little longer, but eventually they too started to kick contemporary butt. There was no one-hour equivalent to *All in the Family*, no breakthrough drama that stood the industry on its ear and proclaimed a new day. Not that no one tried. In 1970 CBS put a show called *The Storefront Lawyers* on the air, its very title letting viewers know that something new was up.

Robert Blake, 1975 (Still Things)

Storefront law offices were springing up throughout the big cities of the U.S. at the time, often amid great controversy. So the show's title made one thing very clear. This wasn't your father's legal show, featuring tired old men yakking, yakking, yakking in court. It was about idealistic young men and women who wanted to help the downtrodden by working out of a storefront office, giving of themselves in the new hippie (and old New Testament) tradition—for free.

The Storefront Lawyers failed. The true mark of its lack of success was that when it returned for a second season it had been renamed *Men at Law*. The storefront element, the element dealing with youthful and relevant hopes and dreams was downplayed, and the series became just another legal show. It never returned for a third year.

The lesson learned here was that trying to increase your viewing audience by straight out catering to rebellious youth wouldn't work.

And how could it? The target audience was out carrying signs and demonstrating in the streets and actively attempting to make a difference in the world. The angry kids of the early seventies just plain didn't have the time to watch television, even if it was about them.

So now some smart guy at a network—or maybe several smart guys at all the networks, because it always seems as though television programming ideas kind of float in the air of any given era and land on the shoulders of a bunch of executives and producers and writers all at once—realizes that the ratings success of *All in the Family* isn't based on a young hip hero with whom the Demonstration Generation can identify (Rob Reiner's "Meathead" character was a supporting player and a dorky one at that). Rather, the big numbers are based on the fact that more members of the existing, older audience are watching because they like seeing the generation gap they're living through as it's experienced by someone else who in many ways is more like them.

Forget attracting an entirely new audience. Just enlarge the old one and hope some newcomers will drop in.

And don't even think that maybe execution of the idea has something to do with the success of a show. That maybe *All in the Family* was cleaning its competition's clocks because it was produced, written, directed, and acted superbly, and *The Storefront Lawyers* just plain sucked.

Gradual change became the order of the one-hour show day. To play the game with a chance of success, the networks decided, they didn't have to write new rules. They just had to loosen up the old ones, which is what they did. One-hour series continued to serve the same old wine of crime and punishment, detection and detention, diagnosis and cure, but they put a little "popcorn" into the presentation and gave us new bottles.

Bottles labeled "relevance."

I don't know what network genius came up with the term, but it was sheer genius. Social and political consciousness crept into cop shows, detective shows, medical shows, and lawyer shows like guerilla fighters out on a raid. Characters who were young and angry, long-haired and rebellious (and bell-bottomed too, which can make for some painful rerun viewing if you ever dressed that way) appeared as villains and witnesses and experts and passers-by, giving one-hour shows a look and a grounding they hadn't had before. Supporting leads became hipper in appearance and outlook on life. But the *alte cocker* heroes and heroines stayed the same, with the added touch of viewing the new generation with a bemused or sometimes jaundiced eye.

How well did this approach work?

Let's put it this way. From 1968 through much of 1972 I was a struggling writer whose economic decisions were based on "What should I do this month? Pay the rent or go to the supermarket?" And from 1972 through 1977 I was one of the (paid!) writers (or even the producer) of

The Interns
The Rookies
The New Land
Star Trek: The Animated Series
The Bold Ones
Genesis II
The Sixth Sense
Ironside
The Six Million Dollar Man
Barnaby Jones
Cannon
Medical Center
Hawaii Five-0
The Streets of San Francisco
Police Woman
Police Story
Gibbsville
Petrocelli
Medical Story
Baretta

These were all one-hour, primetime, network television shows, featuring either drama or action or both.

And why was I so employed?

It wasn't because I was more talented than any other writer at the time (although I sure thought so).

Or because I was smarter than any other writer at the time (although I thought that as well).

It wasn't even because I was more entertaining at the meetings than any other writer at the time (although I was really working like hell to accomplish that).

It was because—

I was *younger* than every other writer at the time.

For one brief, shining moment I was in fact the youngest member of the Writers Guild of America, West.

Right there and then, during the period of relevant programming on television, youth mattered. (Not as much as it does as I write this, but a lot more than people believe, or possibly like to remember.)

Youth was being served. Up.

Will Loren, then the executive story consultant of *Hawaii Five-0*, laid it on the line at our first story meeting. "We need you to be a good writer, and we need you to write something for us because you're the only writer we can find who knows the current slang."

Is that a compliment or what?

The fact is that at the time television was ruled by middle-aged white men. Fiftyish men occupied most of the executive suites. Fiftyish men occupied most of the producers' offices. Fiftyish men occupied most of the writers' hard-backed chairs.

And I was twenty-five years younger than 'em all.

So while other young men and women my age were taking it to the streets, I was writing about the streets. I was talking their talk, disseminating their *Weltanschauung*.

I was popping in the slang so McGarrett and Cannon and Barnaby and Ironside and Pepper and a host of middle-aged series stars (mostly men and all white) could live in and deal with the contemporary world.

I was creating long-haired, radical, and sexually experimental helpers and long-haired, radical, and sexually experimental pals and long-haired, radical, and sexually experimental victims and long-haired, radical, and sexually experimental patients, and long-haired, radical, and sexually experimental perpetrators, and long-haired, radical, and sexually experimental (but innocent) defendants, so that the shows the networks were presenting functioned as mirrors of contemporary life.

Or at least of contemporary life as contemporarily perceived.

I loved it. All of us involved in television production during that era loved it—even those old fiftyish guys. There was a feeling of excitement, of potential, that I haven't felt in television before or since. Sure, there were constraints, but we *were* radicals regardless of our chronological ages (isn't that an essential quality for choosing to make your living in even the most mundane of the arts?), and we were on the *inside*. We could smite the enemy sneakily, secretly, with a line of meaningful dialogue here, an honest portrayal of modern attitude there, and a shocking exposure of hypocrisy wherever we could plant it.

The real seventies weren't anything like *That 70s Show*, my friends. The real seventies were about stirring things up. Causing change. Making the world a better place.

Even for TV writers.

And TV audiences too.

These shows worked. They achieved the ratings goals set by the networks and came very damn close to achieving the creative goals set by their staffs. If we'd only had just a little more time and money—or if Lee Majors had been just a little better actor—those '70s shows would've been every bit as "good" as any other fine drama ever produced anywhere.

And yet—

Until January 17, 1975 something was missing from all this fecund profundity.

Until January 17, 1975 the lesson of *The Storefront Lawyers* was like unto a guidepost before all network eyes.

Until January 17, 1975, it was the supporting actors and guest stars who demonstrated (and sometimes rioted) the searching, rebellious life. Not the leads. *Hawaii Five-0*'s Jim McGarrett, played by Jack Lord, might say "That's not my bag" to a young crook wanting a deal, but he did so with raised eyebrows, and although he might believe in conservation, it wasn't McGarrett who was making the point by well-thought-out acts of eco-terrorism. McGarrett was nailing the idealistic terrorist and saying, "Book 'im, Danno."

Starsky and Hutch's stars, not-so-coincidentally named Starsky and Hutch, were in their twenties and were wild crazy guys, but not rebels. They gave their boss a hard time, sure, but they gave him the same hard time all cop heroes had given their bosses in movies and television since the thirties, by being wiseasses, breaking the rules, and driving too fast in their hot new car. They dressed cool and talked cool, but that was only on the outside. Inside they were *old*. At a time when one of the great social slogans was "If you're not with us you're against us," guess what? Starsky and Hutch were agin.

The heroes of all the shows of that era were good guys, of course, men and sometimes women to be admired. But they were true compassionate conservatives, living their personal and professional lives exactly as they would have if no social revolution was going on, and that was fine and dandy and it worked.

Until January 17, 1975.

And *Baretta*.

Tony Baretta, as played by Robert Blake, was compassionate, all right, but hardly conservative. Nor was he a peace-and-love hippie. Baretta was into love, but the way he proved he loved you was to go nose to nose or punch for punch. At a time when the youth of America were discovering Jean-Paul Sartre and learning that "existence precedes essence," Robert's Baretta was working like a son of a bitch to create a unique essence of his own. He cared about people and wasn't afraid to show it. But instead of turning the other cheek, he fought for the people and ideals he believed in, a modern-day version of an Aristotelian philosopher-king who used might to institute his moral-ethical concept of right.

If Lyndon Johnson's and Richard Nixon's America was "culture," and hippies were "counter-culture," then Baretta was "counter-counter-culture." Definitely his own man.

It wasn't supposed to be that way. When executive producer Roy Huggins (creator of the classic fifties series *Maverick* and many others) and producer Jo Swerling, Jr., recruited me for the show they explained that it was a recasting of a hit they'd had the year before called *Toma*. Tony Masante, the actor who'd played Toma, had walked away from a success because he didn't want to be tied down, and Robert Blake was replacing him. Blake, however, didn't want to be "the second Toma."

"He wants to be his own character," Jo said. "Somebody new. Somebody he's got a hand in creating."

"We're changing the name, but he'll still be Toma," said Roy. "An Italian cop who uses lots of disguises."

Robert, however, didn't quite see it that way. He knew when he was being patronized, and wasn't going for it. I found this out about a week into my job as story consultant-producer of the new show. On that particular day I found Robert in my office when I arrived one morning. He was holding the first few pages I'd written for the second episode of the series. (The first episode had been written by Stephen J. Cannell, who was a protégé of Roy's and producer of *The Rockford Files* at the time.)

"Kid," Robert said, "this ain't gonna fly." He put the sheets of paper back down on my desk. "You're trying too hard to be clever. Don't worry about it. I'll handle the clever. You just gotta make Baretta feel."

"You'll handle the clever?" I said.

"Yeah, I'll fill in the blanks in the dialogue. Nuthin' personal, but I can't leave that kinda thing to anybody else. That's my face up there on the screen, not yours. Millions of people'll be convinced I made up those words and they'll hate me, not you, if the words're dumb. So I'll handle the words. You just write the soul."

"I didn't see all that much soul in the first script," I said.

"The first script stinks," said Robert. "It ain't the character at all. But we're gonna fix that. You and me. We're gonna rewrite the whole thing."

"Have you talked to Roy or Jo about that?"

"Fuck Huggins and Jo. It ain't their show, it's mine." He saw my bewildered look. "I'm takin' over, kid," he said. "Don't worry about makin' those losers happy. Worry about me." Robert went through the other papers on my desk and found what he wanted, my copy of Steve Cannell's script. "Forget your episode for now. We gotta get started on this."

"We" really meant "me." Robert gave me instructions about every scene, lines of dialogue he wanted, cute expressions for Baretta to use. Roy Huggins was out of town, so I talked the changes over with Jo, and his decision, as Roy's second-in-command, was for me to go for it. Keep Robert happy. Do the rewrite.

For two weeks that's what I did, working over Thanksgiving to get the script in that Monday, the day the director of the episode, Bernie Kowalski, was to come in and start preparing to shoot. Sure enough, Bernie came in, and he and Robert went off to Robert's dressing room (that means "trailer" in showbiz talk) to go over what I'd written. Roy Huggins came in too.

At about eleven o'clock that morning Robert walked into my office. "Meetin' time, kid," he said. "You, me, Huggins, and Jo. We're gonna talk about the new script." As we headed toward Roy's office Robert smiled at me reassuringly. "Don't worry 'bout nuthin' no matter what Huggins says. You did what I wanted. I'm right behind you."

Then he opened the door and ushered me in. I took a couple of steps forward. Heard a click behind me. Turned.

The door to Roy Huggins' office was closed.

Robert Blake was behind me, all right.

But on the other side.

Roy and Jo were watching me. The conversation was short. "When I left on my trip I felt very good about our first script," Roy said. "It was good. It was tight. It was *finished*." He held up a copy of the draft I'd just turned in. "Now, however, I find that we're back at square one." And he threw the script onto the floor. The brads holding it together flew off. Pages were everywhere.

"'Square one?'" I said. "There must be some mistake. Robert—"

"Resignation accepted," Roy said.

"Waitaminnit. I didn't resign."

"Meeting over, Larry," Roy said. He turned away.

The meeting *was* over, and so was my stint on *Baretta*. I went looking for Robert, but he was nowhere to be found. Over the next few days I phoned him any number of times, but he never took or returned the calls.

A few months later I read in one of the showbiz trades that Roy

Huggins was no longer in charge of *Baretta*. A few days after that I read that Bernie Kowalski was the new executive producer. And over the months and years that followed I read about this writer-producer and that writer-producer and these other writer-producers being hired and fired and Robert expressing his dissatisfaction with the whole lot of "Hollywood hacks."

Robert Blake *did* take over *Baretta*.

Just not when it would've done me any good.

So why is January 17, 1975, a red-letter date? Why is *Baretta* a turning point? Because of its hero, so admirably idealistic, forthright, rebellious, and strong?

Hell no.

The Tony Baretta character was unique. There hasn't been another one like him. No one but Robert could carry it off. No one else even tried.

Baretta is a turning point because it altered the creative paradigm in a totally unexpected way, changing the balance of power in the television series business. It took creative control of the show away from the Usual Gang of Idiots, the executives and producers and writers, and put it squarely into the hands of Robert Blake. The show was a smash with public and critics alike from its first episode to its last, and every single aspect of it from scripts to casting to sets to costumes to stage crew to office personnel was run by the *star*.

To be sure, in some ways television stars had been *de facto* rulers of the roost for years. Maybe forever. After all, it was their faces up there on the screen, and those of us on the other side have always tried to accommodate them whenever possible—*as long as the accommodation wasn't injurious to the show.*

Who, you ask, defines "injurious"?

That's easy. We do.

Or did anyway.

B.B. Before Baretta.

Before *Baretta* the star of a TV series might be troubled by the writing in a scene or disturbed by the behavior of a member of the crew or just plain be having a bad day. So he or she would throw a hissy fit and sulk in their trailer until the producer or one of the writers came down and made nice. Together the star and the producer or writer would work out a solution to the star's problem, but as they did so they both understood one simple fact.

If the star didn't get back on that set and shoot the scene—and soon—the star was in breach of contract. He could be fired. Or worse, end up with truly terrible publicity because in the eyes of man, God, the court system, *The National Enquirer*, and millions of fans, the star would be *wrong*.

Before *Baretta* facts of life:

On *The Magician*, Bill Bixby could roll his eyes at a script in dismay and announce to the rest of the cast, "This doesn't make sense." But he couldn't refuse to perform, and he couldn't make any revisions without charming the series producer.

On *The Streets of San Francisco*, Karl Malden could mock an actor working for the day because he was bald. But he couldn't have him replaced.

On *The Virginian*, Doug McClure could stagger in after a long night of too much everything. But no matter how much his head hurt or his vision blurred he got to the stage on time, found his mark, and delivered his lines.

A.B.—After *Baretta*—it's a whole 'nuther matter. More and more series stars have producer titles or producer duties written into their contracts. If they aren't happy with the script on the set on Wednesday morning even though they loved it Tuesday night, hey, it's got to be changed. Period. The star has to be satisfied because that's the deal. Casting got the star down? Recast. Now. The star wants everything shot across the street from his house? And all his scenes in his family room? Done. It's the star's way or the highway because he or she is now morally, ethically, and legally in the right.

After *Baretta* facts of life:

On *Baretta*, Robert Blake could grimace at the script, say, "That's not how I want it," and postpone a day's shooting, crossing out whole scenes and penciling in new ones no matter how much it cost.

On *The Fall Guy*, Lee Majors could discover that the week's female guest star didn't think he was as wonderful to hang around with as he did, and fire her before the end of the day.

On *Mike Hammer*, Stacy Keach could insist on having his own writer on the set to change all the dialogue to his specifications without having to consult with anyone else.

Could and can. And will. I observed all this, B.B. and A.B. We are still operating After *Baretta*, and there's no turning back. Who's going to give up absolute power?

For that matter, why *should* anyone abdicate the throne? As many creative genius actors are walking around in the world as genius producers, don't you suppose?

Take Michael Landon, for instance. *Little House on the Prairie* and *Highway to Heaven* were his babies. His was the creative vision. His was the guiding hand, from series concept to each finished episode. Did he drive those who worked for him crazy? Rumor has it he did. Were the shows personal and intense and *good* in the sense that they emotionally involved and moved millions of people?

My take is that they were. Michael's involvement as producer, writer, and director was every bit as valuable—if not more so—than his involvement as star.

The same is true of Roseanne. The concept for her hit series of the same name came from Roseanne and her life, and every aspect of the show was micro-managed by her as executive producer as well as star. The producer and writer dissatisfaction and turnover on *Roseanne* was so great that it reached mythic proportions in the industry. I knew people who bragged about how they were fired.

But Christ! *Roseanne* was a hell of a show. It was idiosyncratic, deliberately so. Nowhere on that series could you find the stale sitcom rhythm of *ba-deep, ba-dop, ba-doop*—set-up, set-up, punch-line. Instead, every line of dialogue was fresh and different and in its way real, a reflection of Roseanne's sensibility. It was an extension of the trailer park weirdness that made her a star in the first place.

So the next time you're watching television and you see your favorite star's face up there on the screen and he or she says or does something really stupid and you want to hate him or her, feel free. Odds are that they've earned it.

But if they say or do something wonderful, by all means go ahead and love 'em for it. Because they've earned that as well.

Note: In 1999 I was sitting in a restaurant in Studio City, California, with a friend, minding my own business as I ate. Suddenly a form swooped down at me. Robert Blake.

"Kid!" he cried. "Brody! You're alive! You survived! I knew you could handle the old sink-or-swim!"

Tough love.

Another note: In 2002 I was sitting at my kitchen table with my wife and unrolled the morning paper to see that Robert Blake had been arrested for the murder of his wife in a situation with remarkable parallels to Steve Cannell's first episode of *Baretta.*

Tough love?

Look Out, America! It's the End of the Bumper and Your Outlook Will Never Be the Same!

*A*nd now for a mini-look at a mini-moment with maxi-repercussions.

Anyone who wasn't a regular television viewer before 1976 probably doesn't know it, but once upon a time the average television show was, in at least one way, significantly less cluttered than it is now. And, in another way, it was no less cluttered at all.

What didn't we have assaulting our TV-trapped eyes and minds prior to America's bicentennial year? We didn't have as many commercials, that's what. Most spots were a full minute long, and during any hour of television-watching time, forty-eight minutes of it would be devoted to the content of the show or shows being aired.

Of the twelve remaining minutes, an average of two would be devoted to "promos," usually four thirty-second announcements by the network and its affiliates (your local station) about other shows we should be watching on the same channel. The other ten minutes would be taken up by ten nationally broadcast commercials, the viewing of which was, as we've seen, the real purpose of getting us to turn on our TV sets.

Nowadays, most commercials are thirty seconds long, and many pop in and out in fifteen. Combine that with the fact that the easing of government regulations allows the typical network television viewing hour to be made up of as little as forty-four minutes of content, and we're sitting or lying or standing there watching between thirty and forty different messages each hour. *Pop!* Here's a segment of a show! *Pop!* Here's a commercial! *Pop!* Here's another commercial! *Pop!* Another one! *Pop!* One more! *Pop!* More of the show! *Pop! Pop! Pop!*

That's a lot of popping. A lot of different sets of related images to have to sort through. A lot of adjusting to new information and new intentions, new thoughts and new ideas. A lot of shifting for a mind to have to do.

Pop!

And the mind-shifting has to be done instantly. With no warning, no overt visual clues that say, "Look out, brain, something new is coming in that's got nothing to do with what you're tracking now!"

Maybe we should think of this not as "mind-shifting" but as "mind-jolting." Some critics might even opt for "mind-numbing."

Before 1976, in those relatively commercial-light days of yore that only old fogeys can recall, the clutter was more subtle. Easier, I believe, to digest. That's because it had no real message. It wasn't on the air for any reason as crass as wanting to sell us anything or as noble as wanting to entertain us. It existed purely to help viewers orient themselves. To make sure they knew where they were and what to expect.

In a sense, the pre-1976 clutter was subliminal. It was something no one paid attention to. Something I, for one, never realized was there and wouldn't have known was gone if I hadn't had my attention drawn to it during one of the many not-so-fun "discussions" (okay, "battles") that go on during the production of the average television show.

What am I talking about?

Bumpers, that's what.

And the five seconds of black that preceded and followed them.

"Bumpers" is actually short for "bumper cards." In times gone by, bumper cards were ubiquitous on television. They were those short (also usually about five seconds) shots of the logo of the TV show we were watching that appeared right after an act of the show ended to remind us of what we'd been watching, before we started watching commercials instead, and then reappeared after the commercials and other announcements that made up a station break to remind us of what we were returning to.

The fade to black before the bumper told our brains they could relax for a few minutes, that the next thing to appear wouldn't be part of the continuity of the show. And the fade from black after the bumper told our brains it was time to settle in again and pick up where we left off before *programmus interruptus* occurred.

Bumpers and fades to black and fades from black had been part of television from its onset. After almost thirty years viewers were used to these smooth, easy, and relatively painless transitions. They were part of the shorthand of the medium. We were conditioned to respond.

But in the mid-seventies someone decided there was a better way.

Not for the viewers.

For the broadcasters and their customers.

The advertisers.

It started with the removal of bumpers at the end of an act break, before the commercials. A small thing none of us noticed. After all, the five seconds of black was still there to alert us that what we were about to see wasn't related to what we'd been seeing, and the bumpers were always in place after the commercials and before the next act of the show.

But five seconds had been saved. Five seconds here, five seconds there, and now there were fifteen seconds that could be used for something else. Not put back into the shows, oh no. Used for something *practical*. A short public service spot of the kind the government required stations to carry. Another network or local promo. Whatever. Over most network hours this meant fifteen more seconds where the medium could be used to *sell*.

But why stop there? If you were a network on a time grab mission, wouldn't you want more? Wouldn't you keep going just to see how far you could get?

Getting rid of all the bumpers and all the little segments of black came next.

But not without a fight.

The way I heard about it was that I heard David Gerber screaming.

Gerber screaming wasn't unusual, as we've already seen. But this time he was applying his full gale force yell to a couple of studio and network executives from Business Affairs. These were the guys who didn't even pretend to be creative, and the Gerb always had fun messing with them. On this particular day in 1976, he was walking through the hall with them and in his anger stopped just outside my office door.

"That's the stupidest thing I ever heard!" Gerber was hollering. His face was flushed. There was no fun in the messing this time. "You can't cut directly to the commercials. The audience can't follow that!"

"David—" one of the suits began.

"It'll confuse 'em completely," Gerber said. "They won't know what's part of the show and what's not!"

"David—" the other suit tried.

Gerber ignored them. His face got redder. "They'll think that happy family drinking Lipton is one of my cops taking a break! Worse than that—they'll think he's the robber!"

"David, it won't be like that—"

"No, no, of course not," Gerber yelled. "You're gonna take out the fades and the bumpers and know what's really gonna happen? Nobody's gonna know when the show comes back on! They'll be sitting and sleeping with their fucking eyes open like everybody does with a commercial and never even notice that some jerk we're paying fifty thousand dollars to for wearing an LAPD uniform for the week is back onscreen rousting suckers and walking right into an ambush!

"As a matter of fact," screeched the Gerb, "your fucking plan is the ambush! You don't know anything about television or movies or stories or audiences. You don't know anything at all!"

"We know we're going to get in another minute of commercials," the first suit said.

"And if you feel so strongly that the audience won't get it," said the second suit, "you can still fade to black and use your bumpers. Only instead of that being on the network's clock it comes out of your storytelling time."

"My storytelling time?! We don't have enough time as it is! What the hell's the matter with you guys?!" Gerber saw me standing in the doorway watching them. And he saw that I wasn't the only one. The hallway was getting pretty crowded. He turned his glare on the assemblage. "What the hell's wrong with you?" demanded the Gerb. "Get back to work! I don't pay you to stand around!"

"Maybe they're thinking, David," the first suit said.

"Not on my goddamn time!" Gerber said. He wrapped his arms around the shoulders of the two men and tromped them up the hall.

And that was how this particular turning point got seared into my mind.

David Gerber, of course, didn't get where he was by giving up anything he thought was his. He didn't give up any storytelling time, but somehow the audience adjusted. Jarring shifts of subject matter, visual and otherwise, became the norm for all television.

Removing the fades and bumpers may have made more time for commercials and given the networks a chance to take in more impact, but there has been a larger impact as well. Without the visual clues of what's coming, the audience no longer can let itself relax. Those of us who watch television now stay primed and ready, and are therefore more attentive to the commercials. We are now active participants in the buying and selling and influencing process. We're *complicit*. We *have* to be. If we don't stay awake, Lord knows what we might miss!

It hasn't ended there. The conditioning process that made fades and bumpers so familiar made no fades and no bumpers just as familiar. Direct cuts to unrelated material have led to a whole new kind of television crowding. At the present time, in addition to more and shorter commercials we have more happening on our television screens at the same time, including:

Network and cable channel logos in the lower corner of the screen throughout the shows.

Coming attractions and promos playing in the other lower corner of the screen throughout the shows.

News crawls along the bottom of the screen throughout news and sometimes even entertainment shows.

Coming attractions and promos bursting onto one side of the screen while squinched-up last moments and closing credits of a show make do with the space left on the other side.

Yes, TV fans, as things stand simultaneity has become the order of the day. There's a little-known rule of television writing that goes "Pile as much crap as possible on your hero's head. And just when you think neither he nor the audience can possibly stand it, dump a whole bunch more."

We write stories that way because we know that the truth is the audience *can* stand it, that the last dump will make the story even more effective than it's been. Similarly, that last, impossible dump of information as we're watching TV seems to be equally effective. Why, I don't know. That's for the neurologists and psychiatrists and experimental psychologists to figure out.

What I do know is that, even without the doctors and scientists for the last thirty years, the television audience has functioned as a kind of collective laboratory rat, with broadcasters experimenting to determine how much information and psychological stimulus they can transmit in the smallest segment of time, and how much of the information and stimulus viewers can absorb.

So far, the amount we can handle is pretty damn impressive. We can do this. We can deal with the ping-pong and razzle dazzle just fine.

But are we enjoying it?

Wouldn't you like—just once—to come home after a hard day's work and turn on your TV set and relax? Know who I think will make a fortune? The man or woman who starts a new cable channel that presents its material in such a way that the viewers can feel soothed and comforted.

Christ! Wouldn't it be great to unwind?

"Hill Street Blues" Enters America's Homes and Primetime Storytelling— and Storytellers—Will Never Be the Same

*M*any critics, viewers, and television insiders believe *Hill Street Blues* to be the best series in the history of television (proving they never watched *I Spy*). Although it was at the bottom of the Nielsen nationals its first season, the show garnered an unprecedented twenty-one Emmy nominations and won eight. When it went back on the air the following season, it did so as the lowest-rated show ever to be renewed.

A cynic might point to the fact that the show's overnights were always high enough to show that the big city audience that buys all the stuff was watching. But why? Clearly, *Hill Street* had something very special going for it, something that resonated with hard-to-impress critics and eventually captured a significant (although still not huge) national audience as well.

That something was *quality*.

In a business where an idea that hooks the audience is considered more important than how well that idea is executed, quality is tough to come by. But *Hill Street Blues*, created and produced by Steven Bochco for NBC, had everything and showed it all off during its 1981 to 1987 run. And, in the process, it changed two television paradigms, effecting not only what viewers would be seeing from

The cast of *Hill Street Blues*, circa 1982 (Still Things)

that time on but the workings of the behind-the-scenes creative process as well.

Here's the first big paradigm shift:

Hill Street Blues was a cop show. Its title referred to the fact that the precinct house was on Hill Street, and the cops' uniforms were the source of the "blues." (The pun on the musical meaning of blues as woes, hardships, and troubles was deliberate, and a key factor in the way *Hill Street* changed programming history.)

The most obvious ancestor of the show was *Naked City*, which first appeared on ABC in 1958. Both shows presented a gritty view of an ensemble cast of police officers (in the case of *Naked City* they were all detectives; *Hill Street Blues* threw in a fine team of uniformed flatfeet and an assortment of lawyers as well), and both showed them doing what cops do—solving crimes.

Naked City, as its name implies, concentrated as much on the inhabitants of that city—New York—and the personal lives, tribulations, hopes, and schemes of the perpetrators of the crimes as it did on the cops' work on the cases. Throughout the fifties, sixties, and seventies, that was the cop show norm.

Shows like *Highway Patrol*, *The FBI*, *The Streets of San Francisco*, *The Rookies*, *Starsky and Hutch*, *Ironside*, *Toma*, *Baretta*, *Police Woman*, *Hawaii Five-O*, *SWAT*, and hundreds of others that were ostensibly about officially empowered crime stoppers actually spent only about half of their forty-eight-minute hours with the good guys. The rest of the time they followed the baddies, presenting their motivations, plans, and, ultimately, crimes. Interspersed throughout was the elephantine *thud* of fist fights and dinosaur death *squeal* of car chases.

To be sure, some shows, including *Dragnet*, *Adam-12*, and *Police Story*, focused almost entirely on the activities of the cops, but these were rare exceptions.

Most television shows about private detectives for the most part operated the same way. *77 Sunset Strip*, *Hawaiian Eye*, *Surfside 6*, *Bourbon Street Beat*, *Checkmate*, *Jigsaw*, *Charlie's Angels*, *Cannon*, *Barnaby Jones*, *Mannix*, *The Rockford Files*, and hundreds of others gave viewers a respite from their heroes by bringing us into the machinations of the villains.

Lawyer shows like *Perry Mason*, *Petrocelli*, and *The Bold Ones* spent almost as much time at home (or on the lam) with clients as they did with the attorneys defending them, and medical shows like *Dr. Kildare*, *Ben Casey*, *Marcus Welby, M.D.*, *Medical Center*, *The Interns*, and *Trapper John, M.D.* focused more on the relationship between doctors and patients than on the day-to-day activities of the physicians who were the leads.

In other words, for all practical purposes the vast majority of one-hour television dramas and action series were almost as much about the weekly guest stars as they were about the stars.

Philip Saltzman, who produced both *The FBI* and *Barnaby Jones*, put it succinctly. "We've got to create really great villains for Barnaby to go up against, because let's face it, he may be a foxy grampa, but he's a pretty boring foxy grampa."

David Gerber was always quick to remind those who worked on *Police Woman* that "You've got to *pow!* over to the good guys and then *wham!* over to the bad guys, because if you stay too long in one place you're gonna come under scrutiny, and no TV script can stand much scrutiny."

Producer Frank Glicksman of *Medical Center* put it more idealistically: "The interaction between [series leads] Chad [Everett] and Jim [James Daly] is an important part of our show, but if we don't give the audience patients they care about whose lives are on the line nobody's going to stick around to see how the doctors are doing."

In feature films there's a saying: "Go with the money." It means that if you're paying Clint Eastwood $20 million to star in a movie you'd better have him in every scene.

In television, until *Hill Street Blues* the opposite was true. Lee Majors may have been getting $70,000 an episode for *The Fall Guy*, but that was all the more reason to cut to the guys his stuntman-turned-bounty hunter lead character was chasing as much as possible and keep him rested.

One genre was the exception to this tradition, and it was a relatively new one back in 1981. The primetime soap opera.

Dallas was the Adam of primetime soaps, going on the air for CBS in 1978 and almost instantly becoming number one in the national and overnight Nielsens. In 1981 *Dynasty* became the Eve. Both shows were about the squabbles between scheming relatives in rich—really, really, really *rich*—families. Interpersonal relationships among the large casts of series regulars were *the* subject matter of both shows, just as on daytime serials, and, just as on daytime serials, the intricate dances of lust, greed, envy, desire, jealousy, and occasionally even true love unfolded over a period of years of real time, each episode merely a chapter in the continuing and pretty damn sordid sagas.

The difference between *Hill Street Blues* and all the cop shows that came before it—all of just about any kind of show that came before it—occurred because Steve Bochco made a decision to "go with the money" and keep the stories centered around the regular characters instead of cutting away to the guests. To make sure this was worth doing and could "stand scrutiny," Steve included among his regulars the kinds of oddballs that Phil Saltzman had saved for the guest stars to play.

And to put the icing on the cake, Steve created elaborate character arcs, developing the personal stories of the regulars over time—a lot of time—so that no *Hill Street* episode ever felt completely finished. *Hill Street* episodes, like those of *Dallas* and *Dynasty* (and the primetime soaps that followed over the years) were just chapters in the ongoing novel that was the tale of the cops known as the *Hill Street Blues*.

Current television viewers know what happened next. As the years went by and *Hill Street*'s Emmy nominations and victories piled higher and higher, and as it was renewed and renewed and renewed, lo, its influence came upon television land. Not all new series could be written or produced or directed or acted as well as *Hill Street*, but, goddamnit, they could all be designed to suck you into the lives of the leads. To be *about* the leads. To develop the leads and string their personal problems along week after week.

To hook the audience and keep it hooked.

By the time *Hill Street Blues* went off the air in 1987 (taking its total of ninety-eight Emmy nominations and twenty-six Emmys with it), the balance of time and attention paid to the regular cast members vis à vis one-time guest stars had done a complete flip-flop.

The Sopranos, Six Feet Under, The Wire, and *The Shield*, premium cable presentations all, concentrate on the lives of their casts. On the network side, no viewer has ever clicked over to *ER* to find out what happens to the patients, or *The Practice* to see if a client will be found guilty, or Bochco's own *NYPD Blue* to see if a stakeout will get their man. Viewers watch to see which doctors are romancing which, which lawyer is going to be disbarred, and what new cross poor, suffering Detective Sipowicz will have to bear.

Is this a good thing?

Are audiences being more entertained now than they were before?

Are more products being sold by the sponsors of shows now than used to be sold before?

Are millions of people paying HBO and Showtime the required monthly subscription price to stay current on the lives of their faves?

Believe it or not, even in a time when huge advances are being made daily in marketing and audience membership, no one can answer all those questions with absolute authority.

Excellence, as we've said before, is of course non-quantifiable.

The degree of entertainment one is receiving is subjective. Even if we use audience size as a determinant, there's a problem because of all the increased competition we've talked about too. Where once a show was considered a hit only if more than thirty-five percent of the entire viewing audience tuned in regularly, and a failure if it received less than twenty percent, at this time we have "hits" with ratings of twelve percent, or seven percent, or even four percent.

On the other hand, many television advertisers say that sales are up, especially among the demographic groups the shows they sponsor target. Premium cable subscriptions are also on the rise, especially for HBO, which specifically credits *The Sopranos*, another high-quality primetime soap opera featuring good guys and bad, albeit with the heroes now those who previously would have been considered the villains.

Trends, trends, trends. That's what television's all about. For my money—and I've got as many bucks to spend on advertised products and subscriptions to cable TV as anyone else—I'd be a whole lot happier if television wasn't so trend-conscious. If programmers weren't all such sheep, trying to give the audience more and more of the new thing, often without understanding what it really is, and almost always at the expense of the old.

Gosh, guys, whatever happened to variety?

And, speaking of money flowing into or out of the pockets of people in the television business, now it's time to turn to the second big paradigm shift caused by *Hill Street Blues*.

A change in the nature of the television creative process.

In the way stories were conceived and episodes were produced.

And in *who* conceived of them and produced them.

From the earliest days of television to the emergence of *Hill Street* as its creative leader, primetime drama series, action series, and sit-coms relied on freelance writers for the great majority of the scripting and freelance directors for an even greater majority of the calls to actors and crew for "Action!"

The office staffs of action and drama shows (as opposed to the production staffs or *crews*) usually consisted of an executive producer, one or two producers, a story editor, and their secretaries. The office staffs of sitcoms were the same, except that there might be two to four story editors instead of merely one because sitcom writers tend to write in teams. And in general, people who create comedy seem to do a much better job of it when they're interfacing with a group.

Executive producers tended to be salesmen-producers who were usually well-connected former executives or, in the earliest days, ex-advertising execs, although there were a few equally well-connected writer-producers.

Staff members with the title "producer" (sans the executive part) usually came up from the nuts and bolts, "below the line," production manager side of things and were experts in scheduling and overseeing, so that the shows shone with a professional gloss and the networks, studios, and production companies got the most bang for their buck.

These early television producers also had a vast knowledge of what worked or didn't work in a script. They couldn't write one to save their lives, but they could spot good writing with their eyes closed, and they knew the clunkers as well.

Story editors, aka "story consultants" or "executive story consultants" (yes, ladies and germs, it's true that title inflation existed from the very beginning) were writers, but they seldom wrote more than one or two episodes a season, whether the season was thirty-nine episodes long or twenty-two. They didn't have time to write because they were much too busy being real editors, just like their equivalents in the publishing world.

Story editors met with freelance writers, told them about the shows, listened to the ideas the freelancers had for episodes, hired the freelancers, and then guided them through the various stages that resulted in finished scripts, a process that averaged approximately six weeks per episode.

Finished scripts more often than not were heavily "edited"—as in *rewritten*—by the story editors as part of their jobs. Just as Maxwell Perkins, who edited Hemingway and Thomas Wolfe, never put his name beside theirs as any kind of "co-writer," neither did the television story editors back in the days of yore.

Directors almost never were part of the staff. Unless the star or executive producer wanted to direct an episode or two, all directors were freelancers who didn't come into the office until there was a script for them to prepare. Most freelance directors worked a total of two weeks on an episode of a series. They spent one week huddling with the production people (the crew) and planning how to shoot the pages they'd been given and another week shooting them. Then they were gone, leaving the assembling and editing of the film in the hands of the producers.

With three networks presenting a total of sixty-three hours of primetime programming a week (with only a few hours to deduct for primetime variety, news, or sports shows, which were all done by in-house staffs) and several more hours of syndicated shows being produced as well, this system offered employment opportunities that are almost mind-boggling. We're talking about a total of from 2600 to 4800 writing and directing gigs a year!

To be sure, the hot writers and directors made "multiples," that is, deals guaranteeing that each of them would write or direct two or three episodes of a specific series a year. But there were, on average, about eighty writers in the Writers Guild of America, West, who qualified as "hot," and most of them were working as story editors, and perhaps forty in-demand, sign-'em-up television directors.

The greatest number of episodes any writer or director would have time to work on during the typical television season was about ten (writers would double up, writing more than one script at a time)—which still left thousands of jobs for those on the way up, those stranded in the middle of the pack, and those whose careers had peaked and were headed down.

At the time, the use of freelance writers worked well for shows, because the new elements being brought into each show each week were the important ones. Freelance writers brought with them interesting new characters for the regulars to interact with and fresh perspectives in terms of the telling of the stories. If (*when*, actually) a freelancer missed the mark characterization-wise in terms of the hero or heroes, the story editor was there to fix it.

The use of freelance directors worked because the visual side of most shows was generic, and television directors became expert at the requirements of those genres. There were only so many ways to shoot car chases and courtroom confrontations and operating room scenes, and the directors who worked the most, and got their full ten freelance assignments each year, were the real pros at staging those kinds of things. If they didn't understand the personalities and interactions of the leads, that was no problemo. The actors knew their parts and made sure their characters' traits and tics were well displayed.

From the late forties to the early eighties, evolution was inevitable. More writers became executive producers. The production experts who would've been called producer often got the title line producer instead and had to share producing responsibilities with writer-producers whose titles ranged from "producer" to "supervising producer" or "co-executive producer" and who ran the entire creative side of the show—casting, sets, costumes, oh, yes, and the scripts too. This meant that in a crunch a producer could help the story editor on the supervisory end and with rewrites, but the number of freelance writers stayed the same. Directors were still hired guns who came in, yelled "Action," and left as soon as they were done.

Hill Street Blues became the big exception to this order of things. It had so many regular characters and such complex continuity that it became clear early on that no freelancers could do the job. The regulars were the characters that had to be serviced by the scripts. The writers needed to be experts in their personalities and quirks, and the only way to insure that the writers were comfortable with the characters and up to date on their individual sagas was to make them part of the daily operation. They had to be put on staff so they had nothing to worry about but *Hill Street* and nothing to do but track *Hill Street* and nothing to care about but making *Hill Street* the best show they could so they could keep their jobs.

Hill Street Blues also had a very identifiable visual style, worked out by Steve Bochco and Bob Butler, who directed the pilot. "We used a lot of low-budget feature tricks to bring everything down and give it a street look no other show had," Butler said to me when we worked together on another project. "The idea was to set a pattern for all the other directors to follow."

The upshot was a credits list containing several story editors who along with Steve Bochco and producer Michael Kozoll did most of the writing, and a small group of directors who, although they were officially freelancers with multiples, did almost all of the directing. This way the characters, the stories, and the look of the show stayed on track. Depth and consistency became hallmarks of the show.

The staffing trend spread, and by the end of the eighties, after *Hill Street Blues* was off the air, more series were staff written than were freelanced and the most successful series used only three or four rotating directors instead of the former interchangeable twelve to twenty-two.

In the nineties, staff writing became the backbone of series production. Most shows had at least half a dozen writers on staff. Some had as many as twenty. Most of the writers were credited with one variation of the producer title or other. Some received a form of the story editor credit. A few—very few—were actually called staff writers. Staff directors came onboard also, with titles like executive producer or producer. Gregory Hoblitt of *NYPD Blue* was there to maintain that show's pseudo-documentary look. Richard Compton set the visual tone of *Babylon 5* and then stayed on awhile to, as he told me during the first season of the show, "make sure the show that's on the air looks like the show they bought."

"Do you do any actual producing?" I asked him.

"Who's got time?" Dick replied. "It's not like all those writer-producers out there are producing anything either, you know."

Currently, staff writing and to a lesser degree staff directing are the order of the day in the television industry. The financial cost of this approach isn't appreciably different than it would've been the freelance way, but the cost in lost jobs for writers and directors has been considerable.

For television writers, especially, the lost opportunities for work are up into the thousands each year. Today's eighty hot writers are working and earning even more than they would have twenty years ago, during television's golden age of employment, and they've been joined by a few hundred more, but the thousands of writers who miss what's called "staffing season" each year have no way to make their car payments except from non-showbiz day jobs.

Still, it's interesting to look over the situation and realize that, at least this once, the reason for a television production trend hasn't been ratings but Emmys. The *Hill Street Blues modus operandi* has triumphed because the industry had a genuine desire to improve the quality of its output, and it's up to the viewers to decide if it has succeeded.

Over a Million U.S. Homes Own VCRs; Let the Revolution Begin!

I bought my first VCR in 1981.

I was working on *The Fall Guy* with Glen Larson, who at the time was famous within the industry not only for his fecundity as a series creator but also for his love of toys.

If you could buy it and play with it, Glen Larson bought it and played with it. He owned seven houses, a literal fleet of limousines, the largest collection of antique slot machines on the planet, and every possible piece of electronic equipment available in that day and age. Glen was one of the first writers in television to work on a computer. And he was one of the first producers to watch dailies (the raw developed footage shot each day) on a VCR.

Sometimes he watched on a TV in one of his limos on the way to or from our offices at Fox. Sometimes he watched on a TV in one of his houses, where he had at least one television set and one videotape recorder hooked up in every room.

Glen was the very model of a TV mogul, drinking the finest of wines and eventually buying his own private jet to fly him wherever his whim demanded that he fly. He was only seven years older than I, and for a time there in the early eighties I wanted to be just like him.

I couldn't afford the houses, though. Or the limos, and certainly not the jet. And the computer terrified me. (What if I forgot to save? What if it ate my masterpiece anyway? How would Lee Majors, our star, know what to say?)

But a VCR I could swing, and even rationalize as a business

expense. So in 1981 I joined approximately one million other people in the country by driving over to Adray's, a Los Angeles–area discount appliance and electronics store where Glen A. Larson had an account, and forking over a check for my very own Panasonic. I got the top of the line, of course, and one of the earliest big-screen projection TVs, a Kloss NovaBeam, as well.

The NovaBeam had a six-foot diagonal screen with an image that dimmed and blurred and vanished unless you sat directly across from the middle of the screen. It cost about $1500 as I recall. Expensive? You bet. Worth the expense? No way. (Not that the Nova-Beam's successors have done much better. The population still hasn't flocked to projection TV. No turning point in television there.)

But the Panasonic PS Whatever Number It Was VCR was something else. With a case of brushed aluminum, two feet wide by almost two feet deep by about six inches high, my first VCR had a genuine electronic remote control, a digital frame counter that automatically marked the beginning of everything you taped so you could go back to the beginning for easy replay, and a running time of one, two, or four hours depending on whether it was in SP, LP, or SLP mode. Its discount price was almost $800 at a time when a new Porsche cost what a new Hyundai costs today.

So yes, it too was *expensive*.

But, unlike the NovaBeam, it was worth it. My Panasonic PS Whatever Number It Was VCR gave me more bang for my buck than I had ever anticipated. Not just in terms of business but personally as well.

And in that I was in good company.

The revolution was underway.

A revolution no one foresaw.

In 1951, when the first video tape recorder, as they then were called, went on the market (funded by crooner Bing Crosby, no less, presumably in his role as an icon of the "recording" industry), the V.T.R. was envisioned as a production tool only. In those days television was ruled by three networks: the National Broadcasting Company, the American Broadcasting Company, and the Columbia

Broadcasting System. Not only were their names hallmarks of nationalism, so were their schedules: Every show they presented in primetime was seen across all of the continental United States. A very big deal at that time.

The broadcasts were live, which was considered the true advantage of television in those days, and they all originated in New York City. This meant that the show a New Yorker saw at 9:00, *Playhouse 90*, say, was seen in Chicago at 8:00, and would have aired in Denver at 7:00 and Los Angeles at 6:00.

I say "would have" because this wasn't the case. Even in its earliest days television was rigidly segregated by time slots. Primetime was 8:00 to 11:00 in the Eastern and Pacific time zones, and 7:00 to 10:00 in the Central area. Mountain time was pretty much on its own. The consumers who were targeted by most television sponsors didn't live in the Mountain zone, so it just got, well, whatever it got.

Within the range of primetime, the earlier hours were considered "family time," with TV fare maturing up to "this stuff is best viewed by grown-ups only" in its last hour. If all shows were broadcast live across the country, L.A. would have been receiving 10:00 fare at 7:00, and advertisers, sensitive souls that they are (not to mention seekers of buyers of specific ages and incomes and tastes even then), didn't go for that.

For this reason, shows were broadcast live in the Eastern, Central, and Mountain time zones, recorded via kinescope, and re-broadcast three hours later in the Pacific time zone. The L.A. audience got what the New York audience got when the New York audience got it, at least by the clock, although not in real time.

And the truth is the Pacific audience didn't really get the same look as the audience in the rest of the country either, because kinescope was dull and grainy and had a look that would make the cheapest, most over-dubbed, over-copied, and under-exposed movie look like *Lawrence Of Arabia*.

Videotape, however, looked great. It was touted as looking "just like live," and for once the hype was true. Even in the fifties it was impossible to tell if a show was live or on tape. This made it perfect for the replay, and by the mid-fifties the Big Three were broadcasting live in the Eastern and Central time zones and on tape in the Mountain and Pacific zones. (The Mountain zone got everything on the same schedule as the Central zone because some genius in the art of demographics decided that Mountain men and Midwesterners were both early to bed and early to rise, a sign of their supposed lack of sophistication when compared to the audiences on both coasts.)

Until the mid-sixties, videotape remained a technology limited to "the biz." It did, however, broaden its base. As the novelty of seeing live performances waned in the minds of the audience (this was helped by the fact that in half the country the performances weren't live anyway), the desire to broadcast tighter, the desire by broadcasters to present more technically proficient shows, increased.

More and more shows that had originally aired live instead appeared "live on tape." Whole genres gave way: variety shows, soap operas, primetime drama, quiz shows, situation comedies (not yet called "sitcoms" but that was coming). By 1966 the rule was this: If it's a series or special broadcast with lots of action of the kind normally associated with feature films, then shoot the show on film. If it's a series or special broadcast that's mainly about people talking or the kind of show that we're used to seeing live, then shoot the show on tape.

Practically speaking, this meant one-hour shows with lots of outdoor scenes were filmed and variety shows and half-hour shows set inside on a stage were taped.

It also meant that all those taped shows now could be rerun. Previously only filmed shows could be rerun in the summer, giving the staffs, casts, and crews a rest while viewers saw the best episodes again. With the advent of "live on tape" just about *everything* could be rerun. This changed the economic situation for producers and networks and established the business model that still prevails at the broadcast and basic cable networks. It did for live shows what Desi Arnaz had done for filmed ones.

It meant they could be rerun.

Up to this time filmed programming had been a sort of loss leader for those who made it. On average, the budget of a filmed episode of any TV series was more than any network would pay for its production. That meant that the only way to approach the break-even point was to get the networks to put out money for a second run—rerun—of episodes that already had been aired.

And to make money the filmed show had to be on a network long enough to amass enough episodes to be stripped, or aired daily, in syndicated reruns on independent or local stations across the country. These stripped reruns were sold in packages of eighty or more episodes, and eventually enough packages of big hits would be sold to pay for the production costs of every series made by a particular producer.

Or maybe not.

Working this way it took—and still takes—years for a producer to get into the black.

Live shows, however, were much less expensive to produce and usually made money, or at least broke even, with their first run. Hell, they *had* to, there wasn't any second run.

Until all the shows started being shown on tape. Now perfect copies of the first airings existed, which meant summer reruns and syndicated reruns as well. In a well-run business this would mean increased profits for very little extra outlay. In the TV business it meant more money could be spent to make bigger and hopefully better taped shows, fronted by bigger and more expensive stars, because now these shows too had the luxury of not having to make back their costs the first time out of the box.

What was the bottom line, turning point–wise?

Just this:

By 1966, within the profession the production pattern that still dominates the industry was set.

And the non-pro, for-personal-use videotape market was just getting started.

Sony was the pioneer here. In 1965 it came up with a V.T.R. machine made for home use. The purpose of Sony's V.T.R. was to play pre-recorded programs on your television set and build a library of favorites.

But the response to the Sony home V.T.R. was a yawn. Its product cost a very pricey $3000 and there were almost no pre-recorded tapes for it to play. Rivals who jumped on the bandwagon fared even worse. The costs of their V.T.R.s ranged from $800 to $4000, and to many buyers these machines seemed to specialize not in playing those hard-to-find videotapes but in *eating* them. As in destroying each volume of the library before it could be put back on the home shelf. The library of favorites instead became the junkpile of wonder if I would've liked that one if I could've seen it.

Sony didn't give up, however, and neither did its rivals. Throughout the remainder of the sixties a host of technical developments took place, including the replacement of the V.T.R. by the VCR as reel-to-reel tape was replaced by cassettes. Video cassette recorders lived, even if they didn't exactly thrive, and in 1975 Sony's Betamax made such a splash among consumers in the U.S. that its rivals intensified their own development and marketing efforts with one goal in mind: to put Betamax out of business by replacing it with their own standard, VHS, or Video Home System.

What began as a research & development war led by Japanese Victor Corporation turned into a P.R. war. Things might have been different if Sony had licensed its technology to other companies, but it didn't, giving the impression that the company was too greedy, that it wanted it all. Sony dropped its prices to well below that of the competition, but it had already blown its chance.

Was Betamax better than VHS, as so many commentators at the time said? We'll never know for sure because it never got the customer base it needed, perhaps because it was always a consumer good and never intended for or used within the biz. In 1981 when I bought my Panasonic I'd heard of Betamax but never even seen a Betamax machine. So it never occurred to me to get one. A VHS VCR was the only way to go. (Yes, it's true. Betamax was eclipsed much the way the Macintosh computer was overshadowed by the PC, but there was no Steve Jobs at Sony to engineer a comeback.)

By 1985 Sony no longer was thinking dominance. Instead the company's VCR division was in survival mode, and it started making VHS recorders as well. Betamax died a lingering death, manufactured until 2002, but by then its sales were nonexistent in the U.S., the format doing business only in Europe.

In 1986 13 million VHS VCRs were sold in the U.S. Forty percent of all homes had one. Over 28 million VCRs were sold in the U.S. in the year 2000, along with 8.5 million DVD players (playing *digital* videotape—the same thing but different . . . what a world!), but the genie long had been out of the bottle. The revolution was in full swing.

Professionally, massive changes in production techniques were made possible by the VCR. College film schools, unable to afford professional quality film equipment—35 millimeter cameras, moviolas for film editing, all those massive lights!—started using videotape in their programs instead. From the mid-eighties on, thousands of students were trained to shoot and edit tape, and the nineties saw a huge change in professional editing techniques as those students took jobs in TV.

For the most part these changes effected filmed shows, including one-hour dramas and action shows and kids' animation. Since the early seventies all television shows have been "shipped" on tape. That means the completely finished show, be it a television movie or a special or an episode of a series, is transferred from the medium in which it's been shot to videotape and sent to the network for broadcast.

For taped shows that's no big deal. For filmed shows it was another step that ate up production and post-production time that otherwise could have been used more creatively. Many people don't realize this, but most TV producers are perfectionists, endlessly tinkering with their shows. When I was supervising producer of *The Fall Guy*, we often were making changes in the soundtrack and such up to an hour before airtime. This was because every change meant having to physically splice and re-splice the 35 millimeter film itself by hand with a scissors and tape. A tedious process to be sure—and dangerous as well, because if the editor made a slip a whole section of film could be ruined.

(In the early seventies I worked on a series called *The Magician*. The staff of which I was a part came in halfway through the season to save the show. We worked on an impossibly tight schedule—filming and editing a new episode every seven working days and airing one every seven calendar days. Think about what that means. Our producer, a wonderful Brit named Paul Playdon, used to joke about the inevitability of eventually missing a deadline so that instead of seeing the episode the audience would tune in and find our star, Bill Bixby, sitting at a desk intoning: "If we'd been able to finish this thing here's what you would've seen," and then reading the script out loud. Fortunately, that never happened. But it was close.)

The hiring of film school graduates with their tape editing expertise changed everything. When Glen Larson asked for *The Fall Guy* dailies on tape, the reaction was one of shock. As of this writing, though, all dailies automatically are transferred to tape. Instead of going to a screening room to watch what was shot on a big screen, producers pop in a cassette and see exactly what the audience will see. They discuss the way they want it edited with the editor at their side, and the editor then goes to work via computer, doing everything electronically. No muss, no fuss.

And, most importantly, speedily.

So now when we want to add a music stinger to the end of a scene at 6:00 Thursday night, when the show is set to air at 7:00, we can do it without sweating—too much. Ain't nobody worryin' about no Bill Bixbys having to sit at no desks turning script pages tonight.

On a personal level, the wide adoption of the VHS VCR and its successor technology created a whole new sense of freedom. In a way it has given all of us who watch television the most precious gift any human being can receive—it has made our time our own. By being able to record TV shows whether they appear on broadcast networks or cable-satellite and rent or buy feature films, we take control of our schedules and free ourselves from having to sit in front of the tube at an assigned time.

As Dick Lindheim (who went from vice president of research for NBC to V.P. of series development for that same network to a founding father of UPN) once said to me, "With a VCR, watching television is the same as reading a book. On one side we lose the 'group experience.' The gang doesn't get together at the water cooler to discuss a show the next day because they haven't all watched it the night before. But on the other hand we gain the chance to watch what we want to watch when we want to watch it."

In the long run, Dick felt, this would lead to creative benefits because the competition for viewers would be thrown wide open. And it certainly has been. In addition to having to compete with each other and with the cable channels and their niche audiences, the broadcast networks now have to vie against the tapes and DVDs viewers bring home from Blockbuster Video or Wal-Mart.

Home VCR use has also helped condition us all to the "A TV show or film is just like a book" frame of mind. All of us, that is, but the production studios, which insist that copying a videotape or DVD is the same as stealing. In a sense the big companies that create TV and feature film entertainment—and music as well—have adopted a mindset that says their customers are all thieves. How else can you explain the FBI "Do Not Copy or You'll Get Busted" warnings that appear on every videotape and DVD? And the lawsuits against users who make copies available over the Internet? How this battle between creators' rights and users' rights will end no one knows. But it's going to keep a lot of lawyers employed.

Another aspect of the VCR revolution involves pornography. Great thinkers ranging from economist Noam Chomsky to columnist Jonathan Alter to pornmeister Larry Flynt have pointed out that before home VCRs pornography was a rather small business with an audience of, as stripper Blaze Starr once said, "old men in raincoats" who had to go out in public to movie theaters to see the kind of action they wanted to see. Home video made the porn industry into a giant. Anyone could watch anything in complete privacy.

In fact, as Chomsky has pointed out, so rich has the porn industry become that it now literally drives technology. Chomsky has even made the argument that both the home computer business and the World Wide Web are porn-driven, with bigger hard drives, faster micro-processors, and all the business functions of the Web created in order to accommodate the needs of porn creators and porn users.

If you trace all this back to first causes the conclusion is inescapable—Larry Flynt, Bill Gates, and Netscape founder Marc Andreessen owe their billions to the VCR.

Frankly, I don't know how valid this line of thinking is, but I do know of at least one case in which the professional and personal uses of VCRs were linked together by porn in a way that actually *saved* a TV series in danger of being canceled.

In the nineteen nineties I was co-creator and supervising producer of what might well be the worst children's show ever aired in first-run syndication by anyone. Halfway through the first season we saw that we were in ratings trouble. But the executive producer of the series had a plan.

One day Exec. Prod. came into my office and indicated the monitor we used for watching our taped dailies. "I know how to get us renewed for next season," he said. "Send your assistant to the local video store to buy some Ginger Lynn tapes. [She was *the* major porn star of that era.] Our corporate exec loves Ginger Lynn but isn't the kind of guy who'd ever get those tapes on his own, so we'll have one of them playing next time he comes into the office. And then you can magnanimously give him the whole 'collection' when he leaves."

I must've looked astounded because Exec. Prod. laughed. "Trust me here," he said. "This'll work."

I couldn't resist wanting to know what would happen. I got the tapes but left my job on the show before the plan was put into action. A year later I read about the series beginning its second season of production.

Did Mr. Exec. Prod. use the tapes? Did they work?

Let's put it this way. I also read that among the guest stars scheduled to appear on the show in the coming season was—Ginger Lynn.

Now there's a real television turning point.

The Infrared Remote Control Takes Charge and the Revolution Rolls On!

*A*nd now for another mini-look, this time at a mini-object with maxi-repercussions.

The infrared remote control.

Bye-bye *ka-chung*.

Hello, silent little red light. You look like a phaser from *Star Trek: The Original Series*. But you're really a teeny command chair, and you make me as powerful as Captain Kirk. Thanks to you, I can conduct my voyage of discovery through the universe of television instead of through outer space.

The history of the remote control is almost as long as the history of television. The first remote was developed by Zenith in 1950 and was connected to the TV set by a cable. As a kid, I heard tales about such a device, but never knew anyone who had one. It seemed mystical and wonderful to six-year-old Larry, yet also sort of foolish. Why would you need a remote when all you had to do was get up, walk over to the TV set, and *ka-chung* for yourself?

In 1955, responding to complaints about people tripping over the remote control cable, Zenith introduced the first wireless remote control. I never saw one of those either, and while I regarded the concept as very cool I still didn't see where it was necessary. To me it was just another frivolous way for people who had more money than my parents did to show off.

A year after the first wireless remote appeared, Zenith announced

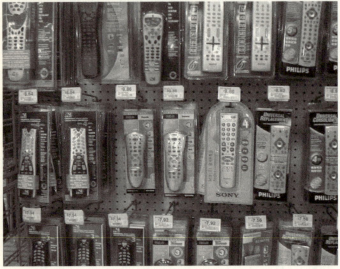

Remotes for all, 2004 (Cloud Creek Institute for the Arts)

a major improvement, a remote that functioned through the use of ultrasonic sound. Credited to Zenith researcher Dr. Robert Adler, the ultrasonic remote fixed an annoying flaw in the earlier version—the tendency of the TV set to change channels "on its own" when in bright sunlight. (Its operation was based on four photo cells embedded in the set, and if the light hit them just right they went way wrong.)

This particular technological advance also had no real effect on me, nor, judging by the sales figures, on many others. Its main contribution to our culture was the introduction of the term "clicker" as a synonym for remote control because of the clicking sound that was made when the remote was, well, "clicked."

This wasn't a very big deal unless you were much younger than I was. In fact, the only close encounter I ever had with one of those ultrasonic clickers was at my neighbor Neil Friedman's house. His six-year-old brother, Robbie, was captivated by the sound of the remote that had come (for another hundred dollars or so) with their big console, and he clicked the hell out of the thing until it stopped working. It's what resulted after Robbie broke the clicker that I still remember—Mrs. Friedman yelling about the spanking he was going to get.

Remote-controlled television sets continued to be regarded as toys, and no further improvements were made for about twenty-five years. And why should there have been? The least objectionable program principle of programming was still in full operation. With limited channels and choices viewers still had no overwhelming need to stay on their duffs when watching television. We only had to think about what we were going to watch once every hour, or half-hour if we were into sitcoms, and it was still no big deal to rise, shuffle over to the set, and turn the knob.

All that changed in 1981. Throughout the nineties the television and computer industries talked about "convergence," a melding of their two technologies that they claim is destined to create truly "interactive" television programming, and that may well be. But in 1981 another kind of convergence had occurred, resulting in the degree of interactivity we have today.

What? You didn't know we were already interactive? You missed that development?

Here's what happened, and how.

The year 1981 was, as we've seen, a pivotal one for the VCR industry, the year in which over a million homes possessed VCRs and therefore the ability to record anything being shown on their TV sets and then choose when to see it, either again or for the first time.

1981 was also the year in which the number of households equipped for cable increased by over thirty-three percent, the beginning of a time of meteoric growth. From 1981 to 1999 the number of cable households almost tripled. As we've also seen, the early eighties in particular were a key time for cable channels themselves. That's when HBO and Showtime started producing their own TV movies, with a resultant doubling of subscriptions.

Both these situations are major turning points in television. But what helped them along—no, more than that, what I believe made them possible—was the invention in 1981 of the infrared remote control.

The *ubiquitous* infrared remote.

Unlike their predecessors, the new remotes worked almost all the time. Point and click technology at its finest. Not only that, the new remotes started coming with all new TV sets because how else could you make use of the ninety-nine channels that were now being built into the UHF dial? Get up and walk? Not now.

The new remotes also started coming with many new VCRs because how else could you go back and forth between recording and viewing live and then viewing what you recorded and then going back to viewing live? Get up and walk? Not now.

And the new remotes became available with all cable set-top boxes because how else could you make use of the potentially infinite number of cable channels now available from your local supplier? Get up and walk? Uh-uh. Not now.

As the eighties advanced toward the nineties, the remote became a necessity. Only by using a remote could you utilize the full potential of your cable package and your VCR. The remote converged with the other technological and programming advances to create viewing that was interactive because it put the viewer in total command, even while lying in bed or exercising on our stair-climbers or cooking. Even while making love, or breaking up.

Using your TV set as the prime source of entertainment right now? Don't like what you're seeing (or hearing, in the case of the all-music channels now available to replace your stereo system's radio receiver)?

Click—silently now—away.

Using your TV set for background and finding that what's on is interfering with instead of enhancing your life?

Click silently away.

I love my remote. It takes such good care of me that I'm ashamed of myself for constantly losing it as I do. (Maybe one of these days I'll have trained myself to put it on top of the set when I'm finished instead of under the pillow or amid the blankets or in the nightstand or under the bed.)

The invention of the infrared remote control by Zenith is a turning point because it helped other turning points. The remote completed the creative uprising caused by the development of cable and satellite channels and the VCR. It empowered their revolutions. Without it the staggering number of channels we have access to would be precisely that, *staggering*.

This also makes the infrared remote significant in another respect:

It has completely changed the way we watch television. And by doing so it has also changed the way television shows are conceived and produced.

"What?" you say. *"Again?* What the hell's wrong with this business? Can't TV ever think for itself?"

No, of course it can't. Television was, is, and probably always will be firmly rooted in pop culture. As an aspect of pop culture, it must be about the *now*. The strength of the television medium in terms of creativity is that even when it's not trying for significance (remember "relevance?") television always reflects what's happening in society one way or another. At one level of execution or another, television always gives back to its audience what its audience demands.

This aspect is a weakness as well. Even though the paradigm only changes under special circumstances, the way the paradigm is played out changes constantly, its ebbs and flows mitigating against the creation of art that can last. No matter how good the intentions of those involved, television isn't about shows that will endure for all eternity. Television programming as "product" always takes over in the end.

As a product, then, television is doomed to react to consumer demand (even in its highest mode, the one where the viewer is treated as the consumer). Giving the viewer—whether the viewer be customer or product—a remote has meant having to take the existence of the remote into consideration all through the producing process.

In the seventies it was fashionable among certain educators to blame the otherwise highly regarded PBS children's series *Sesame Street* for shortening our attention spans as a society. The idea behind this was that all the short sequences and quick cuts from one series element to another trained young viewers to expect all entertainment to be just as short and fast.

This may well have been true, but from the eighties on, another force has been at work to limit our attention spans.

That's right. The remote.

Comic book publisher-editor-writer-creator *par excellence* Stan Lee once wrote (in the first story about Spider-Man) that, "With great power comes great responsibility." Those who toil in the fields of television production look at it another way:

"With great power comes great impatience."

Since its creation in 1981, the infrared remote has conferred great power on all viewers. I know that the minute I got one I started watching television differently. Instant gratification became the order of the day for me because I no longer had to put up with slow spots or dull dialogue or even commercials. One press of my thumb and the Red Eyed Commander of the Television Cosmos would whisk me away. As a viewer, I was spared from having to see even two seconds that I didn't like.

I wasn't unique. Impatient viewers everywhere did the same thing. I learned this in 1982, during a meeting about some new scripts being planned for *The Fall Guy*.

Peter Roth, who has since gone on to become president of several production companies including Warner Brothers Television, was ABC's executive overseeing the show at the time. When he came into my office to discuss where we were headed I expected the worst. Instead, Peter was a happy camper.

"These scripts are terrific," he said. "They're just what we need. They move so fast they don't give anybody time to think." I thought of David Gerber and his requirement that scripts should move along so they couldn't be subjected to scrutiny, but said nothing.

"We've got to remember to keep everything going," Peter continued, "because more and more people are sitting there with those damned remotes, and the minute you give them an opening they're gonna click away. And who knows if they'll ever come back?"

"This is a fact about the remotes?" I said. "Or just your opinion? Or your fear?"

"We've got the research to prove it. So keep these fuckers moving. Go!"

In 1988, when I was supervising producer of CBS's *Mike Hammer*, Anthony Barr, vice president for Current Programming, took it a bit further.

"You've got a bump here," he said, pointing to a passage in a script. "A place where you stop and explain what's going on."

"I figured it was about time everyone knew," I said.

"It doesn't matter if they know," Tony said. "Our research shows that the minute the momentum stops everybody out there clicks the remote and ends up so lost in the maze of channels that even if they want to they can't find their way back."

Eight years later the influence of the remote was explained this way by Marvel's Avi Arad as we went over a *Silver Surfer* script:

"Too much talk," Avi said. "The kids are sitting there with the remotes in their hands, ready to punish you the second the fighting stops. We need eye candy everywhere or they'll click the TV off and put on their Nintendo box instead.

"Know what's wrong with the world today?" Avi added. "Fucking kids are over-empowered!"

Adults with remotes. Kids with remotes.

Producers and writers and directors and actors and animators working in fear of losing their audience at any time. Speeding up the storytelling and the images, emphasizing the action and the laughs.

That's why, no matter how soapy the emotions behind *ER* get, what you see on the screen is a frenzy of medical activity at almost all times. That's why, in the words of Theodore J. Flicker, co-creator of the classic seventies sitcom *Barney Miller*, "There are no set-ups anymore. Everything's just punchline, punchline, punchline."

Glen Larson was correct when he said television was talking heads separated by action—for that time. Now, though, the balance has reversed. It's action separated by talking heads.

And many feature films, knowing they're headed for television either via cable, satellite, VHS, or DVD, use their bigger budgets to eliminate the talking heads altogether. What other excuse is there for *Dude, Where's My Car?*; *Charlie's Angels*; *Mission: Impossible*; *The Mummy*; or any Vin Diesel film?

As I write this, infrared remote controls have spread well beyond our TV sets. One universal remote can operate all the stereo, video, and computer equipment you have. Many experts say that the primary purpose of clicking on the TV set no longer is to find a show and watch it. Rather it's just to look around. Channel surfing is the activity, an end instead of a means.

Even my wife, Gwen, known to one and all as the most patient of souls, watches television with a "backup" channel programmed so that whenever what she's watching gets the slightest bit tedious she can switch to something else she knows she wants to see.

Sometimes when we're in bed and she does this I'll protest. "Hey, what're you changing for? That one was good!"

That's when she honors me with her most patient look. "The other one might be better," she'll say.

Wonder what HBO's going to do about *that*.

The Writers Guild of America Goes on Strike, Planting the Seeds for the Reality Genre

*I*n March of 1988 I embarked upon what was intended to be a little trip to Santa Fe, New Mexico. The Writers Guild of America, West, of which I was and still am a member, and the Writers Guild of America, East, had joined forces on March 7 in a strike against the Alliance of Motion Picture and Television Producers, and I figured I had a week or so to go someplace I'd never been and learn about a part of the country that had intrigued me for several years.

The trip lasted through the first week in August.

So did the 150-day strike.

It was the longest entertainment union walk-out up to that time. (Only the 2001 strike by commercial actors has lasted longer.) And what did it achieve?

It gave broadcast networks and cable channels alike a whole new outlook, that's what it achieved. It taught them not to be so dependent on those uppity screen and television writers and on the kinds of programming that used them.

It caused entertainment business executives to do what had heretofore been impossible for them—to think out of the box. To question traditional ways and approaches.

It encouraged more production companies to become what we call "non-signatories" to the WGA's Minimum Basic Agreement.

And it set the stage for a rush of non-scripted (or supposedly non-scripted) television series, also known as reality shows!

To understand how this happened, how we stumbled into a turning point no one ever envisioned and very few have ever admitted they would have desired, it's important to understand the players and their history. So:

In this corner, ladies and gentlemen, we have the Alliance of Motion Picture and Television Producers, a trade organization made up of most major network, studio, and production companies in the United States. The AMPTP represents 350 different companies and is show business's equivalent of a 500-pound gorilla. For all practical purposes it's the Company, gang. The Boss. Management.

And in this corner we have the Writers Guild of America, with branches in both Los Angeles and New York, a trade guild made up of about 9000 writers and writer-producers at the time of the 1988 strike, and consisting of close to 12,000 members as I write these words. For all practical purposes the WGA is the Union. Employees. Labor.

In the earliest days of Hollywood the studios that comprised management were dead set against unions of all sorts. They fought the unionization of writers tooth and nail, even starting their own sweetheart union, which dominated the industry until 1939 when, acting under the provisions of the National Labor Relations Act, what was then called the Screen Writers Guild began collective bargaining with producers.

The first contract didn't take effect until after World War II, which is a good indication of how well the parties got along, and bargaining between the two sides has never really gotten much easier. By 1988 the WGA had achieved some major successes, the kind any union could be proud of. It provided its members with an excellent, employer-paid pension program, one of the best health insurance policies in the country (also employer paid), and minimum wages that were and are mind-boggling to those not in the entertainment industry.

(Writers don't see it that way, and here's why. A minimum wage of $1500 a week, which is what it was for writers in 1988, *is* a hell of a lot of money, until you take into consideration the very disconcerting—hell, it's *frightening*—fact that in a business where the hunt for and existence of *talent* underlies every employment opportunity and contracts can last for as little as six or seven weeks there is absolutely no security whatsoever, making it necessary to in effect pull in your lifetime's earnings from every, or any, job. This same situation applies to actors and directors.)

The WGA's record hasn't been as good when it comes to issues that are peculiar to creators of literary material. Historically, management has showed very little respect for writers, assuming that audiences pay to see the stars and that having people actually plot out stories and write dialogue is nothing but a necessary evil. From the beginning of films, creative control has been in the hands of management and its designated beneficiaries, directors, with writers being put on and taken off projects like workers on an assembly line.

The reason for this is that although authors who write for publication and the stage are the owners of the copyrights of their material, and therefore the controllers of it both creatively and financially, films, and later television, dismissed all that up front. A writer with an idea for a screenplay or television series has to sell all the rights to it to a studio, network, or production company and then do the writing on the project as an employee. A writer who writes a complete screenplay must sell it to a management entity in order for it to be produced and loses all rights to it from that point on.

The fact is that as long as writers are willing to work within a system that buys their children and is then free to entrust them to any surrogate parent it desires, there's no reason to respect those writers. Ain't no leverage there, my word-processing, sometimes-wealthy, always-emasculated friends.

In 1988 the WGA and the AMPTP sat down at a bargaining table to discuss their expiring deal, known as the Minimum Basic Agreement, that existed at the time. The main issues were oldies but goodies: A bigger piece of the pie and more respect. The sub-issues were higher minimums; more ancillary rights; further strengthening of the pension and health care systems; an end to what's called the "possessory credit" for directors (that business at the beginning of a film where it says, "Robert Altman's Whatever-the-Title-Is," or "A Mike Figgis Film") because it implied that the director made up the whole damn thing instead of working from a script by someone else; the right to rewrite one's own work before being fired in favor of another writer; and various rule changes to the "Written by" credit-awarding procedure.

None of this stuff was new. The writers and the producers had been arguing about all of these topics since that very first time they sat down together in 1939. But this time, after several months of talks, both sides walked out with statements to the press that meant the same thing: "Fuck you."

Guild members voted for a strike, the first since 1981, figuring that like that one this strike would last only a few days. After all, March was the month in which television networks started planning their programming schedules for the season to begin the following fall, with April the month in which the selections were always announced so that production could begin in May and both new and returning series could be ready to go on the air in September. AMPTP would have to come up with something acceptable pretty damn quick.

Only it didn't. The Association took a stand.

And whupped writer ass.

For five months, the writers were out.

Five months of, in my case, traveling. In the cases of some others, of writing what they really wanted to write. (April Smith, who had been the writer-producer of CBS's *Cagney & Lacey*, wrote a hell of a detective novel and never looked back at television again.) Other writers rediscovered—or discovered—old and new personal relationships and hobbies. Others rediscovered—or discovered—the joys of working in other fields.

It became a big summer for mortgage brokers, not only because a lot of writers had to refinance their homes in order to survive but also because a lot of them decided that was a pretty good field to go into. The ranks of real estate brokers also swelled.

I mean, five months on strike is a fucking long time. Especially for a group notorious for living above its means. As the Everly Brothers could've put it, "Bye-bye, savings, bye-bye."

In August of 1988, when the strike was finally settled and a new Minimum Basic Agreement (not appreciably better in any way than the one that had expired) had been ratified by the members of the WGA and the AMPTP, everyone involved expected things to resume where they left off.

Okay, the '88 fall season would be starting late and maybe be a few episodes shorter per show (which meant less money for all, not merely for the writers who'd already been "giving" for five months), but that could be handled. "We gave it a shot," Cal Clements, Jr., said to me philosophically. "It's like poker. When you go for a big pot you've got to be prepared to pay up if you lose."

It didn't turn out that way.

The members of the Writers Guild of America, both West and East, didn't just lose what they'd bet.

They lost more.

It wasn't a matter of fewer episodes but the same number of shows. It became a matter of fewer *shows*.

Fewer dramas. Fewer sitcoms. Fewer series that relied on WGA members for personnel.

Fewer writing jobs.

Not as many as had been lost throughout the decade by the creation of mostly staff-written shows, but, over the years, thousands of jobs.

During the 1987 to 1988 television season ABC's *20/20* and Fox's *Ten O'Clock News* were the only primetime non-entertainment shows.

During the 1988–1989 season, the first one after the strike, CBS's *48 Hours* and *West 57th* joined the club. These were newsmagazine shows, legitimate descendants of *See It Now*. The 1989–1990 season saw the addition of another primetime newsmagazine, ABC's *Primetime Live*, and the first wave of reality shows, including *Rescue 911* on CBS, *Unsolved Mysteries* on NBC, and *America's Most Wanted*, *Totally Hidden Video*, and *Cops* on Fox.

This wasn't an accident. The broadcast network executives knew what they were doing. They were minimizing their risks. None of the new reality shows was literally "unscripted" or "unwritten." They just looked that way.

As host of *Rescue 911*, Bill Shatner brought his Captain James Kirk authority to re-enactments of real emergencies responded to by paramedics from all over the country, but someone had to write the scripts for the re-enactments and the verbiage on the cue cards Bill glowered at during the segment introductions and sum-ups.

On the long running *America's Most Wanted*, John Walsh isn't ad-libbing, he's saying words written for him by a writer.

But not a WGA writer. Not a professional storyteller and purveyor of fiction. Not a man or woman who went out on that 1988 strike or could go out on another one.

"The '88 strike showed the networks that they couldn't stay dependent on Writers Guild shows," former CBS president Kim LeMasters said to me in 1995. "An alternative was needed. News shows were an easy segue, but they were still expensive. Then along came the reality series, where not only could you hire new guys right out of college as writers, you could save a fortune on production costs by using handheld cameras and shooting on the fly."

Peter Steckelman, vice president of Business Affairs for Kids WB described the situation a little differently to me when he held that same job at Saban Entertainment, which was a partner in both the Fox Family Network and the Fox Kids Network cable channels, as well as one of the primo production companies for family entertainment until being absorbed by Fox and Disney at the turn of the 21st century.

"In order to do business as efficiently as possible," said Peter, "Saban has formed hundreds of production entities for the purpose of deal-making. Almost all of them are non-Guild [WGA], non–Directors Guild, non-SAG [Screen Actors Guild].

"When you write or direct or act for one of those companies you get a fair salary but no benefits or residuals or royalties, because if we had to figure those things into the budget we couldn't afford to be in business.

"This situation applies to most new cable channels as well," Peter said. "They produce shows on budgets that are less than a tenth of those of the networks because otherwise they couldn't create any programming at all. If they had to pay all the fringes they'd never survive."

The first wave of reality shows wasn't a huge success in terms of attracting the audience. Cable channel ratings increased by over thirty percent during that time, at the broadcast networks' expense. But the costs of reality programming were often less than half those of conventional entertainment shows, which made a second wave inevitable.

During the nineties and into the 21st century, *Rescue 911*, *Unsolved Mysteries*, *America's Most Wanted*, *Totally Hidden Video*, and *Cops* begat a line of progeny that includes such neo-classics as

American Candidate
Playing It Straight
Newlyweds
My Big Fat Obnoxious Fiancé
American Idol
Survivor
Average Joe
The Apprentice
Todd TV
Real Life
The Surreal Life
The Simple Life
The Real World
Big Brother
Joe Millionaire
Last Comic Standing
The Bachelor
Who Wants to Be a Millionaire?
Are You Hot?
Extreme Makeover
The Bachelorette
The Osbournes
Temptation Island
Boot Camp
The Amazing Race
The Mole

And more and more and more and more every thirteen weeks, or so it seems. Cable and satellite channels have joined with the networks on this because going any other route would make it just about impossible for them to afford to produce original material. The cost of one episode of *The Sopranos* is approximately $2 million. A series like *Trading Spaces* can be done for $25,000 per half hour.

If you were the CEO of a television production company, responsible for its financial well-being, which would *you* choose?

To be sure, all so-called reality shows are not alike. *The Bachelorette* doesn't have all that much in common with *Boot Camp* or *The Simple Life*, and even less in common with *Who Wants to be a Millionaire?* or *World Championship Poker*. But all these shows are linked by the fact that their crews can be "new guys right out of college" and they "save a fortune on production costs" as a result.

There are game shows and lifestyle shows and hidden camera shows and tragic re-enactment shows and celebrity self-gratification shows and talent shows and how-to shows and fish-out-of-water shows and oh-baby-humiliate-me-please shows and has-been shows and never-will-be shows and oh-god-I-hope-so shows. An infinite number of sub-genres, like the million and one flavors of Baskin-Robbins ice cream, compared to the old one-hour action-drama and half-hour sitcom, akin to the old corner grocery store's chocolate and vanilla.

And how are the ratings this time around?

Better, thank you, especially in view of the fact that expectations are lower than before. Many of these shows, including *Who Wants to be a Millionaire?* and *Survivor*, have started out knocking the Nielsens dead but then faltered considerably. That, however, is made up for by the fact that many of the shows have a built-in curiosity factor that just won't quit.

The "stars" of these series, after all, for the most part aren't stars at all. They're just plain folks like you and me and mom and dad and Aunt Dorothy and Uncle George and cousin Alan Smiley. Only now, suddenly, they're *famous*. They've got perks up the wazoo and fans down the ying yang. Newsmagazine shows like *Entertainment Tonight* cover this cycle's Bachelor or Joe Millionaire with the same gushing intensity they use when reporting on Alec Baldwin's divorce or the latest escapade by any singer whose last name is Jackson. Supermarket tabloids print pictures taken during their "private moments" by paparazzi who otherwise would be getting punched by Sean Penn.

This kind of coverage sells a lot of commercial spots, and attracts an ample number of cable and satellite subscribers.

Years ago, an L.A. disk jockey friend of mine named Dave Hull (a hot topic himself once upon a time for being the first deejay in Southern California to play the Beatles) said, "Owning a radio station is like having a license to print money." Nowadays, getting the right reality series on the air does the same thing.

In all their diversity, and for all their crassness and cynicism, today's reality series are bringing an enthusiasm and openness and even spontaneity to television that hasn't been there since the live and live-on-kinescope days of the early fifties. And with the five hundred plus networks and channels we all have to choose from, there are still plenty of the old standby hours and half-hours left.

Which brings us to one more question. How do those we could call the "victims" of this particular television turning point feel about how things have turned out? What do the working, or hardly working, or no-longer working writers who were WGA strikers back in 1988 have to say?

Current and former Writers Guild officers haven't commented much about the matter on the record. But others haven't been quite so reluctant.

Cal Clements, Jr., is still philosophical. "The hell with it," he says, and, paraphrasing Harry Truman speaking about his opponent, Thomas Dewey, during the 1948 presidential campaign, "If that's what the audience wants, it deserves what it gets."

Stan Berkowitz, a story editor on the CBS series *Houston Knights*, which was canceled to make room for *West 57th*, says, "The popularity of reality shows would affirm my lack of belief in humanity if I believed for a second that popularity had anything to do with them being on the air. It's about cheap production, and in that department we're like the old coach builders put out to pasture by Henry Ford. We can't compete."

And then there are the words of Dick Wolf, creator and executive producer of NBC's franchise, *Law & Order, Law & Order: SVU,*

Law & Order: Criminal Intent, and a host of other one-hour shows. Dick is the most successful of current WGA-affiliated writer-producers, a former employee of Steve Bochco and current bearer of Steve's mantle of high acclaim. When asked what he thought about the possibility of another long Writers Guild strike, Dick spoke straight to the matter: "This has to be settled or we're looking at the end of network television as we know it."

As for myself, I'm painfully aware that my career never really recovered after 1988. But the reality I found during my sojourn into the Southwest during the strike has meant more to me than any television show.

During those five months *real* reality hooked me, and turned out to be better than *Howdy Doody, I Spy, Police Story,* or even *Hill Street Blues.*

Although, come to think about it, *World's Funniest Animals* has really become tough to beat. . . .

The Telecommunications Act of 1996 Paves the Way for Big Media and the Corporate Outlook

$\mathcal{T}$o some people in the television business the Telecommunications Act of 1996 was an act of salvation.

To others in the TV business it was the work of the devil.

Just about everyone who earns a living in one aspect of broadcasting or another has an opinion on it—even though most were completely ignorant of its existence or clueless about its meaning when the Act was signed.

Yes, here we are again, eyeball to eyeball with another turning point that no one expected or foresaw. It's not often something sneaks up behind your back and looks you straight in the face, but television seems to have more than its share of these unlikely occurrences. (Just the opposite of a complaint once voiced by David Gerber: "That guy looked me right in the eye and stabbed me in the back!")

The first act regulating what later became the telecommunications industry was passed by Congress in 1934. The Communications Act, as it was called, was a straightforward bill giving the Federal Communications Commission the power to create a regulatory plan that would ensure that government licenses given to broadcasters would be used in the "public interest, convenience, and necessity."

Review of compliance was on an *ad hoc* basis. When a person or corporate entity applied for a license or for the extension of a license, the best interests, convenience, and necessity of the public would be taken into consideration in deciding whether or not to grant the request. Similarly, when someone complained about a license holder, these same three aspects would be weighed in any proceeding about whether or not a license should be revoked.

The specifics of the Communications Act, however, aren't what's significant here. What's significant is the state of mind it represented—one that considered it not only prudent but supremely *important* to establish standards for ownership. Standards based on the public good.

This state of mind also manifested itself in the way the federal government came to look at what was called "vertical integration" in the feature film business. Throughout the thirties and early forties, motion picture studios took advantage of the economic difficulties of the time to buy their own chains of movie theaters, thus "vertically integrating" themselves as suppliers, with themselves as direct conduits of their product to the public.

Concerned that this situation was "anti-competitive" in that it could keep independent theaters from showing the best films and new producers from getting their work distributed, in 1948 the Department of Justice filed a conspiracy suit against seven major motion picture studios and won, forcing the studios to divest themselves of their theater holdings.

The message sent by the lawsuit and its success was clear: The government believed that encouraging competition and diversity in the field of entertainment and communications was its obligation— because competition was in the *public good*.

In terms of the motion picture business this situation lasted until the mid eighties, when the government looked the other way as Columbia, Paramount, and MCA (the parent company of Universal Pictures) bought controlling stakes in major theater chains. A new era of vertical integration was now at hand.

The relaxation of the anti–vertical integration mindset showed itself in terms of television at the same time. Broadcast networks and cable channels alike opened production companies to supply themselves with television series and movies of the week, and merger mania began as the major players in the field jockeyed for position and control. It was up to the Securities and Exchange Commission to determine whether or not such mergers were anti-competitive (and therefore not in the public interest), and up to the FCC to decide if the broadcasting licenses of the stations involved should stay in place.

Guess what? Just about every move made by the big companies was approved. Where in 1983 fifty corporations controlled the majority of news media in the United States, including television holdings, newspapers, and radio stations, by 1992 ninety percent of the country's mass media were owned by only ten different companies.

That's hundreds of television networks and television stations and television channels and television syndication companies and television production companies and television hardware companies and radio networks and radio channels and radio production companies and radio syndication companies and radio hardware companies and film studios and film production companies and theaters and newspapers and magazines and publishing companies, owned by less than a dozen big corporations.

The backers of the Communications Act of 1934 must've been spinning in their graves, along with the Justice Department lawyers who fought the good fight in 1948.

The Telecommunications Act of 1996 was the icing on the cake or, depending on your point of view, the final nail in the coffin. In the Act, Congress ordered the FCC to establish a biannual review of its broadcast ownership rules "to determine whether any of such rules are necessary in the public interest as the result of competition" and "to repeal or modify any regulation [the FCC] determines to be no longer in the public interest."

Translation: "Now that we're no longer encouraging competition you've got a chance every two years to look over what may be standing in the way of more media consolidation and get rid of it."

The *Columbia Journalism Review* put it another way when writing about the deal in 2002 in which Westinghouse/CBS (which had already merged) bought the Infinity Radio Broadcasting and Outdoor Advertising Group for almost $5 billion:

"This deal is mainly a result of the Telecommunications Act of 1996, which heavily deregulated the media industry and allowed a company to significantly increase the amount of . . . stations it could own."

If this isn't a major television turning point then nothing is.

In the late nineties the companies we have since learned to call "big media" (Ted Flicker prefers "mega-media" because it has stronger connotations, but then Ted Flicker is a writer, director, and producer to whom such connotations mean much more than they do to the big-mega-media companies themselves) became the big lovers of the Telecommunications Act of 1996.

And those who feared those companies and their potential influence and power over viewers and listeners and readers became the Act's demonizers.

It was a hell of a situation.

And it hasn't improved.

In 2003 a lot of time and money and *angst* were spent bemoaning the fact that the FCC had voted to ease multiple-ownership rules and make it easier than ever for the big corporations to dominate media—especially television. But if "the thought is father to the deed," then the Telecommunications Act of 1996 had already done the job.

According to a study done by the FCC, in 2002 fully eighty-eight percent of primetime television programming was supplied by ten studios. According to *The Nation* magazine the odds were good—very good—that those ten studios were owned by one or more (in varying percentages and combinations) of only *six* big-mega-media corporations that have dominated the industry since the year 2000. Specifically:

Time-Warner
Disney
General Electric
News Corporation
Viacom
Universal

Th-th-th-that's all, folks. Six major players running the show.

Can this be true? What about all those different company names we see everywhere? All those media logos?

Here's the tally of media companies owned by News Corporation as reported by Consumers Union in December of 2003, shortly after the FCC approved a merger of News Corporation with satellite operator DirecTV:

Thirty-five broadcast television stations including two each in New York, Los Angeles, Dallas, Washington, D.C., Houston, Minneapolis, Phoenix, and Orlando.

Fox News Channel, Fox Kids Channel, FX, Fox Movie Channel, Fox Sports Network, Fox Regional Sports Networks, Fox Sports World, Speed Channel, Golf Channel, Fox Pan American Sports, National Geographic Channel, and the Health Network.

Twentieth Century-Fox Film Corporation, Fox 2000 Pictures, Fox Searchlight Pictures, Fox Music, Twentieth Century-Fox Home Entertainment, Fox Interactive, Twentieth Century-Fox Television, Fox Television Studios, Twentieth Television, Regency Television, and Blue Sky Studios.

Finally, *The New York Post, Weekly Standard,* HarperCollins Publishers, Regan Books, Amistad Press, William Morrow & Company, Avon Books, and Gemstar TV Guide International.

News Corporation also has a few sports holdings, including a piece of the action of the New York Knicks, New York Rangers, L.A. Kings, L.A. Lakers, Staples Center, and Madison Square Garden. (News Corporation had also owned the Los Angeles Dodgers in their entirety as well as a percentage of Dodger Stadium, but that didn't last.)

Can holdings like these be good for anyone other than News Corporation? Do similar holdings by the five other companies benefit anyone other than those companies?

No matter how many channels there are to choose from, be it 300 or 500, if most of those channels are controlled by the same people—the same decision-makers—it follows that although the choices offered to viewers may appear to be many, they will in fact be limited by the imaginations, creativity, talent, craftsmanship, and special interests of those at the top and the employees they hire to speak and act for them.

Similarly, although the illusion may be that viewers are receiving 500 different points of view, the reality is that the only points of view they are actually getting are those authorized by the decision-makers and their employees as well.

It's a managerial truism that, in the words of Professor Jack Feldman, "like hires like." Otherwise boss and employee become just too damn uncomfortable to get any job done, and, as my mother would have said, it's "So long I met you." In other words, "Hasta la vista, boychick."

The square peg employee is gone.

And so is that employee's point of view.

The multitudinous perspectives of individuals are sacrificed to the hive mind perspective of the Corporation Man.

Think I'm exaggerating?

I wish I were.

Once upon a time, when giants walked the earth and kissing a frog was romantic instead of perverse, show business, including television, was all about oddballs. Writers, directors, and producers were at best a wacky lot.

As Rod Serling would have said on *The Twilight Zone*, "Case in point:"

Bob Clampett, creator of *Beany and Cecil*, one of the most beloved children's shows of all time, was said by his friends to be so shy that he always wore his Cecil the Seasick Sea Serpent hand puppet and talked to people through its mouth instead of his own. It's from his life that we get the infamous phrase "Talk to the hand."

But regardless of what he was like, Bob Clampett wrote, directed, and produced a classic.

Then there's my short-term employer, Roy Huggins. Rumor had it that he taped everything said in his office, and had his secretary monitor employee phone calls. Going through a script with a writer and throwing each page on the floor as he finished it, only to demand that the writer then prostrate himself before Roy's desk and pick it up was Roy's standard procedure, and a reason Jo Swerling said of him, "Don't worry about Roy holding a grudge against you, Larry. He has so many enemies he's forgotten them all."

But Roy Huggins gave us the character called *Maverick* and had the brilliance to cast the perfect actor, James Garner, in the part.

And there was a writer named Leon Takatchyan, a wild man whose conversation at meetings could never be steered to the script. Leon had too much to say about his latest adventures outraging tourists on the little island in Northern California where he lived.

But he created *Lou Grant* and gave it not only meaning but *soul*.

Another writer, Jack Hanrahan, didn't walk, he staggered. His favorite reply to just about anything said to him was, "If you've got writer's block all it means is you're not drinking enough."

How good a writer was he? Hell, Jack turned in pearls even Gene Roddenberry wouldn't have revised—and he was one of the mainstays of a little magazine called *Mad*.

These men were *artists* who got their starts because they pushed through the doors and demanded attention. The writers shoved their samples into the faces of those in charge and said, in effect, "I dare you not to hire me." The directors turned out the lights and put on their reels and by God the results were worth watching.

These guys worked because they were good at what they did. Whether or not they got along with anyone else didn't matter. What did was that they *delivered*—not necessarily on time but always extraordinarily well.

Know how new writers and producers and directors get started in the big-mega-media age? They go to work for the corporations. As assistants.

They make coffee at Time-Warner. Run out for lunch for the boss at Disney. Distribute mail at General Electric. Deliver scripts to guest stars for shows owned by News Corporation. Wash the executive producer's car at Viacom. Pick up new sunglasses for some execs at Universal.

And if the coffee's good and they always get the lunch order right and put the mail in the correct slot and the scripts reach the actors' houses on time and the producer's car shines so brightly she doesn't have to pay to have it detailed and if the sunglasses are the right style—then, and I swear, *only* then someone might say, "Hey, how'd you like to be a writer? A producer? Ever think about directing?" Or "Doris the Development Girl came down with this bad rash. How'd you like to become a creative exec?"

That's right. The criteria for a new person's suitability for a creative job have become exactly the same as for every other corporate position.

"I like you."

"You make me feel good about myself."

"You haven't screwed up too badly so far."

And out trots the corporate ladder, waiting to be climbed.

In the words of Paul Weitzman, an agent at the Preferred Talent Agency in Encino, California, "When I'm approached by somebody who wants to be a new client I look to see if they're already working as an assistant somewhere in the business because if so they've already got the most important part behind them. It's easier moving *up* than it is moving *in*."

Whatever you do, though, don't piss off anyone on the top rung. Because all those top rungs are interrelated. Make an enemy of the number three guy at Viacom and you've screwed yourself with the CEOs of CBS *and* UPN.

After all, they're one and the same.

Be a getalong guy who shares the *Weltanschauung* of a top exec, though, and odds are you can run show after show no matter how low-rated, short-lived, and critically disdained. Because you're running just the way he would if he only had the time. You're a corporate cog now, and "like hires like."

Who needs talent when what's important is that you're giving the audience the choices and points of view the corporation has endorsed?

Ah, but can it be that choice is overrated? Could it be true that limited points of view are all audiences want or need?

Sure . . . We all love surfing with our remotes and passing seventeen variations of "Look At How We're Gonna Fix Arnie's House," and two dozen versions of "A Series About a Good Cop Torn by Bad Impulses," and a hundred takes on, "Big Mouth Commentator Takes on Three Jerks with Opposing Opinions."

Of course, we're just crazy about seven different Disney Channels showing seven different episodes of *The Cosby Show* simultaneously while E! and VH1 and Biography serve up "The Life and Times of Your Favorite One-Hit Wonder and How She Shook Her Drug Habit but O.D.ed Anyway."

Yeah. Right. Nothing's better than half a dozen different versions of *Law & Order* and *CSI*. Or seeing Tony Soprano as Tony Soprano on one channel while another has the same character as a tough cop, and another serves him up as a hood of Colombian instead of Italian descent.

If we love limitations so much, if we're so content with being handed whatever big-mega-media wants to give us, then why are fewer and fewer people watching television each year? Why are the ratings going down?

Oh, that's right. Statistical error. Faulty testing. Funny how no one complained about the way the Nielsen folks worked their magic when it showed viewers on the rise.

Telecommunications Act of 1996, I salute you. You've put the power out there nakedly, for all to see.

Time-Warner.

Disney.

General Electric.

News Corporation.

Viacom.

Universal.

Knock yourselves out, big guys. Go ahead, eat each other. Grab it all.

Maybe someday one of you will be the Supreme Ruler of the Media Universe.

With an audience of, oh, let's say "one."

Which Wonders of the Future Are the Turning Points of Today?

*I*n a time when futurists, psychics, science fiction writers, and prognosticators of all sorts have by and large earned public disdain for the failure of their visions of tomorrow to stand up for themselves even long after tomorrow has become yesterday, it seems foolish for anyone, let alone me, to even try to rattle off the next major television turning point.

Especially when you consider how difficult it was to see most of the turning points we've already discussed coming. Hell, I've barely figured out the game of hindsight, and feel much more comfortable as a television viewer or writer or producer than as a Nostradamus or Edgar Cayce.

However—

There's a hell of a lot of new stuff going on. New technology. New social attitudes (aided and abetted by new technology). New methods of creation and presentation (founded in, of course, new technology) for creative work of all kinds. To ignore the strides and the baby steps being taken would be to take the coward's way out, and while many people might argue that cowardice is television's way—even more than it is any other entertainment medium's—it would be hypocritical of me to advocate courage and change while keeping myself in the same old, same old straitjacket big-mega-media has laid out for the executives, staffs, and viewers of its product.

In terms of entertainment technology I can think of no better era to be living in than the first couple of decades of the 21st century.

Flat screen, wide screen, big screen, plasma screen, High Defin-

Hi-tech at low prices, 2004 (Cloud Creek Institute for the Arts)

ition Digital TV sets that can hang on walls! (Only—what?—maybe forty years behind the futurists' schedule.) Dolby Surround-Sound systems that can shake the house down! (Only—what?—thirty years after stereo mavens started jury-rigging and kludging their TVs to their tuners to get rid of that God-awful tinny sound.)

These new sets are really something, aren't they? Images so clear that not only can we not tell if it's real or Memorex, we've got no reason to care. They can be hung out of the way, so we can pretend television doesn't exist as we timelessly furnish our *Architectural Digest* masterpiece of a room. True motion picture theater ratio images, making television a full brother to feature films instead of the bastard relation it was. Moving sound we can chase in a circle and, with enough speakers, all through your house, apartment, loft, studio, restaurant, or dance club.

And don't forget Tivo! And Replay! And the media PC! Talk about no longer being bound by the schedules of the broadcast networks and cable and satellite channels! With these babies we're finally severed from any and all commercials as well! What could be better than being able to create instant DVDs?

Our Tivos and Replays and media PCs act as "timeshifters." (Sony's description back in the mid-seventies, according to *Wired* magazine in October of 2003—a great word, a wonderful word, a word almost as powerful as the act of timeshifting itself.) Via this timeshifting technology we can watch anything we want whenever we want to regardless of when it was broadcast, cutting out commercials and announcements and scenes with actors we don't like. We can speed things up or slow 'em down. Store our favorites forever on massive hard drives or delete 'em and suck in something new. We can answer the phone without fear of *televisionus interruptus* because when we're done we can go right to the place where we stopped—even if we were watching in real time—and not worry about screwing up the recording the way we had to with VCRs.

The technology has plugged right into society's cultural attitudes as well. As this is being written the Academy of Motion Picture Arts and Sciences and the Recording Industry Association of America are rattling their sabers and flexing their subpoenas, and bellowing the kinds of threats that would've made Gene Autry and Hopalong Cassidy and most certainly Paladin reach for their guns.

The ones being sued and put out of business aren't rustlers or train robbers. Rather, they're the customers of said Academy and

Association. They're the file-sharers and file-sharing web sites, the rebellious viewers and listeners whose outlooks are a logical extension of "If you build it, they will come," i.e., "If the tech exists for me to do something, then I should."

Are the file-sharers and their enablers right or wrong? Are they acting in a morally or ethically responsible way? Frankly, I can stand up at any podium and do twenty minutes either way. Equally frankly, I don't believe the propriety or impropriety of availing yourself of the results of someone else's creative impulses and talent (and investment of time and money) matters anymore. What matters is that if something can be done it *will* be done. If I have to predict anything here, then this is it:

Big-mega-media's not going to be able to stop what it calls "piracy." Every time it plugs a hole, legal or technological, five other people are going to drill five new ones each. The "theft" of intellectual property of all kinds will continue until someone who is every bit as intelligent as Einstein, as pragmatic as Bill Gates, and as of this moment in our culture as Elvis and the Beatles and Bruce Springsteen once were comes up with a brilliant new business model whereby copyright holders can still become richer than the aforementioned B.G. while our sons and daughters continue to copy and trade content of all kinds for free.

(Yes, I said "continue," because let's face it. Even if our little teenage darlings are denying any involvement in the dread downloading they're still doing it. Just as they deny having sex or trying drugs—oh, oh, better stick your fingers in your ears if you can't face the truth—yet still do those too.)

Want proof? It's available in dozens of places, based on the same kind of testing television networks do so well. "How many of you kids out there think file-sharing's a perfectly reasonable thing to do? Hmm, I can't see any faces anymore. They're blocked out by all those raised hands. . . ."

In the nineties, the first users of the World Wide Web had a slogan: "Information wants to be free." Big-mega-media didn't listen. It tried to co-opt the web and make it a vehicle for advertising and for paid services. And in just a few years big-mega-media got creamed. Some of us remember when *Time* magazine had a regular section devoted to the Internet and all the Time-Warner-controlled content that was either available or about to be. This section extolled the wonders of the Web and predicted that it would take over where all previous mass media left off.

By the early 2000s this section was gone. Not because the Web wasn't living up to its promise, but because the Time-Warner presence hadn't lived up to its promise. No point in trumpeting a medium where you're not making any money and don't seem likely to anytime soon.

With exceptions that accounted for a very small percentage of Web usage, information remained free. Now the slogan's a little different: "Entertainment wants to be free." And, like Commander Riker and Lt. Worf and the other personnel on *Star Trek: The Next Generation*, Internet users are making it so.

Hey, drinking alcoholic beverages and smoking cigarettes and snorting coke are in all likelihood a lot worse things to do than trading digitized copies of *Turning Points in Television* on the web, but no one's ever been able to stop them either.

New tech has had a significant impact on production and legal distribution of content as well. When a production company shoots a television series like *The Sopranos*, utilizing traditional equipment, sound stages, and guild and union personnel, the costs can average out to more than a quarter of a million dollars per shooting day, with reality series, as we've said, running at about one-tenth that amount.

New technology, however, has rendered most of the elements that comprise those costs obsolete. For $2500 you can buy a professional quality video camera. For less than that you can buy a computer packed with film editing, special effects, and music composition and editing software. Add a few lights and some sound equipment and you're in for five to seven grand. For equipment that can be used over and over, even after it has become obsolete, giving whoever owns it the kind of amortization CPAs would kill for.

Personnel can be obtained even more cheaply. No one sets out on the road to success saying, "I'm gonna work for free!" but actors, writers, directors, and composers, even budding cinematographers and film and video editors, know the value of volunteering, and of trading services on each other's projects when they're starting out. And the men and women who work in what we call "independent film" (which is just that, film or video made independently of big-mega-media and its bucks) have made wages ranging from low to zero a lifestyle in their labors of love.

Oh, and if you're talented enough to write and direct and hold the camera and edit what you've shot (or you learned all about how to do it in one of the thousands of high school—that's *high school*—film and video classes that have sprung up in school systems all over the country), then all you need are some actors who can double as gofers-crew members-*shleppers* as well.

Seven thousand dollars, some videotape, and some time and you've got yourself anything from a half-hour reality show about fly fishing in your backyard or a conversation with your state senator, to a play-by-play of the only game your local football team won all year, or even a two-hour movie about a big dumb guy who wants to prove he can go fifteen rounds with the champ, or short, chubby elves trying to keep the world from ending.

(And, speaking of fantasy, if you're into animation the cost of a good computer animation program is about the same as one for video editing. Or if you don't mind risking a lawsuit or two you can download all the creative software you'll ever need for free.)

This can be $7000 for the entire run of a whole *series*, by the way. Depends on how dedicated you can be, and how well you can support yourself at your day job.

New tech gets your work to an audience after it's finished too. The interactivity that was a kind of Holy Grail in the nineties—the interweaving of television and personal computer so viewers could interact with the shows they were watching in real time via the Web—hasn't happened yet, probably because big-mega-media's big-buck Web ventures got them so badly burned. But whether it does or not (and I think it will even if viewers end up having to do it themselves), the Web is the closest link any artist has to an audience in this day and age.

Want your sixty-three-part series about how your dog digs up gophers to be seen? Put it up on the Web and let the file-sharers take it from there. Sell a DVD version from your Web site as well. A longer version with something no one can get if all they do is download (how about your autograph on the cover?) will do.

You can peddle your masterpiece to a home video distribution company so your neighbors can buy it at Wal-Mart too. Or maybe you'll get lucky and a big-mega-media honcho will see what you've got and decide it's just *got* to be on the broadcast network or cable or satellite channel that's paying him while he's out shopping or surfing the Web.

What? That's not a likely enough chance? You want to make absolutely sure that before they die your grandparents will see the twelve-part series you put together out of their old photo album on real, honest-to-God professional TV? Send it to your local broadcast station or the nearest cable company's local access station. (You can *lease* access too, but we're trying to keep costs down.) Local broadcast stations are always looking for programming. They want it for free, of course, but who knows? If it's well received, a company with real money may want to pick it up.

You still want more? The way you see it, it's broadcast network or cable or satellite channel or nothing? Man, you drive a hard bargain, but guess what? The existence of all those new outlets has changed the development end of the television business so much that an unknown creator has almost as good a chance of selling his or her work as one of those old-time experienced agents.

Here it is, from the mouth of Mark Lichtman, a founding partner of the Shapiro-Lichtman Talent Agency. Over the years Mark has represented an assortment of big names and been instrumental in making the deals that got about a dozen of the shows created by Glen Larson on the air.

"It used to be that I could call a guy up and tell him about a project, and then meet him for lunch or dinner or even breakfast and wrap up the deal," Mark said to me during the writing of this book. "Because it used to be that we were all in L.A., and on the same side of town at that.

"Now," Mark said, "most of the new players are somewhere else. Atlanta. Baltimore. DC. We can't get together, and they don't want to talk on the phone. They want me to e-mail them about what my client has in mind. If they like the idea they e-mail me back and ask for a sample of the show. If they don't, I don't hear from them again."

Well, hell, just about anyone can send out an e-mail and not get a reply. You can. I can. New tech—e-mail—levels the playing field. More new tech—your own inexpensively shot pilot episode—keeps it level. All it takes is some *chutzpah*.

It'll help if you know what you're doing creatively. If you've identified the right niche and produced something that other people will agree fits right in.

Hmm . . .

Looks like I've stumbled onto a prediction of sorts even though I didn't want to make it.

Looks like the answer to "What's the next turning point in television?" is, "It's already here."

That turning point isn't merely something dependent on the technology that has been constantly developing from the last decade of the twentieth century to this minute right now.

The turning point *is* the new technology. Because the new tech has broken down the great barrier of true interactivity and made it possible for the viewer and the creator to be one.

Any viewer with a dream can now present that dream to others in a form that's as "professional" and worth watching as anything else.

Any viewer with a dream can get up from the sofa or out of the bed and move from in front of the television screen to behind it.

Any viewer with a dream can put down the remote and pick up the video camera and share that dream with the world.

Not since the days of Homer, when anyone who had a story could walk down the road or stand in the *agora* and tell that story to an *audience*, has there been so much opportunity.

I know the kind of show I want to make.

I've got the camera and the computer.

Excuse me while I go out and find me a puppeteer.

Sources

Most of the information in this book is from the author's personal experiences, conversations, and recollections. However, in providing and/or verifying certain facts, the following Web sites were valuable.

espn.go.com
i-spy.150m.com
usinfo.state.gov
www.consumersunion.org
www.earlytelevision.org
www.ee.washington.edu
www.familyeducation.com
www.fiftiesweb.com
www.howdydoodytime.com
www.imdb.com
www.latimes.com
www.lucylibrary.com
www.memorabletv.com
www.museum.tv
www.netreach.net
www.nick.com
www.pbs.org
www.remote-controls-online.co.uk
www.time.com
www.tripletsandus.com
www.tvacres.com
www.tvhistory.tv
www.tvparty.com
www.tvtome.com
www.wired.com

Index

About the Author

LARRY BRODY has been profiled in such national magazines as *Esquire, Entertainment Weekly, Starlog, People, Electronic Media, IndySlate*, on Web sites such as *TechTV*, and of course in *TV Guide*.

He has written over 500 hours of network television, including episodes of *The Huntress, Diagnosis Murder, Star Trek: Voyager, Walker, Texas Ranger, Heaven Help Us*, and *Star Trek: The Next Generation*. Larry was Executive Creative Consultant on *Spider-Man Unlimited*, and the highly acclaimed *Silver Surfer* and *Spawn* animated series. *Farrell for the People*, one of the many TV movies Larry has written, won a Women In TV & Film Award for Best Drama. Larry is the winner of the Humanitas Certificate and the Population Institute Award for his outstanding work on *Medical Story*, and was nominated for both an Emmy and a Writers Guild Award for Best Dramatic Writing on that groundbreaking series.

Larry also produced *Super Force*, as well as *Baretta, The Fall Guy, Automan, Partners in Crime, Mike Hammer*, and *Police Story* (which won an Emmy as Best Drama Show 'way back when and for which Larry won the Nosotros Award).

As a student at Northwestern University, Larry Brody majored in English and practiced his craft writing dozens of short stories, poetry and essays. Being an avid science fiction fan, he started writing in the genre, and by the time he graduated he was selling stories to *The Magazine of Fantasy & Science Fiction* and various men's magazines on a fairly regular basis. After graduation he took a major career diversion by going to law school but quit after one year and enrolled at the University of Iowa, which was well-known for its Writers Workshop. During that first school year Larry sold his first novel. Armed with confidence from the book sale, LB and his first wife pulled up stakes and moved to L.A. in 1968. His first big break came through a chance meeting with Sammy Jackson, star of the series *No Time for Sergeants*. The two struck up a friendship that would ultimately launch Larry's career.

A strong believer in the social responsibility of not only the artist, but of the media as a whole, Larry has for years crusaded to raise standards so that productions will be meaningful as well as entertaining. To that end, he has established TV Writer.Com (www.tvwriter.com), the most highly regarded and visited television writing site on the Web, where he shares his experience and insight into the business and artistry of TV writing today.

In the summer of 2002 Larry moved with his wife, Gwen, and teenage daughter, Amber, to St. Joe, Arkansas, to establish the Cloud Creek Institute for the Arts (www.cloudcreek.org), a non-profit charitable corporation dedicated to the advancement of the arts. The mission of CCIA is to foster and advance creativity and interest in all the arts by helping new artists develop their talents and skills, and to create an environment of respect, appreciation, and support for the arts in the community at large. He's written two e-books, nine novels, six books of poetry, and *Television Writing from the Inside Out: Your Channel to Success*, published in the fall of 2003. Currently, Larry is a regular columnist for *Screentalk* magazine, offering words of advice to struggling young screenwriters, all hoping for their first big break.